Dear Carole —
This book is so
beautifully written
and illustrated. It
brings back memories of
the many antiques of
antiques you & collected the
& hope it brings you home of
pleasure

With Love
your from
Christmas, 1975

HOUSE & GARDEN'S

ANTIQUES:

Questions & Answers

LOUISE ADE BOGER

SIMON AND SCHUSTER · NEW YORK

FIRST PRINTING

SBN 671-21506-x
LIBRARY OF CONGRESS CATALOG CARD NUMBER: 72-93514
DESIGNED BY EVE METZ
MANUFACTURED IN THE UNITED STATES OF AMERICA

Contents

HOUSE & GARDEN'S

ANTIQUES:

Questions & Answers

Preface

THE PURPOSE OF THE BOOK

This book is a collection of the most interesting columns from the popular monthly feature "Antiques: Questions & Answers," which has appeared for more than ten years in *House & Garden* magazine. It is the first book on antiques consisting entirely of questions and answers. The more than 900 fully illustrated items are conveniently arranged in categories: furniture; pottery and porcelain; silver; pewter; glass; clocks and watches; musical instruments; pictures; sculpture; lighting; heating equipment; toys and games; items on wheels; weapons; food service; utility items; and decorative-useful items.

The book is directed primarily to the readers of *House & Garden* magazine who use the "Antiques" column to identify their objects and have asked how they can obtain issues of the column. It will, however, be equally useful to others interested in antiques. The questions and answers and accompanying illustrations are well worth a collector's attention. No one even moderately curious about antiques can remain immune to the great variety of subjects and the human interest in collecting and possessing found in these letters. In principle the book is written by collectors, and in this respect it is unique.

THE LETTERS WE RECEIVE

There is a reason for every letter selected to appear in this column — no question and answer appears by chance. At the present time no "little book" on antiques covers such a variety of subjects from so many different countries.

I have been writing the column since November, 1966, and especially rewarding to me are the many letters received from *House & Garden* readers expressing their warm thanks for the service the column offers. Quite a number of letters come from readers who are not inquiring about the age and origin of their antiques but have learned to use the column as a source of identification—which is one of its chief values. For this reason the majority of letters chosen are concerned with the popular antiques made in the nineteenth century after about 1840, because not only are they of greatest interest to our readers but also relatively little study, until very recent times, has been done on this era. Then too, the antiques law that became effective on February 1, 1967, states that objects one hundred years old are now designated as "antiques," superseding the earlier rule that set 1830 as the cut off date for labeling objects antiques. This has noticeably made the nineteenth and even the early twentieth centuries much more attractive to young collectors, who must decide what will be desirable twenty-five to fifty years from now. Letters from newlyweds say that they find my column useful in getting started, since I look ahead and do not close shop at a particular date.

Pride and sentiment associated with heirlooms account for the questions in numerous letters. A writer will state, for example, that she was told by her mother that her "plain oak chair came over on the *Mayflower*" or her "handsome china plate belonged to Napoleon," and she asks whether this could be true. Generally the information is not sufficient for establishing a historical background. Recently, however, I received a letter from a reader stating that a plate made by Minton was given to her husband's grandfather when he was American consul at Stoke-on-Trent, England, in about 1890. It was said to be from Queen Victoria's china set. Could this be true? Yes, it was true. Minton identified her plate as part of a dessert service it had made that was used by Queen Victoria at Balmoral Castle, Scotland. This particular service was first produced in December, 1878. Minton kindly sent me one of its old brochures showing an illustration and reference to the service. This reply gave great pleasure not only to the owner but also to me, as I was able to establish fact from what almost always must necessarily remain fiction.

Finally, a type of question and answer selected to appear occasionally in the column is intended to broaden the readers' horizons or to provide an opportunity for a "link article." In a link article I might describe a Chinese Ming chair whose features were partly adopted in the characteristic early-eighteenth-century English Queen Anne splat-back chair; an eighteenth-century Louis XV style chair that became the prototype of the popular curvilinear Victorian rococo chair; or a sixteenth-century Elizabethan court cupboard of which versions were made during the Victorian Renaissance revival, when Renaissance ornament and forms became widely popular. If I want to make my readers more familiar with exotic objects, I might choose a question about a Chinese Dog of Fo, a Japanese inro, or Japanese sword ornaments—the menuki and tsuba. And because I always have my readers in mind, they write that they find the column educational, or that everything they know about antiques they have learned through my column.

HOW TO LEARN ABOUT ANTIQUES

Readers who wish to travel beyond my column to richer sources, to turn the matter into an educational project, ask where to start to learn more about furniture and antiques. In order to become more knowledgeable, it is of great importance to look at as many antiques as possible. Certain early Colonial cities in America, such as Boston, New York, and Philadelphia, offer a rich assortment of source materials—in museums, exhibitions, galleries, historic houses, and auctions. Most of us do not live in these cities, but it is good policy never to miss the opportunity of visiting one when traveling.

The museum field is expanding in everyone's favor. In the second edition of the *Museums Directory of the United States and Canada,* printed in 1965, are listed 4,956 museums; well over one thousand of them have been established since 1950. Even more significant is the increase in annual museum attendance, which passed the two-hundred-million mark in the early 1960s—a figure that had more than doubled since 1950. This attendance includes participation in the organized and cultural programs that 91 percent of our museums now provide for their communities. They also have traveling exhibitions, which seem to reach every corner of our country.

Museums always provide a special visual delight, for in the objects displayed we rediscover our past; we are reminded that although we have changed, we are still the same: the modern is the outcome and inheritor of the ancient, the old visibly influencing the new. To know the story behind what you see—its origin, history, and social significance—increases your appreciation immeasurably.

With all modes of observation, the eye will see only what the mind brings to it, for as the Spanish proverb (quoted by Dr. Johnson) runs: "He who would bring home the wealth of the Indies must carry the wealth of the Indies with him." For those who travel the antiques trail, books are the principal source of wealth. The need for a basic library cannot be overemphasized. It can begin modestly with a single book and grow as one's affluence and interest increase. For this reason, I am including a selective bibliography of reference works in special fields. These books offer sound scholarly information and fuller bibliographies, including references to periodicals, bulletins of museums, and other sources. Fortunately, many fine out-of-print publications have been reissued in recent years as paperbacks. Some of these I have also listed.

Bookshops have for your convenience *Books in Print* in three volumes: Volume I, author index; Volume II, title and publisher index; Volumes III and IV, *Subject Guide to Books in Print,* for those not familiar with title or author. Paperbacks are also listed in the three volumes, but a more extensive listing of these appears in *Paperbound Books in Print,* comprising author index, title index, and subject guide in one volume. These books are published yearly by the R. R. Bowker Company, New York, and you can find in them exactly what is available on any particular subject. If you are very up to date you may want to consult the catalogues that the R. R. Bowker Company issues three or four times a year as supplements to its latest publication of the four-volume *Books in Print*. An excellent, though often neglected, source for information on such utility items as typewriters and sewing machines is a good encyclopedia.

Without such a home library, the chances for successful collecting and the ultimate pleasure in a collection are greatly decreased. The well-prepared collector knows that the chase and victory of acquisition and the enjoyment that follows are inextricably connected with an understanding of the factors embodied in the object itself, whatever it may be. These factors may be good design, craftsmanship, and an appropriate use of the medium. An object should always reflect in a logical and reasonable manner the spirit of the era in which it was made. Origin, history, and social significance are other elements to be considered. Recognition of these features distinguishes the collector from the accumulator.

Finally, to learn about antiques, I heartily recommend that one handle as many as possible of the objects he intends to collect in order to get the feel of them.

ANTIQUE COLLECTING BECOMES FASHIONABLE

In about 1865 the Empress Eugénie, wife of Napoleon III, seized with a passion for everything that had been connected with Marie Antoinette, decorated her apartments with furniture made for Marie Antoinette, and for her personal use ordered exact copies of certain pieces. From about this time onward it became fashionable to collect antiques and to make copies of them. The fashion spread to England and America, where the interest in antiques had its origin at the time of the Philadelphia Centennial Exposition of 1876. So it can be no surprise that books on antiques first began to appear about 1900. It is only in very recent times that objects made after 1830 have engaged the interest of writers as antiques, since it was difficult to forget the requirement "before 1830," the year that marked the beginning of the machine age and essentially the decline of the individual craftsman working in a tradition handed down from master to apprentice.

THE ART OF FAKING

As soon as the buying of antiques became a fashionable occupation, the fine art of faking became sufficiently profitable for the forger to enter the field. There are many ways in which deception may be practiced in the various crafts. For example, factory marks on pottery and porcelain do not necessarily guarantee age and origin. Certain marks, such as the crossed swords of Meissen and the crossed L's of Sèvres, have been widely forged. It is said that probably more than half the porcelain purporting to be Sèvres owned by private collectors is partly or entirely false. Such clues as the difference between old and modern gilding cannot as a rule be readily detected in a photograph, so that even topflight experts really have to examine the object itself to be able to make a definite determination.

In silver, a frequent fraudulent practice is to take the marks from an old piece of little value and put them into a piece of modern manufacture which, if it were old, would be expensive. For example, the part of a handle of a teaspoon on which the marks occur may be transferred to a large tray.

Late in the nineteenth century, English and French cabinetmakers were fond of enriching plain pieces of old furniture to make them look more decorative and therefore more salable. The *Pall Mall Gazette* (1875) writes on the subject:

> Throughout the last century every piece of furniture, however common, was made in the same style and on the same general design as what is now known as "decorative" furniture, and there are still great quantities of it to be bought at a lower price than the same goods could be made for. These common chairs or tables or cabinets only need the addition of appropriate ornament and exhibition in a fashionable dealer's rooms to take rank and value as fine old Chippendale or marquetry furniture.

> There are many workmen in London who are mainly or wholly employed in "enriching" goods for the old furniture market . . . The vendor probably tells his customers but the truth. He says that the furniture is old; and so it is. There is nothing new about it except the bits of decoration here and there, which do not make up a hundredth part of its bulk, though they increase its price twenty fold.

Many of the pieces, both English and French, that were given this treatment a hundred years ago are extremely deceptive, and their decoration has often passed as original.

These words on fraudulent practices should remind collectors that caution is necessary. "The Buyer needs a thousand eyes; The Seller but one," writes Herbert Cescinsky in his book *The Gentle Art of Faking Furniture* (London, 1931). No matter how excellent the workmanship, a fake never measures up to an original. Probably the only real defense against the skillful fake is a very broad knowledge of genuine antiques. Even the cleverest of forgers will slip up somewhere, and generally because of lack of knowledge of the history of the craft. For example, in English silver, if a matching tea service comprising a teapot, sugar bowl, and creamer bears a hallmark of, say, 1775, all or part is false, as tea services of uniform design were not introduced in England until about 1790. When in doubt about the authenticity of an antique, consult an expert; payment for his opinion will be your cheapest investment. It goes without saying that antiques should be purchased from an unquestionably reliable dealer.

Authentic reproductions—any handmade piece that is genuine—will in the ordinary course of time increase in value. Of first importance in determining the value of an authentic reproduction is the accuracy—the exactness in duplicating the craftsmanship and materials of the original model. An exact copy of an original antique is known as a fake only when it was skillfully made with intent to deceive. "Fake" is a rather unpleasant word and should not influence the choice of people who buy reproductions. In the early twentieth century, when many wealthy Americans were building princely mansions and yearned for the furniture of Versailles to fill them, they settled for authentic reproductions. In American furniture, the era of quality reproductions made for commercial distribution was initiated in the 1930s.

FACTORS AFFECTING VALUE

Though I do not give values, an understanding of the factors that determine the value of an antique is helpful. Of first importance is age or scarcity value. Associated with the scarcity factor is supply and demand. Style, craftsmanship, and intrinsic beauty are contributing and important factors affecting the value of an antique. If you think of the word "antique" as meaning "original," you will have solved many problems of value. For example, the value of a Currier & Ives print is noticeably impaired when it bears a stain, or its original margin has been trimmed, perhaps to fit into a particular frame, as it is no longer in its original condition. If the original finial on a grandfather clock has been lost and a new one has replaced it, the value as an antique will be that of the piece without the addition. A silver tray on which engraved ornament has been added at a later date loses its full value as an antique.

THE CARE OF ANTIQUES

One of the greatest concerns to anyone interested in antiques is how to care for them properly. It is the responsibility of an owner to see that antiques are handed down to future generations with as little change as possible. And it is a wise person who can decide what he should undertake himself and what he should leave for experienced hands to do. Truthfully, one should do little more than basic cleaning. Silver, for example, should be cleaned regularly with an approved, standard polish or paste that will in no way be harmful. Essentially, the formula for good silver polish has changed little over the past two hundred years. It is generally compounded of some kind of abrasive chalk dissolved in an alcohol solution. Naturally, the coarser the abrasive, the more superb the luster—but the more damaging it will be as well. In a word, use the least abrasive polish possible.

Silver should never be left to tarnish to such an extent that it is necessary to have it buffed, for buffing alters the entire outer surface and ruins the natural patina. Then, too, the marks may be obliterated. When storing silver, it is prudent to wrap each piece in an antitarnish flannel bag, which will serve as a means of protection. If silver is displayed in a glazed cupboard or cabinet, a small cake of refined camphor placed inside the case will help to retard tarnish. One way to prevent tarnish from building up on the surface of silver is to wash it often; use soap and warm water, rinse thoroughly, and dry with a soft cloth. If the water in your vicinity is full of minerals, distilled water is suggested. Detergents, either for dishwashers or for washing dishes by hand, should not be used, for many contain phosphorus or sulfur compounds, which may cause unsightly staining. Salt corrodes silver badly. For this reason, silver saltcellars should be emptied after each use and, together with their spoons, washed thoroughly. Gilt salts are safe until the gilding wears off. If the corrosion is a mild case, then jeweler's rouge is effective; otherwise it requires the work of a silversmith. Bruises and dents should be hammered out only by a skilled craftsman who knows how much stress the metal can take. Ornament is best cleaned with ammonia and French chalk—gently brushed into the crevices, if there are intricate surfaces, and then rubbed briskly with a soft cloth. Certain new liquid cleaners are safe provided the directions are followed exactly and the silver is thoroughly rinsed and dried. They possess the advantage of speed and avoid abrasion.

No one has ever come forth with better instructions for the care of silver-gilt than the great English silversmith Paul de Lamerie (1688–1751): "Clean it now and then with only warm water and soap with a sponge, and then wash it with clean water, and dry it very well with a soft linen cloth, and keep it in a dry place for the damp will spoil it." According to French authorities, white wine or champagne may be used in place of water. Always avoid any sort of abrasive powder, strong detergent, or a brush.

Gold can be washed with good results in a weak solution of liquid ammonia or other detergent and polished with a soft cloth. Gold is softer than silver and requires very gentle handling.

Pewter is considerably softer than silver, and for this reason is more readily bent, dented, or scratched. To clean pewter, wash it in water and a little washing-up liquid, rinse, and wipe dry with a soft cloth. To restore the original luster after lengthy use, one pewter dealer, who is generally considered America's foremost authority in the field, cleans his pewter in an enameled basin or bowl filled with a solution of lye and water (one-half can of lye and five gallons of water, thoroughly mixed). The solution must cover the pewter to at least one inch from the top; if any part of the pewter is exposed above the solution, it acquires a stain that can never be removed. The pewter can soak in the solution several hours or several days. *When working with lye it is very important always to wear rubber gloves.* If the pewter is not pitted or corroded—when it is commonly called "sick pewter"—it will probably be clean in one or two hours. Remove, rinse, and dry thoroughly. Then rub with quadruple-ought (0000) steel wool. For best results when cleaning a round article, rub around it, not up and down.

If the pewter is sick, it must remain in the solution until all the corrosion has been eaten away. Depending upon the seriousness of the corrosion, the holes that will result may or may not go all the way through. The holes may range from pinpoint to thumb size. The latter is relatively uncommon. The question of whether or not to solder the holes depends upon use and value. The soldering must be done by a skilled workman, and the cost may be greater than the value of the piece. If a piece of sick pewter is put with healthy pewter, the latter will in time—perhaps in two or three years—become sick, as this disease is contagious. For example, if a sick pewter plate is stacked with healthy pewter plates, the latter will in time catch the disease. After pewter is polished it will not all have the same degree of brightness and luster, for modern pewter with a high lead content was originally more dull and dark in appearance; it will always look bluish.

Furniture should be cleaned with a paste wax. Before applying the wax, clean the surface with a damp cloth. Then, with a pad or damp cloth, apply the wax to a space about two feet square. Wipe immediately with a clean, dry cloth until a luster begins to show. Finish by wiping with another dry cloth until a hard, glowing surface is obtained. Always avoid an accumulation of wax on carved and inlaid pieces. For seat furniture upholstered in leather, a saddle soap is an excellent cleanser and softener.

The first caution in caring for pieces of glass and china is: Don't drop them! At all times handle such articles with loving care. Always wash glass and china with a mild detergent. It is best never to use ammonia on glass. The temperature of the water should be approximately the same as that of the glass itself; briefly, never wash cold glass in hot water. Never put the glass stopper into a fine glass decanter until the decanter is thoroughly dry, as the stopper seals it and prevents the moisture from evaporating. In time this will cause discoloration, generally known as "sick glass." For the same reason, do not store liquor or wine in fine glass decanters. The only remedy for sick glass is grinding, and if the glass has surface decoration it will be lost.

Glass bottles with a residue from medicine, liquor, or other liquids always present a problem because of their narrow necks. Some glass experts recommend the use of dry rice poured into the bottle with water; others have luck with a handful of buckshot or BB shot and warm soapy water, or with shredded newspaper and water. Vinegar and washing soda each has their followers. Regardless of what you use, fill the bottle with warm water, shake occasionally to loosen the sediment, and always allow the solution enough time to work—at least overnight. If the results look favorable, repeat several times and the residue may disappear completely. The drying of glass is best carried out with lint-free paper towels.

In the end, the chief concern of anyone who has antiques is to keep them as much the way they originally were as possible. This involves the dual effort of preservation and restoration.

RESTORATIONS

Restorations, repairs, and refinishing necessary to renovate objects can cause serious dilemmas. For example, should one replate plated silverware when the thin layer of silver is entirely worn away, thus exposing the base metal? Silver-plating will as a rule reduce the value; but without replating, the article has an appearance it was never intended to have, and one that definitely lessens the value of the piece.

In the preface of the catalogue entitled *Nineteenth-Century America, Furniture and Other Decorative Arts* — for an exhibition in celebration of the hundredth anniversary of the Metropolitan Museum of Art, April 16 through September 7, 1970 — Thomas Hoving, director of the museum, writes of the problem of restoration confronting the staff in the presentation of this important exhibition: "An immense amount of work has gone into the renovation of the objects — cabinetmaking, reupholstery, regilding, repainting — to make them as close to their original condition as possible — and also as beautiful, for we must not forget that beauty is one of the things that art is about."

THE YOUNG COLLECTOR

Since more than 45 percent of the United States population today is less than twenty-five years old, it is inescapable that the age of the young collector has arrived. Indeed, auction galleries now advertise sales for young collectors. Enhancing this trend is the stimulus furnished by a greatly increased awareness of and interest in all aspects of American history and its arts and crafts, as well as an awareness of primitive, ancient, European, and Far Eastern arts and artifacts. This has been due chiefly to the increased activity and enlivened programs — since the end of the Second World War — of museums, historical societies, and organizations responsible for historic sites. The direct effect of these programs has served to make the younger generation much more conscious of their heritage and to instill in them a desire to be part of it. It is only reasonable that this desire should find expression in the collecting of antiques.

HOW TO START A COLLECTION

How should one begin to acquire a collection? The answer depends on the kind of person you are, for any collection you make, costly or not, will be guided by your personal likes and dislikes. To attain success in the assembling of a collection, however modest, the young collector must be a willing student of the subject in which he is interested. The beginning collector must train eyes and mind to recognize the qualities of good design, workmanship, and a suitable use of the specific medium, for these are the factors that consistently increase the value of antiques through the years.

Collecting is a fascinating pursuit, but it is work. And as in all work, one wishes to be successful, and to be successful one must be right much more often than wrong. The key to business success is the development of skill and knowledge, preferably in specialized fields that have been overlooked by others. The same principle applies to collecting. Since the finances of most young collectors are limited, and many antiques are very expensive, this problem should be recognized at the beginning and accepted in a practical way, but it should in no manner discourage the beginner. The search for objects less rare that nevertheless possess attributes of aesthetic quality, good craftsmanship, and historical significance affords as many challenges and satisfactions as the quest for masterpieces.

The knowledge required for judging can be acquired only through training and repeated experience. In order to develop sound judgment and a discriminating eye, one must examine and handle as often as possible objects one is interested in; consult books; make frequent visits to museums; attend seminars and forums devoted to antiques and art sponsored by various museums and universities; make friends of other collectors; get to know dealers; browse in antique shops and fairs; and attend auctions. Never bid for objects at auction without having carefully examined them beforehand. Always heed the ancient warning, *caveat emptor*—let the buyer beware.

After starting a specific collection, one seldom changes to another field. Through the ensuing years the collector will continue to acquire knowledge, and as he becomes more experienced, he will constantly upgrade his collection. He will analyze the fitness of each piece in the context of the whole, and weed out from it the weak, for a collection, like a chain, is no stronger than its weakest link. Briefly, less can be more.

I wish you years of happy hunting along the antiques trail. Once the traveler's feet are set on the right path, the rewards of collecting extend far beyond the collection itself, as they give a zest for living that will reach into every activity of life.

FURNITURE

American

CHIPPENDALE TESTER BED

I recently inherited this tester mahogany bed from an aunt who collected antiques. What can you tell me about my bed? How old is it?

F.R. — Seattle, Wash.

Your bed having two front cabriole legs with ball-and-claw feet is in the Chippendale style and was probably made at Newport, Rhode Island, around 1760–1770. Though a few high-post beds in the Queen Anne style have been found in America, the story of fine American beds essentially begins with the Chippendale style. The drapery adds greatly to the appearance of such a bed.

AMERICAN SLEIGH BED

Any information about this mahogany sleigh bed will be appreciated.

J.W. — *Ashland, Ky.*

Sleigh beds were made by American cabinetmakers about 1820–1840. They are in the Empire style; usually the headboard and footboard roll over in a form somewhat resembling that in the "rolled-over" sofas of the period. Properly, they were to be placed lengthwise against the wall, generally with a dome-shaped canopy extending from the wall.

NEW ORLEANS TESTER BED

How old do you think our bed is, and where was it made? We know it has been in Missouri for four generations. It is of mahogany, handmade and carved. The posts have been cut down some, so we know it was once taller than its present 9 feet.

C.W.H. — *Springfield, Mo.*

Your tester bed is similar to those designed for the handsome mansions of the lower Mississippi valley. It was probably made by a cabinetmaker working in New Orleans around 1830–1840, the late years of the American Empire period.

VASE-TURNED BEDPOSTS

We have always called our black walnut bed a "spool bed," but have never been able to find out anything about this type of bedpost. Can you help?

M.A.G. — *Lake Charles, La.*

The turnings on the post are not spools but a series of baluster, or vase-shaped, forms separated by rings. Your tester bed probably dates around 1840 to 1850.

HIGH-POST BED

Could you tell me when and by whom this mahogany bed was made? I recently bought it at an antique shop.

R.W.P. — Mt. Vernon, Ill.

Your bed is late American Empire or early Victorian. It was probably made to order by an excellent cabinetmaker. High-post beds of this type, showing classical influence, were commonly used in Southern plantation mansions about 1835–1850.

NEW ORLEANS FRENCH BED

Could you furnish me with any information about this bed—where it was made and how long ago?
D.W.B., Jr. — Hamlet, N.C.

We believe your bed with high octagonal posts and paneled headboard is of the kind made by cabinetmakers trained in France, working in New Orleans around 1840–1860.

AMERICAN LOW-POST BED

Can you tell me the approximate age of my walnut "cannonball" bed? It has round wooden pegs in the posts and oblong pegs in the rails.
D.B.H.—Walnut Ridge, Ark.

The pegs in the bedstock indicate that the support for the mattress was made of canvas and rope. A perforated bedstock with ropes drawn through the holes is much more common. Your type would be found on a more sophisticated bed, a "city" bed, and was probably made between 1825 and 1840.

CANNONBALL HEADBOARD

Can you date this bed from the headboard? The side rails have pegs along them.
P.S.—Saint Marys, Pa.

The knobs on the two turned posts of the shaped headboard are a variation of the cannonball finial. The shaping of the headboard, so clearly shown in your snapshot, is a typical feature of this type of bed. It probably dates around the 1830s.

VICTORIAN RENAISSANCE HEADBOARD

The headboard pictured is part of a three-piece set which belonged to my great-aunt. The wood could be cherry or walnut with maple inlays. The headboard is 8 feet 9 inches tall, with a figurehead and plumes carved at the top. We would like to know how old the set might be.

K.S.S.—Brookings, Ore.

Your bedroom set is a fine example of Victorian Renaissance, made in the United States around 1865–1880. Although once scorned, furniture in this style is coming back into favor and is increasing in value.

VICTORIAN CHILD'S BED

I would appreciate any information on this walnut child's bed, especially in regard to the unusual canopy.

B.L.K.—Jefferson City, Mo.

Your bed is in the Victorian Renaissance style, 1860–1880. This type of canopy has been freely adapted from the French *lit à la Polonaise,* in fashion around 1750–1785.

MFA'S BENCH

AMERICAN EMPIRE BENCHES

I am enclosing a photograph of a window bench that I purchased from a dealer in New York State several years ago. One of the photographs of the Rosedown restoration in the January 1964 issue of House & Garden *includes a bench that appears to be almost identical to mine and that is identified only as an "1810 mahogany bench." I would be most grateful for any further information you can give me.*

M.F.A. — Fayetteville, N.C.

Your bench is indeed similar to, although not quite identical with, the one at Rosedown. These American Empire benches were known as "cornucopia" benches because each end is shaped to follow the contour of a stylized version of that symbol of abundance and prosperity. Fruits and flowers are carved at the mouth of the cornucopia, while the horn continues in a broad unbroken curve to form the seat rail. The motif was most widely used from 1820 to 1830, which is probably when your bench was made. In the most graceful examples (including yours and the one at Rosedown) there is enough space in the curve below the upholstered top for a small bolster or "squab." The curator at Rosedown believes their bench to have been one of the earlier ones, made in New York about 1810.

THE BENCH
AT ROSEDOWN

REVOLVING BOOKCASE OR BOOKSTAND

Please give me any information you can about this turntable. It is an attractive piece, which we treasure a lot.

J.R.M. — Boca Grande, Fla.

You apparently have an American revolving bookcase, made in a furniture factory sometime between 1895 and 1910. This variety of furniture, which was introduced in England around 1800, was designed to hold books for ready references.

COLONIAL REVIVAL BREWSTER CHAIR

This chair has been in my family for many years. I was told it is a Governor Carver chair. Is this so?
F.H. — Columbia, Mo.

Your chair is a Brewster chair, not a Carver. Both were named after Pilgrim Fathers, who are reputed to have brought them over on the *Mayflower*. The Brewster has many more vertical spindles than the Carver, which usually has only three. Many of these chairs were made until about 1700. Subsequently copies appeared, and judging from your snapshot, your Brewster chair seems to date from the last quarter of the nineteenth century, when a Colonial revival was fostered by the Philadelphia Centennial Exposition of 1876.

SLAT-BACK CHAIR

I am fifteen years old and just inherited this small chair from my grandmother. In Wallace Nutting's Furniture Treasury *I found a similar chair labeled "The earliest Pilgrim slat back—1620–1630." I would like to learn more about my chair so I can do a report on it for my American History class.*
D.R.—*Springfield, Mo.*

Although your slat-back side chair and the Pilgrim chair in *Furniture Treasury* may appear to be similar to an untrained eye, actually there are several noticeable differences. Your chair was probably made about 200 years later (1820–1830). These country chairs of marked simplicity have retained their popularity from Pilgrim times.

NEW ENGLAND SLAT-BACK ARMCHAIR

Could you please give me any information about the chair in the enclosed picture? The rockers seem to have been added, and the arms are slightly curved, with posts set halfway back.
N.D.—*Natick, Mass.*

Your five-slat-back chair with recessed arms is of late eighteenth- or very early nineteenth-century vintage. It was probably made by a New England country chairmaker. The shaping of the rockers suggests they were added not later than 1825.

BANISTER-BACK CHAIR

I inherited this maple chair from an aunt who bought it at auction. It is supposed to be very old. What can you tell me about it?

S.T.—Portland, Ore.

Judging from the photograph, your banister-back armchair was made in Pennsylvania around 1700–1725, when this type of chair came into general use. These chairs with rush seats were usually made of maple, and were very popular for many years, particularly in the country districts. The ornamental cresting, the so-called heart and crown, on your chair greatly enhances its appearance.

QUEEN ANNE SPLAT-BACK CHAIR

Please tell me what you can about this walnut chair. Underneath it is the information that it was "reconstructed by Jean B. Hassawer, 1918, U.S.A."

T.H.—Fort Worth, Tex.

Your splat-back walnut side chair is typically Queen Anne, of New England origin, probably Massachusetts, dating around 1740. As it has been reconstructed, it is not possible to determine accurately from a photograph how much is original. The profile of the chair back shows clearly how it conformed to the shape of the sitter's back and explains its remarkable comfort.

QUEEN ANNE CORNER CHAIR

I think my antique corner chair was made in America rather than in England. What do you think?

M.E. — Palm Springs, Cal.

Yes, your Queen Anne style corner chair having cabriole legs ending in club feet was made in America around 1740–1750. These popular chairs were introduced in the early eighteenth century in England, where, it is generally believed, they were used in the library for reading or writing. Hence they are often called writing chairs.

AMERICAN QUEEN ANNE WING CHAIR

My American Queen Anne chair has stretchers. Is this right? Also, when were ball-and-claw feet used on these chairs?

T.T. — Ellensburg, Wash.

Yes, American Queen Anne style wing chairs were made either with or without stretchers. The shape of your stretcher is typical of the style. In America the ball-and-claw foot is generally identified with the Chippendale style. However, in England this foot was apparently first used on later Queen Anne chairs. The Queen Anne wing chair having the wings and arms appearing as one continuous unit is one of the choice pieces of eighteenth-century upholstered furniture.

CHIPPENDALE SPLAT-BACK CHAIR

I recently inherited this handsome mahogany chair, but was unable to learn its history. Perhaps you could help. The seat cover had several layers of material, including the original handwoven linen.

J.S.V.A. — Binghamton, N.Y.

It is American and was probably made by a Philadelphia cabinetmaker around 1765–1780. Chippendale style splat-back chairs such as yours were designed with either cabriole legs and no stretchers, or straight legs and stretchers, the latter preferred for dining.

CHIPPENDALE SPLAT-BACK CHAIR

This handmade chair has been in my family for several generations. My great-grandmother thought it to be an original. Can you tell me its age?

B.C.L. — Woodbury, N.J.

You have an American Chippendale chair, dating about 1760–1780. It is identifiable by the pierced splat and the cabriole legs terminating in claw-and-ball feet, and resembles other chairs known to have been made by Philadelphia cabinetmakers.

HEART-SHAPED CHAIR BACK

I recently inherited this mahogany chair. What style is it, and does the back have a name?
                                S.N. — Seattle, Wash.

The back, known as heart-shaped, and the two front square tapering legs finishing in spade feet tell you that the chair is in the Hepplewhite style. Hepplewhite is perhaps best known for his numerous designs of chair backs. Of these the heart-shaped back comprising interlaced ovals is one of the most popular and graceful.

DUNCAN PHYFE CHAIR

What is the style of my chair? I recently inherited a pair of them.
                                F.R. — San Francisco, Cal.

Your chair is in the manner of Duncan Phyfe, dating around 1800–1820. Properly the word "style" cannot be given to Duncan Phyfe furniture, as he did not develop a new style, but appears to have used wholly or partly one of the three styles that were popular during the period in which his finest furniture was made — about 1800–1825. The styles were Sheraton, Directoire and early Empire. In your chair the Sheraton style is recognized by the curule type crossbars in the back, the rounded seat, and the round, reeded and tapering front legs.

EMPIRE GONDOLA CHAIR

Any information on this chair will be appreciated. It has a separate original horsehair seat and Roman numerals on the back made with a gouge.
                                R.B. — Albuquerque, N.M.

Yours is a mahogany side chair of the American Empire period. Chairs like this were made in considerable quantity from 1820 to 1835. This type of chair with a concave top rail joined to the front legs by a concave curve derives from the popular French Empire style gondola chair.

AMERICAN CORNER CHAIR

As you can see, this Early American corner chair has crudely wrought back slats and appears to have the original rush seat. Please tell me its age, origin and rarity.

M.G.A. — Abilene, Tex.

From about 1800 to 1835 craftsmen in small chair shops from Maine to Pennsylvania, and as far west as Kentucky, lathe-turned all the parts for these chairs except the handshaved back slats. Your chair's turned finials make it rarer than most such chairs sold in rural antique shops.

DIRECTOIRE CHAIR

Will you kindly tell me the age of this chair? With the exception of the round stretchers, it is made of walnut and is rather heavy.

D.I. — Fayetteville, Ark.

Your sturdy chair with its elongated S-shaped uprights and saber legs is in the American Directoire style, which flourished from around 1805 to 1820. However, the round stretchers indicate that it was made later, probably around 1850 — unless, of course, the stretchers are not original.

EMPIRE SWAN-NECK CHAIR

We wish any information you can give on this chair. The woman we bought it from told us it had been brought to Texas by the daughter of an early governor of Tennessee, who had ordered it from France. Will having the chair refinished decrease its value?

B.A.F., Jr. — Corpus Christi, Tex.

Your armchair is called a swan-neck chair because of the shape of the arms, a detail common to both the French Directoire and Empire styles. The winged leg and animal foot are believed to suggest the winged griffin — a motif found in ancient Egyptian furniture and again in the Empire period, around 1810 to 1830. The value of an old piece is always greater if it still has the original finish. If you consult an expert finisher, he will know how to refurbish the old finish by merely rubbing and cleaning.

AMERICAN EMPIRE CHAIR

I would like to know the period and origin of this chair. The seat is caned.

C.J. — New York, N.Y.

Your chair is American, probably maple, made in the late Empire style around 1825–1840. These chairs were usually made in sets of six or twelve for dining rooms. If the stretchers are original, the chair probably dates around the mid-nineteenth century.

FANCY CHAIRS AND SETTEE

This set of furniture has been in the family since 1800, perhaps earlier. Someone suggested that it is Chippendale. What is your judgment?

L.L.L. — Claremont, Cal.

AMERICAN

Your chairs and settee are examples of American Sheraton, made by an American "fancy chair" maker about 1800–1820. They are not Chippendale.

FANCY CHAIR

When I bought this chair the dealer told me it was old and good of its type. Can you tell me what kind of chair it is and just how old?
P.D.E. — *Naples, Fla.*

Your chair is a pleasing example of a Sheraton style "fancy chair." It is American, probably made in Baltimore, and dates from around 1825.

HITCHCOCK TYPE FANCY CHAIR

I would certainly appreciate your identifying this chair for me. We have a pair of them and they are decorated with colorful fruit and gold acanthus leaves. They have been in our family for years.
V.R. — *Plainview, Tex.*

Your chairs are American Hitchcock type "fancy chairs" and were probably made around 1820–1850. From your description of them, they seem to have retained their original decoration, which is most unusual.

CONNECTICUT CHAIRS

"G. Brown, Warranted" is stamped on this chair, one of a set of four. What can you tell about them?
D.B.S. — Hanover, N.H.

These chairs are typical of those made by various Connecticut chair shops between 1820 and 1835, although checklists of known American cabinet- and chairmakers do not mention G. Brown. The best-known of the Connecticut chairmakers was Lambert Hitchcock of Hitchcocksville. Such chairs have solid wooden or rush seats.

AMERICAN PAINTED CHAIR

We refinished this chair and another like it. Someone said they are primitives, made before 1820. Is this true?
E.R. — Bedford, Ind.

I don't consider them primitives, but they are good examples of the painted chairs made in considerable quantity in American chair shops from New England to Ohio about 1815–1840.

VICTORIAN GONDOLA CHAIR

This chair is one of a pair that I own. They are said to be called William Penn chairs. Can you date them?
J.W.F. — Westport, Conn.

Although your side chair is strongly reminiscent of the splat-back "gondola" chair of the American Empire period, details of the arched top rail indicate that it is early Victorian, probably dating around 1840–1850. I have never heard of a chair of that period being called William Penn.

BELTER-SCHOOL CHAIR

My uncle, a collector of antiques, left me this chair. The back is carved out of two solid pieces of a hard wood like ebony and has quite a curvature. Any information about this kind of chair would be welcome.

E.A.R. — Northfield, Ill.

Your chair is in the revived Rococo, or Victorian Louis XV, style and belongs to the distinctive Belter School of cabinetwork. The name derives from German-born John H. Belter (1804–1863), who worked in New York around 1840–1860 and created a local style, which is highly esteemed. Your chair dates from about that time.

"LOUIS XIV" VICTORIAN CHAIR

Can you tell me anything about this chair, which is one of a set of five that I own?

J.M. — Garden City, N.Y.

Your set of Victorian parlor chairs was probably made between 1850 and 1870. The principal sources of inspiration for the design were the French Louis XIV and Louis XVI styles.

RENAISSANCE CHAIRS

Any information would be welcome as to age and style of my identical chairs. They are made, I believe, of mahogany.

N.F.M. — Washington, D.C.

Your side chairs with their arched crest rail and turned tapering legs are in the Victorian Renaissance style, probably dating around 1850–1875. The treatment of the backs is a pleasing and unexpected touch.

VICTORIAN SIDE CHAIRS

When were these chairs made? The backs are one piece of wood, handcarved.

W.D. — Danville, Va.

These side chairs are American Victorian, dating about 1855–1865. A Mathew Brady photograph of Mrs. Abraham Lincoln shows her beside such a chair.

VICTORIAN RENAISSANCE

Can you give me any information on the period and style of this chair? It was given to me recently, and the previous owner said it is at least 150 years old.

M.T. — Wood-Ridge, N.J.

Your parlor chair is not quite as old as its previous owner supposed. It is in the Victorian Renaissance style popular around 1850–1875. Incised ornament was typical of that period.

VICTORIAN SIDE CHAIR

Will you please advise me if this chair was made by a recognized cabinetmaker? It is one of a pair from my great-grandmother's parlor at Gaysport, Pennsylvania.

H.T.C. — Tyrone, Pa.

No, this is a factory-made chair, a Victorian parlor side chair, widely manufactured by the better American factories from 1865 to 1885. Well-appointed parlors always had a pair or two of these occasional chairs.

SLAT-BACK SIDE CHAIR

What is the age and style of my solid walnut dining chairs?

C.R.O. — Oakland, Cal.

Your Victorian side chairs were made by an American furniture factory between 1870 and 1885. Although manufactured in quantity, chairs of this sort interest collectors of late Victoriana, perhaps because they possess several of the features of the early country, or rustic, furniture.

STEER-HORN ARMCHAIR

My husband's family has had this chair, made of matching steer horns, for over forty-five years. Is it rare?

W.L.S. — Levittown, N.Y.

Steer-horn chairs, tables, stools, and hatracks are known to have been made by several factories in Denver about 1880 to 1900, usually for wealthy ranch owners. Your chair must be one of those.

ARROW-BACK ROCKER

This chair supposedly came by mule train from Massachusetts to New York, and once belonged to President Adams's family. I would like to know the age and origin of the chair.

M.E.W. — Oneida, N.Y.

Judging from your snapshot, this arrow-back rocking chair is American in origin, dating from around 1840. The local cabinetmaker who made the chair had a nice feeling for style, as the tall back is quite pleasing.

HUBBARD ROCKER

Branded on the seat of our rocker is "J. C. Hubbard, Boston." The parts of the chair are numbered in Roman numerals. Any information would be appreciated.

N.M.T. — Perkasie, Pa.

Hubbard, a Boston chairmaker, had Roman numerals marked on the parts to guide the workmen in assembling the chairs. Your rocker dates between 1825 and 1850.

BOSTON ROCKER

The finish and workmanship look to be old on this chair I bought in Athens, Ohio. But most old rockers have more than six spindles. Is it an antique?

M. McD. — Parkersburg, W.Va.

Yours is a Boston rocker typical of those made by chair shops in the Boston area. Makers varied the number of spindles to suit their fancy. This one dates about 1830–1850 and seems to retain its original stencils. Yes, it is an antique.

PENNSYLVANIA DUTCH ROCKER

I'd like very much to know what I have in this old Boston rocker, which is different from any I have seen. We bought it in the Ozarks.
W.H.B. — Independence, Mo.

Yours is not a Boston rocker, but of a type made in the Pennsylvania Dutch country about the same time — 1840–1860.

PLATFORM ROCKER

Approximately fifty years ago my father bought this platform rocker at an auction. We think the carving and brass trim are very unusual and would be pleased to know the age and origin of our chair.
R.Z.C. — Midwest City, Okla.

Platform rockers such as yours were popular in the 1880s. It is generally believed that they were developed to save wear and tear on carpets. These rockers were made by many furniture factories throughout the United States.

WILLOW ROCKER

I bought this rocker at an auction because it was unusual. It is handmade from bent tree limbs. Can you tell me anything about it?

F.G. — Old Forge, Pa.

This style of late-nineteenth-century American willow furniture was created in a period when there was great interest in bentwood furniture. (The most sophisticated designer was Michael Thonet of bent-beechwood fame.) It was often found in the Midwest, where it was popular as porch furniture.

NEW ENGLAND WINDSOR

Is this Windsor chair an antique? Also, can you tell where it was made?

B.H. — Santa Clara, Cal.

Your New England Windsor armchair appears to be an antique, dating around the late eighteenth century. This type of Windsor originated and was chiefly made in New England. The distinctive feature is that the top rail and arms are combined in one piece of bent wood.

LOOP-BACK WINDSOR

Could you tell me if this Windsor chair is an antique and where it was made? It has a seat of solid pine, hickory spindles, mahogany arms, and maple legs.

B.H. — Santa Clara, Cal.

Yes, your loop-back Windsor chair is an antique, made by an American chairmaker between 1750 and 1800. Using mahogany for the arms was a refinement characteristic of Pennsylvania chairmakers. This type of Windsor, having the bent rail of the back continued down to the seat, is also called a bow-back. At first they were made without arms as a companion to the New England Windsor, and in this form they were very popular.

LOOP- OR BOW-BACK WINDSOR

I understand that Windsor chairs are given certain names depending on the type of back. If this is true, what is my Windsor chair called?

C.K. — Seattle, Wash.

Yes, this is true. Windsor chairs are best classified according to the designs of the back. However, all writers on the subject occasionally use different names for the same type, which may cause some confusion until you learn more about Windsors. Then, too, there are the variations of the principal types, often all conveniently classified as Windsors. Your type is called a loop-back or bow-back. Nine spindles are the usual number for this kind of back.

STENCILED COMB-BACK WINDSOR

I know this is a comb-back Windsor chair, but I don't know its age. The stenciling is barely visible. Should I refinish it?

J.B. — Corvallis, Ore.

Your Windsor armchair with comb piece was probably made in New England about 1800–1820. As some of the stencil decoration is still visible, I would not refinish it. Any antique should, if possible, be left with its original finish.

HOOP-BACK WINDSOR

Friends have told me that the back of my Windsor chair is too high. What can you tell me?

M.M. — Mobile, Ala.

As a rule this type of Windsor chair, called a hoop-back or bow-back, has a lower back. But when the back is high — and it sometimes is — the general appearance is more graceful and it acquires a certain air of importance. Briefly, it becomes less practical but more decorative.

HOOP-BACK IRON WINDSOR

I recently purchased a chair that looks exactly like a Windsor chair, but is made of iron. Is it unusual?

V.B.P.—Verona, N.J.

When iron garden furniture began to appear around 1840 it was often made in imitation of popular wooden furniture designs. Windsors were a logical selection, as they were already advertised in late-eighteenth-century Philadelphia newspapers as "fit for piazzas or gardens." Your hoop-back Windsor chair probably dates around 1850–1870.

COMB-BACK WINDSOR

When I bought this Windsor chair the antique dealer told me that it was an eighteenth-century comb-back Windsor. What do you think?

P.T.—Swarthmore, Pa.

Yes, you have an eighteenth-century American comb-back Windsor, and, as the name implies, in this type of chair the "comb" is the special feature. The "ideal" number of spindles for this type of Windsor is nine. However, the general appearance of your Windsor with seven spindles is notably pleasing and graceful.

BLOCK-FRONT CHEST OF DRAWERS

This chest originally belonged to my great-great-grandmother's aunt, who died in 1797. Can you tell me more about it?

B.S.W. — *Grosse Pointe Farms, Mich.*

Your Chippendale style, block-front chest of drawers was made in Massachusetts around 1760–1770. Almost all block-front furniture was made in New England. A block-front was often cut from a single piece of wood. It is said, however, that in some cases the raised flat surfaces were applied with glue.

HEPPLEWHITE CHEST OF DRAWERS

I inherited this chest of drawers from my mother's family, who came from New England. The front of the chest is curved. Where was it made, and about when?

R.B. — *Lee, Mass.*

Your bow-front chest of drawers is in the Hepplewhite style and was made in America, probably New England, in the late eighteenth century. Hepplewhite chests of drawers have either a bow front or straight front. The latter were by far more plentiful, no doubt because they were less expensive to make. The valanced base curving into French bracket feet is a marked feature of the Hepplewhite style.

CHIPPENDALE STYLE CHEST OF DRAWERS

Can you give me any clues as to the origin of this chest? The inlaid plaque on the top drawer has these words: "Engl Glory" and "By Shearer to Mrs. Elizth Richards."

D.M.S.—Bethesda, Md.

Your mahogany chest of drawers with its serpentine front, blocked ends, and ogee bracket feet is in the Chippendale style. It was made in the late eighteenth century either in England or the United States, and the inscription indicates that it was made specifically as a presentation piece. If it is American, it was made in the South. For any further authentication you should have the chest of drawers examined by an expert.

AMERICAN EMPIRE STYLE CHEST OF DRAWERS

I would like to know the place and time this cherry-wood chest of drawers was made. I inherited it from my grandmother, who acquired it in Ohio.

J.H.M.—Alexandria, Va.

Your chest of drawers probably dates from about the 1830s and appears to be the work of a regional cabinetmaker. The overhanging top drawer supported by detached ring-and-spiral-turned columns at each corner immediately identifies it as being in the American Empire style.

AMERICAN EMPIRE CHEST OF DRAWERS

I was told this chest of drawers, which was given to me as a birthday gift, is about 200 years old. Is this true?

G.M. — Roselle Park, N.J.

Your chest of drawers with freestanding columns supporting the overhanging top drawer is typical of the American Empire period, so it could not have been made 200 years ago. It is a fine piece of cabinetwork, dating between 1825 and 1835.

QUEEN ANNE LOWBOY

I recently inherited this lowboy. How old is it and what style is it in? How was it used?

B.L. — Buffalo, N.Y.

Your kind of oblong side table, known as a lowboy in America, is in the Queen Anne style and was probably made in America around 1740–1750. It was a very useful piece of furniture, as it combined the advantages of a small chest of drawers and a table. Because of these features women found lowboys useful as dressing tables, and on the flat top was placed the characteristic dressing mirror mounted on a box stand. However, it was not convenient to sit at all of these tables, as the drawers were too low. When this was the case, the lowboy was used as a side table wherever it would be most useful. The word lowboy, like the word highboy, is purely an American term.

QUEEN ANNE BONNET-TOP HIGHBOY

*Some years ago I inherited this Connecticut high-
boy made of cherry, with some of the brassware
replaced. The name "David Butler" appears under
one of the drawers. I would appreciate any information about it.*

F.C.T. — Delray Beach, Fla.

You have a good example of a Connecticut scroll-top highboy in the
Queen Anne style, probably dating about 1770. We cannot identify
David Butler; he could be the original owner. The scroll top came into
fashion about 1730, but flat-top highboys of the previous era continued to be made for many years after that date. In many of the scroll-
top pieces the scroll extends from the front of the highboy to the back,
as in your example, and the word "bonnet-top" is used to describe
them.

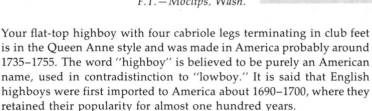

QUEEN ANNE FLAT-TOP HIGHBOY

*I would like some information about my highboy,
which I recently inherited through my husband's
family.*

F.T. — Moclips, Wash.

Your flat-top highboy with four cabriole legs terminating in club feet
is in the Queen Anne style and was made in America probably around
1735–1755. The word "highboy" is believed to be purely an American
name, used in contradistinction to "lowboy." It is said that English
highboys were first imported to America about 1690–1700, where they
retained their popularity for almost one hundred years.

CHIPPENDALE STYLE HIGHBOY

I recently inherited this mahogany highboy. Can you judge from the photograph what period it is of and where it was made?

W.P.A. — Montgomery, Ala.

You have a fine example of a Chippendale style, scroll-top highboy. The shell carving of the drawers in the lower section and the cabriole legs with claw-and-ball feet persuade me that it was made in Philadelphia about 1765–1775. Philadelphia cabinetmakers were famous for their fine Chippendale highboys, many of which are now in museums.

AMERICAN TALL CHEST OF DRAWERS

Can you tell me the age of this chest of drawers and where it was made?

C.M.C. — New York, N.Y.

Your tall chest of drawers dates about 1760–1775, and is American of the Chippendale period. If the wood is walnut, it was probably made in Pennsylvania; if cherry or maple, it could be a piece from a New England cabinetmaker. The ogee bracket feet are a marked feature of the Chippendale style.

AMERICAN CHEST-ON-CHEST

I purchased this mahogany chest-on-chest at an estate sale but was unable to learn its history. What do you think of it?

J.G. — Dallas, Tex.

You have a fine American piece of the Chippendale period, made by an eastern cabinetmaker about 1760–1775.

AMERICAN CRADLE

I am enclosing a picture of a cradle that I possess. I was told that it dates back to 1609. Can you verify this and give me any further details on its origin?

R.G. — Norwalk, Conn.

Your cradle with heart-shaped handholes and wide carved rockers is American, dating either from the last half of the eighteenth century or the first quarter of the nineteenth century. It looks as if it had been made by some Pennsylvania Dutch cabinetmaker. This cradle could not date back to 1609, for cradles like this were not made in this country or in Europe before the eighteenth century.

PENNSYLVANIA CRADLE

Can you tell when and in what part of the country this walnut cradle was made? The openings in the headboard and footboard are heart-shaped.

D.M.W. — Prairie Village, Kans.

The heart-shaped handholes could indicate that this is a Pennsylvania Dutch cradle. It was probably made by a country cabinetmaker in eastern Pennsylvania in the latter part of the eighteenth century. A turned rocking post at each corner is a useful detail, and one of very early origin.

AMERICAN HOODED CRADLE

This cradle was purchased as an antique. I would like to know if you can tell me its approximate age and probable origin.

R.P. — Mamaroneck, N.Y.

It is an American hooded cradle and might date as early as 1760 or as late as 1820. If it is made of maple or some other soft wood, it was probably the work of a country cabinetmaker. It appears to be a New England piece.

BENTWOOD CRADLE

I would like to know more about this old cradle, which has circular ends made of bent pieces of wood.

D.H. — New Berlin, Wis.

AMERICAN

This type of late-nineteenth-century American cradle was created in a period when there was widespread interest in bentwood furniture, spawned by the work of Michael Thonet of bent-beechwood fame.

THONET CRADLE

Do you know who made my son's cradle? I would also like to know when it was made and if it is rare.

C. McI. — *Jackson, Miss.*

Your charming bentwood swing cradle was almost certainly made in the Vienna factory of Michael Thonet (1796–1871), who in 1856 perfected a process for steaming and bending solid lengths of beechwood to form long, curved rods. Your cradle was probably made in the 1890s. Models of this type are indeed scarce.

VICTORIAN ROCKING CRADLE

We are most interested in finding out about this cradle, which my husband bought locally. I've looked in several antique and furniture books to try to learn the name. Someone told us that it is a "Jenny Lind" cradle. Is this true?

D.C.McG. — *Schenevus, N.Y.*

Spool furniture, which is a popular kind of country furniture, was made at the beginning of the nineteenth century in small shops and turned on a lathe. Later it was mass produced in factories. Many pieces of spool-turned furniture were named for Jenny Lind, because the Swedish singer toured America when furniture of this kind was widely popular. The Jenny Lind spool-turned cradle and bed, dating about 1850–75, featured rounded corners on the headboard and footboard, such as are found on your cradle.

JENNY LIND CRADLE

Enclosed is a photograph of our black walnut cradle. Do you know to what period it belongs?
W.D.M. — *Wooster, Ohio*

Your American spool-turned cradle with rounded corners is popularly called a Jenny Lind cradle. It probably dates around the 1860s.

AMERICAN SPINDLE CRADLE

What information can you give me about my antique cradle?
P.B. — *Aurora, Ill.*

The turning of the spindles, the netting support and the over-all design indicate that your cradle is American Victorian, made between 1860 and 1870.

AMERICAN CRADLE

We are restoring this cradle and want to know if it ever had a canopy. It used to have a foot pedal to rock it with, but this unfortunately was discarded.
R.R. — *Camillus, N.Y.*

We doubt that American Victorian cradles like yours ever had canopies. They date about 1865–1875; some of them did have iron rocking pedals.

AMERICAN

CARRIAGE CRIB

I would very much appreciate any information you can give me as to the age and origin of this cradle.

W.F.W.—Carlisle, Pa.

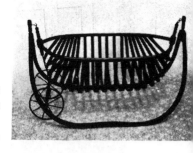

The Marietta Chair Company, Marietta, Ohio, made your cradle about 1880–1890. Their catalogue called it a "Chicago carriage crib."

CHIPPENDALE CORNER CUPBOÅRD

I would appreciate information regarding this corner cupboard. It is either applewood or pine, is in two sections, and has brass hinges.

A.M.S.—Lexington, Ky.

Judging from the snapshot and information in your letter, your Chippendale style corner cupboard was probably made about 1760–1775 by a cabinetmaker working in or near Philadelphia. The broken S-scrolled pediment terminating in rosettes and the ogee bracket feet are marked features of the Chippendale style.

AMERICAN CHINA CUPBOARD

My cherry cupboard is very old, with the original glass, which looks handblown. Could you perhaps tell its approximate age?

D.M.L.—Louisville, Ky.

Your two-part cupboard showing classical influence was probably made by a New England regional cabinetmaker around 1800–1820. The glazed upper section could have been used for books or china. We favor the latter possibility.

AMERICAN DRESSER

This piece of furniture is either walnut or cherry, with holes in the edge of the top two shelves for spoons. It came from a plantation house in South Carolina. Can you tell its age and origin?
                                 R.N.S.—Charleston, S.C.

Your dresser with a recessed superstructure of open shelves was made by an American regional cabinetmaker around 1780–1820. This type of dresser appears to have been in common use throughout Europe in the eighteenth century (and in some cases earlier) and always possesses a singular provincial charm.

VICTORIAN ÉTAGÈRE

My rosewood étagère has been in our family for over 100 years. I am anxious to know something of its origin and period.
                                 W.E.P.—Birmingham, Ala.

Your étagère is in the Victorian Renaissance style dating around 1860–1875 and is American in origin. The Victorian love for bric-a-brac made the étagère an almost indispensable piece of parlor furniture.

AMERICAN WHATNOT

The lady I bought this piece from said it belonged to her grandmother and was at least 100 years old. Could you estimate its age?
                                 R.C.S.—Warren, Mich.

AMERICAN

It is an American corner whatnot, or étagère, of the Victorian period, made by some furniture factory around 1855–1870. Such pieces were generally of black walnut, occasionally of mahogany.

FIRE-SCREEN DESK

We saw a desk similar to this one—which has been in our family for seventy years—at Williamsburg, and were told it was a soldier's field desk. When and where was it made?
H.S.R.—Washington, D.C.

This kind of fire screen provided with a shelf that could be let down to receive a cup of tea, an inkwell or needlework bag was introduced in France around the mid-eighteenth century. Your interesting example is American in origin, dating around 1840–1860.

CAST-IRON FOOTSTOOL

Dealers don't seem to know the age or origin of our iron footstool, which I have sketched. Can you help?
J.O.—Webster Groves, Mo.

A number of iron foundries made such furniture around the late 1860s and 1870s for use in both house and garden. Your stool is American in origin.

SHERATON STYLE MIRROR

Can you tell me anything about my mirror, which has fifteen balls around the top and painted decorations?

E.M.A.—Macon, Ga.

Your overmantel mirror, decorated with an *églomisé* panel, is in the Sheraton style. It is of English or American origin, made probably between 1810 and 1820. The French term *églomisé* is given to a decorative method for ornamenting glass by drawing and painting on the underside and backing the ornamentation with metal foil, generally gold or silver leaf. The word is derived from Jean Glomi (d. 1786), French designer and framer, who is usually given credit for inventing the method.

AMERICAN EMPIRE MIRROR

A friend gave me this mirror in 1953, saying that her father had acquired it from someone in Connecticut many years before that. There is a primitive painting at the top, and the dark wood looks hand carved. The mirror is clouded with age. When I received it the back was covered with overlapping shingles held by small handmade nails. Can you estimate its age?

A.E.S.—Concordia, Kans.

Your wall mirror is in the American Empire style, dating around 1820–1840. Interesting design elements are the cornice and columns that usually appeared on the earlier Sheraton style wall mirrors, giving the frames an architectural appearance. The columns on your mirror, however, are larger than those generally found on Sheraton designs, and the delicate reeding of the earlier mirrors has been supplanted by carved leaves and rings.

AMERICAN TOILET MIRROR

Can you approximate the age of this shaving stand? What type of drawer pulls did it have originally?

T.H. — *Powhatan, Va.*

You have an American Sheraton toilet mirror, dating about 1800–1815. The original knobs were small, mushroom-turned, of either mahogany or ivory. The always popular swinging toilet mirror mounted on a box stand, the mirror being supported on uprights by swivel screws, was introduced in England around 1700. This type of mirror was intended to stand on the top of a dressing table or chest of drawers. Cosmetics were placed in the row of small drawers in the box stand.

WESTERN PIE SAFE

This pie safe has been in our family for at least seventy-five years. The cabinetmaker who restored it said he had never seen an inlay like the tin front of the safe. Can you tell us anything about it?

L.L.McO. — *Cincinnati, Ohio*

Your pie safe, also known as a kitchen safe, seems to be of mid-nineteenth-century design. The pierced tin doors are typical of the safes made in western and midwestern United States. These country pie safes are valued chiefly for the skill shown in piercing the tin. Yours may originally have had porcelain knobs.

AMERICAN HEPPLEWHITE SETTEE

Could you please give me any information regarding this love seat that I recently acquired? I believe the inlaid frame is mahogany. Is the curved seat unusual?

E.C.L. — Rochester, N.Y.

We consider that your bow-front small settee is American of the Hepplewhite period, around 1790–1800. Its inlaid mahogany frame with pendant bell flowers indicates it may well have been made by one of the Baltimore cabinetmakers. You apparently have a fine antique.

AMERICAN LYRE-FORM SOFA

What can you tell me of the origin of this sofa, similar to some I have seen pictured? Carved acanthus leaves edge the entire back, and the legs are carved dolphins. The wood is walnut, with its original finish.

E.C.N. — Gaston, Ind.

Your American lyre-form sofa, influenced by the French Directoire style, was made by a very skillful cabinetmaker around 1815–1820. Sofas similar to yours, but without a full back, were sometimes known as "Grecian" sofas. However, your sofa is, no doubt, a variation of a Grecian sofa, with a longer back to lean against.

AMERICAN

AMERICAN TRANSITIONAL SOFA

Could you tell us the style and age of this couch?
We think it was made around 1860.
L.T.H. — Belmont, Mass.

Your sofa is transitional, marking the change in style from the late American Empire to the early Victorian. As such, it dates between 1840 and 1850, and may be regarded as early Victorian Classical. It is interesting because the type is far from common.

AMERICAN EMPIRE SOFA

I inherited this sofa from relatives who had inherited it from their father, born in 1766. It has a brass inlay in the rosewood back strip. When the sofa was first restored we found the claw feet had a Chinese stain. Can you possibly tell me more about the piece and determine its date?
J.B.L. — Pasadena, Cal.

Your sofa, designed in the Grecian manner, is in the American Empire style, dating around the 1820s. With its graceful lines and bold carving, it represents the finest quality of workmanship of that era. The sofa was probably made by a New York cabinetmaker.

NEW ORLEANS FURNITURE

I would appreciate information regarding my lovely old armchair and love seat that came from New Orleans. There is also a small side chair belonging to the group.

H.B. — Danville, Ind.

Your armchair and love seat are typical of the work of French-trained cabinetmakers who made this kind of furniture in New Orleans between 1840 and 1860. The design follows that of the Louis-Philippe period.

REVIVED-ROCOCO SOFA

I bought this sofa some time ago, and I would like to know its style, age and origin.

B.H. — Odessa, Tex.

Your sofa is in the Rococo Revival, or Victorian Louis XV, style. It is an American piece and was probably made around 1860. This sofa with a triple-crested back was an innovative furniture form dating from the mid-nineteenth century.

VICTORIAN TRIPLE-BACK SOFA

Could you possibly tell the approximate age of this sofa? It came to me from a family who had owned it for many years. The frame is walnut.

G.F.S. — Camptown, Pa.

AMERICAN

You have an American triple-back sofa in the Victorian Louis XV style. This one was probably made by a fine eastern furniture factory and dates around the early 1860s.

VICTORIAN PARLOR SET

What information can you give me on the period and style of my antique sofa and chairs? Could you also tell me when and where they were made?
S.H.—Dayton, Ohio

Your triple serpentine-arched sofa with carved crestings and matching arm and side chair are in the Victorian Louis XV style. They are American in origin and were probably made around the 1850s. Unless such a set bears the maker's label it is impossible to identify.

DOUBLE CHAIR-BACK SETTEE

I recently inherited this sofa. My grandfather bought it at an auction in New York City approximately 100 years ago. Can you give me an idea of its date and style?
M.C.C.—Boonton, N.J.

Your interesting double chair-back settee is in the Victorian Louis XV style and was made in America about 1855–1865.

KELLOGG LOVE SEAT

The decoration on my love seat is a woman's head, with "C. L. Kellogg" printed below. Did she own it?

V.H. — *Rosenberg, Tex.*

Clara Louise Kellogg (1842–1915) was the first American-trained opera star. Your love seat dates between 1865 and 1875, when many manufacturers used her likeness because of her popularity.

VICTORIAN RENAISSANCE SOFA

This sofa has been in the family of the man who sold it to me for 300 years. The frame is rosewood, the face on the arms is that of Queen Elizabeth I. Can you tell me anything more about the sofa?

E.W.B. — *Little Rock, Ark.*

The man who sold you the sofa was evidently misled as to its age. It is in the American Victorian Renaissance style and was probably made around 1850–1870. You have a fine example of the best furniture of that time. The principal source of inspiration for its design was the French Louis XVI style of the eighteenth century. A guest room in Washington's Blair House, the President's guesthouse, has just been refurnished in the American Victorian Renaissance style (see *House & Garden,* January 1968).

EASTLAKE SETTEE

My love seat is handcarved walnut and has four matching chairs. Any information about it will be appreciated.

D.D.S. — *Plano, Tex.*

Your upholstered parlor settee with its turned and tapering front legs is in the so-called Eastlake style, which was widely popular in the U.S. in the 1870s. Charles Lock Eastlake's book *Hints of Household Taste,* published in England in 1868, was responsible for the demand for this type of furniture.

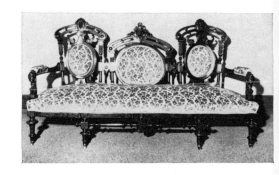

VICTORIAN SETTEE

What is the style and age of this settee? It has five carved faces of women — each of them with a different expression — in the walnut framework.

E.R. — *Hartford, Ky.*

Your unusual chair-back settee is in the nineteenth-century revived Renaissance style popular from about 1850 onward. Your settee appears to have the look of the Rutherford B. Hayes era, 1877–1881.

AMERICAN SHERATON BOW-FRONT SIDEBOARD

*I would appreciate your opinion of the approxi-
mate age of this buffet, which my family has
owned since about 1920. Our understanding is
that it was made in Danvers, Massachusetts, between 1800 and 1840. I do not believe the brass
pulls are original.*

S.H.V.D. — Louisville, Ky.

Your Sheraton sideboard is an excellent example of American cabinetwork, probably dating around 1800–1820. The four slender columns
placed at the angles of the sideboard and extending the entire height
are one of Sheraton's favorite devices, and one of the chief differences
between Sheraton and Hepplewhite, who never used projecting columns.

SHERATON DEEP-END SIDEBOARD

*My sideboard once belonged to my great-grand-
mother in Annapolis, Maryland. I wish to know
if it is a Sheraton piece. Do you think it came from
England?*

W.D.H. — Fayetteville, N.C.

Your sideboard is in the late Sheraton style and was made in America
around the first quarter of the nineteenth century. In this type of sideboard the cupboards on each end are deeper than those in the earlier
examples. For this reason it is often given the descriptive name "deep-
end" sideboard by American experts.

GUSTAV HERTER SIDEBOARD

*We inherited this sideboard from my husband's
family. It is oak except for ornamental veneers on
the doors and drawers. The base has a brownish-
coral marble top. "G. Herter, New York, New
York" appears on a label on the back. What more
can you tell us about this piece?*

G.D.M. — Memphis, Tenn.

AMERICAN

Your carved sideboard in the Victorian Renaissance style was made around 1860–1870 by Gustav Herter, whose cabinetwork was represented at the Crystal Palace World's Fair exposition in New York in 1853. It was shortly after 1850 that sideboards such as yours began to be designed with rounded ends, a high back, and a base resting directly on the floor.

AMERICAN EMPIRE SIDEBOARD

A friend left me this mahogany sideboard. The knobs are pressed glass—very intricate—with brass screws through them. It is in original condition. Is it a valuable piece?

E.H.T.—Elkins, W.Va.

You have a fine example of an American Empire style sideboard, probably dating about 1815–1825. The knobs are like those made by the Boston and Sandwich Glass Company. The overhanging top drawers supported by columns are a feature of the Empire style.

VICTORIAN PEDESTAL SIDEBOARD

Could you give me any information about this buffet, which has been in our family for many years?

A.O.L.—Newton, N.J.

Your American early Victorian sideboard with a projecting center flanked by pedestals probably dates around the 1840s. The shaped backboard protects china or silverware that may be leaned against it. The pedestal sideboard was popular in England in the early years of the nineteenth century; Sheraton gave a design for one in his *Cabinet-Makers and Upholsterer's Drawing Book,* published in four parts between 1791 and 1794.

EASTLAKE SIDEBOARD

What is the period and age of this refinished side-board? The wood is very light walnut; the glass doors are red-plush lined.

J.O'G. — Santa Monica, Cal

This is a Victorian sideboard in the Eastlake style, dating about 1870-1880. It was probably made to order rather than factory-produced.

AMERICAN SHERATON CARD TABLE

This table was made for a Bath, Maine, family many years ago. Can you tell me anything about it?

K.L.S. — Newport, R.I

Your folding-top card table with outset rounded corners is in the American later Sheraton style, 1815–1830. In fact, this type of leg, carved in a heavy spiral form, is a feature of the American Empire style. But the outset rounded corners are a marked feature of the Sheraton style.

AMERICAN DROP-LEAF BREAKFAST TABLE

This table belonged to a woman who would now be ninety-five. She claimed that it was her grandmother's. Can you identify it further?

J.K.VW. — Allendale, N.J.

AMERICAN

Your drop-leaf breakfast table with rope-turned legs is in the American Empire style and was made around 1830.

HEPPLEWHITE CARD TABLE

I just purchased this table at an estate auction and should like to know its age and type.
P.H.P. — Forty Fort, Pa.

You have a folding-top Hepplewhite card table, dating about 1785–1800. It was probably made by a cabinetmaker working in New England, possibly in Salem, Massachusetts. Square tapering legs are especially identified with the Hepplewhite style.

BUTTERFLY TABLE

What can you tell me about my butterfly table? We think that it is very old.
D.M.Z. — Chicago, Ill.

Yes, your butterfly table appears to be an antique, and was probably made in New England in the early eighteenth century. It was given its modern name from the supposed resemblance of the wood brackets that hold up the leaves to the wings of a butterfly. The butterfly table is in fact an early form of drop-leaf table.

"LOUIS XIV" CENTER TABLE

When my mother bought this table—about thirty years ago—it had a green felt top. Is it possibly a game table, and can you date it?
P.McK.—San Antonio, Tex.

Your kind of table was generally placed in the center of the Victorian parlor and as a rule had a marble top. (The green felt was probably put on at some later time.) Its chief purpose was to be decorative. It is in the style the Victorians loved to call "Louis XIV" and is probably of American manufacture, dating around the 1860s.

AMERICAN CONSOLE TABLE AND MIRROR

We have just acquired this handcarved antique table with mirror. The mermaids are about 3 feet tall, the mirror nearly 5 feet, and all in beautiful condition. Any information on its age and origin will be appreciated.
E.C.McC.—Springfield, Mo.

Your console table with carved caryatid supports is probably American of the Directoire period, 1810–1820. The mirror seems of the same period.

EMPIRE CONSOLE TABLE

My mahogany console table is 37 inches high and 51 inches wide. I believe the dolphins that anchor the top are handcarved; they are in two sections

held together by wooden dowels. Is it possible to tell me the style of the piece and when and where it was made?

M.M.M.—Dallas, Tex.

Your console table is in the American Empire style, dating about 1815–1825, and is the work of a talented cabinetmaker. Did you ever think about filling in the entire back under the tabletop with a looking glass?

VICTORIAN CONSOLE TABLE

In our home this table was in the reception hall, but I use it as a dressing table. It is made of mahogany. Is there any significance to the mirror beneath the tabletop? I would appreciate anything you can tell me about it.

A.C.M.—Evanston, Ill.

Your console table is in the Victorian Classical style, dating from the 1840s and manufactured in America. In the late eighteenth and early nineteenth centuries the console table was sometimes provided with a looking glass under the tabletop at the rear of the table, extending its entire length. Sheraton, commenting on this practice, notes that the glass, by reflection, makes the table appear double.

CHIPPENDALE RECTANGULAR DINING TABLE

What can you tell me about my drop-leaf dining table?

K.S.B.—Moscow, Idaho

Your dining table with square flaps supported on swing-out cabriole legs is in the Chippendale style and was made in America around 1755–1775. Originally it may have been one of a pair that could be placed together when required.

LATE SHERATON COUNTRY TABLE

I have never seen a tavern table without stretch-
ers and wonder if this one might be a rare type.
It is maple, has wooden pegs instead of nails, and
the bottom of the drawers are chamfered.
                              C.M. — Albemarle, N.C.

Your stretcherless table with round tapering legs in the late Sheraton style is unusual, but it appears to be the work of a rural cabinetmaker, and country pieces often did not follow any set pattern. Your table was probably made around 1820–1830.

QUEEN ANNE OVAL DINING TABLE

I recently bought this table with two semicircular
flaps at auction. It was described as a dining table.
How did they manage a large dinner party?
                              I.F. — Fort Lee, N.J.

In England, rooms set apart for dining came into general use among the upper classes late in the seventeenth century. It became the fashion to serve meals at several small tables, varying in number from about three to eight. However, there were few tables in the Queen Anne and Chippendale styles identified as dining tables exclusively. During this period in America all tables appearing to be dining tables have drop leaves, such as your Queen Anne style table, dating about 1750.

AMERICAN SHERATON DINING TABLE

Our old banquet table has been in our family for some time. Made of cherry, with bird's-eye maple insets, it has three sections and opens to 10 feet. Any information about it will be appreciated. Is it unusual?

R.L.S. — Arcadia, Cal.

Complete three-part tables like yours are rare. It is a fine example of the American later Sheraton period and dates between 1815 and 1825.

SHERATON DROP-LEAF TABLE

My family believes this old table to be genuine Sheraton. Is it? The outside edges of the leaves have indentations as though for attaching other leaves.

G.C.W. — Oak Park, Ga.

Yes, your American drop-leaf table is of Sheraton design, dating about 1815–1825. The indentations strongly indicate that it was originally the center section of a three-part dining table.

AMERICAN EMPIRE DINING TABLE

What is the period and approximate date of my pair of mahogany banquet tables? I wonder if you could also tell me where they might have been made?

R.N.B.—*Oshkosh, Wis.*

Two-part dining tables, each having a drop leaf, similar in principle to your example, were in general use from the Hepplewhite period—late eighteenth century—up to the early years of the Victorian era. Your two-part table is in the American Empire style, dating about 1820–1830, and was probably made by a skilled rural cabinetmaker working along the east coast.

VICTORIAN DRESSING TABLE

Could you give me any information about this dresser that I inherited?

M.D.A.—*Needham, Mass.*

This is a handsome Victorian piece in the revived Renaissance style and was made by one of the better American furniture factories somewhere between 1860 and 1875. It was, no doubt, part of a set of bedroom furniture.

VICTORIAN DRESSING TABLE

I would like your opinion on the age and origin of this dressing table.

R.L.W.—*Little Rock, Ark.*

Your ornately carved Victorian dressing table with scrolled supports was made in America, probably around 1850–1870. The decorative device centered in the stretcher is supposed to represent a shepherdess's wicker basket—a pastoral motif occasionally used by eighteenth-century cabinetmakers working in the French Louis XVI style.

HEPPLEWHITE DROP-LEAF TABLE

I bought this inlaid mahogany table years ago from my great-aunt, who was an antique dealer. She said it was an original Virginia antique. Could you verify this?

D.H.M.—*Newburgh, N.Y.*

It is a Hepplewhite drop-leaf table dating about 1790–1800. The inlay on the tapering legs indicates it was made in Baltimore.

GATELEG TABLE

What is the true age of this walnut table? My great-grandfather, in a notebook dated 1844, stated that it had been in the family for almost 200 years.

O.F.H. — San José, Cal.

This is a New England gateleg table dating 1700–1725. The gateleg table, which is a variety of drop-leaf table, was popular in America from about 1650 to 1725, when it was to a great extent supplanted by drop-leaf tables, in which the leaves are supported by swing-out legs without the gate feature. A large gateleg table was generally used as a dining table.

SHERATON DROP-LEAF LIBRARY TABLE

Is this a Duncan Phyfe table? It is of Santa Domingo mahogany, with hand carved claw feet, and was brought here ninety years ago.

E.R. — Indianapolis, Ind.

Your table is not really in the Duncan Phyfe manner. This variety of drop-leaf table is often called a library table and was made chiefly in the later Sheraton period and style, after 1800, and continued to be made in the early part of the Empire period. Your pedestal table with four concave legs terminating in brass paw feet and casters is in the late Sheraton style, dating around 1810–1820.

REVIVED RENAISSANCE OCCASIONAL TABLE

Can you identify my table? Is it an antique or just an old table?

M.D.J. — Ft. Mitchell, Ky.

To be officially considered an antique, an article must be at least 100 years old. Your center table in two tones of walnut with marble top is typical of the popular version of the revived Renaissance style. It probably dates around the 1870s.

LATE SHERATON LIBRARY TABLE

My great-grandfather bought this table in the early nineteenth century from a family on their way west from Maryland. The center section is solid mahogany, with handmade brass screws. Can you identify it further?

F.E.S. — Leawood, Kans.

Your pedestal drop-leaf table with its splayed quadruped base ending in brass paw feet and casters is in the late Sheraton style. It was made in America sometime between 1810 and 1830.

AMERICAN SERVING TABLE

Anything you can tell me about my small cherry sideboard with acanthus-carved skirt and legs will be appreciated.

W.S.C. — *Valparaiso, Ind.*

Your serving table, a kind of side table, has features of the Sheraton style and was probably made in America around the 1820s. Side tables, in distinction to center tables, are intended to be placed against a wall, and therefore the back surface is left unfinished.

SHERATON STYLE SEWING TABLE

I would appreciate any information you can furnish as to the age, origin, and style of this cherry sewing stand that originally belonged to my great-great-grandmother.

I.W. — *Durham, N.C.*

Late Sheraton is the style of your sewing table mounted on a turned pedestal with four splayed supports. The table was made in America, probably around 1810–1830. Though some sewing tables were made in the Hepplewhite style, by far the great majority were made in the Sheraton and Empire styles.

ANTIQUE MINIATURE

Is this little mahogany table an antique? It has been in my husband's family for years.

G.F.G. — *Philadelphia, Pa.*

You have an antique miniature sewing table of the American Empire period, dating about 1825–1835.

DUNCAN PHYFE SEWING TABLE

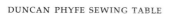

Is my sewing table, which my mother bought at auction, Duncan Phyfe, and would a label make it authentic?

P.McC. — *New York, N.Y.*

Your handsome sewing or worktable with lyre support is in the Duncan Phyfe manner, and was made in New York City probably around 1820. The presence of a label is frequently regarded as positive proof of the genuineness of an article, but care should be taken not to rely entirely upon a label. Your sewing table belongs to the so-called Martha Washington variety, because the upper portion has certain distinctive features. It is oval in form with a hinged top, and is in three sections, a center section with drawers flanked by semicircular bins.

TEA TABLE WITH BIRD-CAGE DEVICE

Could you tell me the approximate age of my bird-cage table? And what do you call that type of foot?

A.F. — Salem, Mass.

Your tilt-top tea table of tripod form is in the American Chippendale style, dating around 1760–1770. The cabriole legs terminate in snake feet. The bird-cage device surmounting the pedestal permits the top to revolve and tilt.

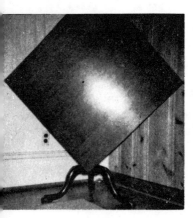

CHIPPENDALE TRIPOD TEA TABLE

Can you tell me where my cherry tilt-top table was made?

L.F. — Norwalk, Conn.

The design of your tripod tea table suggests that it was made in New England about 1770–1780. It is impossible to tell from your snapshot, however, whether the table actually dates from the eighteenth century or is a fine twentieth-century reproduction of a table in the Chippendale style.

EMPIRE TILT-TOP TEA TABLE

What can you tell me about my grandmother's mahogany table, which was a wedding present in 1850 and was said to have come originally from England? It has carved acanthus leaves on the base of the pedestal.

H.M.B. — Bala-Cynwyd, Pa.

Your tilt-top tea table supported on a turned pedestal with quadruped base is in the late Empire style. The details of the design indicate it was made in America and probably dates between 1840 and 1850.

CHIPPENDALE TILT-TOP TEA TABLE

My mother purchased this table in 1922 in Brooklyn from two elderly ladies who said it belonged to their grandfather. We believe it to be very old. What do you think?

M.C. — Manchester, Vt.

Your Chippendale style, tripod piecrust table with a tilt top may be of New York or Southern origin. If so, it was probably made around 1765–1780. Since it is not possible to identify it definitely from your snapshot, we would suggest you consult an expert on American antiques. Larger tea tables were often made to tilt so they could be placed against the wall when not in use.

VICTORIAN WASHSTAND

Under the marble top of this cabinet is written "Rothschild, made to order." What style is this piece?

E.P. — Lorain, Ohio

Your special-order washstand is in the American Victorian Renaissance style, dating about 1865–1875. The marble top and marble splash rail suggest that it was more than an ordinary washstand.

PORTABLE DESK

I believe this old box to be an antique lap desk. Can you give its age and original use?

H.J. — Decatur, Ala.

This is an American or English small portable desk dating about 1800–1830. The user opened the box and wrote with a quill pen on the slanting velvet panels. Small portable desks were in use throughout the Middle Ages, and they were often extremely elaborate. They retained a measure of popularity throughout the eighteenth century, but they gradually lost their decorative quality, the majority being made of plain mahogany.

NEW ENGLAND SLANT-FRONT DESK

When I got this maple desk fifty years ago it was painted black. It has handmade nails and dowels. Can you tell me about it?

N.M.H.—Elkins Park, Pa.

Your slant-front desk mounted on straight bracket feet is in the Hepplewhite style. I would say it was made in New England around 1780–1790. The oval brasses may be replacements of the originals.

CHIPPENDALE SLANT-FRONT DESK

I recently inherited this desk. Can you tell from the photograph what style it is in and where it was made? We think it is made of birch.

S.N.—Washington, N.C.

Your slant-front desk is in the Chippendale style and was made in one of the New England states around 1755–1785. Your kind of desk is the most usual type of desk and is in reality a chest of drawers with a writing section above. It could be of birch, as this wood was used for entire pieces of various kinds of furniture.

HEPPLEWHITE SLANT-FRONT DESK

Could you kindly tell me about how old this desk is? It has been in my husband's family for a number of years. It was originally made without nails — all the joints are dovetailed or pegged.

G.B. — Pluckemin, N.J.

Your slant-front mahogany desk is American Hepplewhite, dating between 1785 and 1810. Lion's-head-and-ring drawer pulls, if original, indicate the latter date. The bracket feet must have once been 4 to 6 inches high; they appear to have been cut off. You should have a skilled cabinetmaker repair them.

PSEUDO-GOVERNOR WINTHROP DESK

What are the essential characteristics of a Winthrop secretary? Here are photocopies of two different desks, both, I think, in this style.

F.J.C. — San Juan, P.R.

Essentially, there is no such thing as a Governor Winthrop desk, because those we call by that name were made long after the two governors Winthrop died (John Winthrop, 1588–1649, Massachusetts; John Winthrop, 1607–1676, Connecticut). The lower portion in your two illustrations corresponds to what we like to call a Governor Winthrop desk, which is always designed in the Chippendale style, in fashion around 1750–1780. The so-called Governor Winthrop desk, however, never has an upper section with either glass or wood-paneled doors, as in your examples.

AMERICAN

VICTORIAN SLANT-FRONT SECRETARY-BOOKCASE

Enclosed is a picture of a secretary that has been in our family for seventy-five years. What is its style and how old do you think it might be?
B.C.R. — Waukesha, Wis.

The design of your slant-front secretary marks the style transition between American Empire and Victorian. Its leaf-carved drawer pulls and use of rippled molding are characteristic of pieces made by our early furniture factories from 1840 to 1860. This popular variety of writing furniture, designed in two sections, was introduced into England from the Continent late in the seventeenth century. The upper section was placed in the narrow shelf at the top of the slant-front desk. In a word, the secretary was born.

AMERICAN HEPPLEWHITE SECRETARY

This highboy belongs to a friend of mine. It is 8 feet tall, and was bought in 1936 at a New York gallery. The piece had been restored, and my friend is under the impression that it is Early American. Is there a possibility that it was made in England?
H.H. — Lafayette, Cal.

Your friend's secretary with fall-front writing drawer and valanced base curving into French bracket feet is in the American Hepplewhite style and was made around 1790–1800, probably in Baltimore. The oval panels and inlaid decoration are typical of Baltimore cabinetwork of that period. It represents the highest quality of American craftsmanship.

MASSACHUSETTS SECRETARY-BOOKCASE

Will you please tell me anything you can from this photograph of my cabinet?

M.C. — Rome, Ga.

Your secretary-bookcase with a fall-front writing drawer is in the Hepplewhite style, and typical of those made in Massachusetts around 1790. To be absolutely certain, however, you should have it examined by an expert, because it is difficult to make exact identification from your photograph.

AMERICAN SECRETARY

Could you tell me the style and approximate age of this desk? The bookshelf is not fastened to the desk part.

P.V.L. — Gadsden, Ala.

Your mahogany secretary having a large overhanging top drawer that pulls out and lets down, serving as a desk, is in the American Empire style, dating around 1825–1830. The bookcase upper section was probably added at a later time. However, the many panes of glass, mostly diamond-shaped, often occur in this style of Empire secretary. Properly, it should have a straight molded cornice.

AMERICAN SECRETARY-BOOKCASE

We know our solid mahogany secretary is at least seventy-five years old — do you think it might be older? It is in two sections but has no identifying marks.

L.L.B. — Fort Worth, Tex.

AMERICAN

Your secretary-bookcase with a hinged folding lid, which may be opened to form a writing surface supported by two pulls, appears to be in the American late Empire style, dating from around the 1830s. This type of secretary, with a folding writing flap, belongs to a characteristic class of writing furniture.

AMERICAN EMPIRE SECRETARY

This desk, probably made in Philadelphia around 1815–1820, is on view at Decatur House, Washington, D.C. When was this kind of writing furniture first introduced?

V.H. — New York, N.Y.

This type of tall secretary with a drop front was introduced about the middle of the eighteenth century in France. The great French *ébénistes* expended their talents in decorating the ample surface of these desks, which were always luxury pieces. One of the most celebrated is the secretary by J.-H. Riesener, dated 1790, made for Marie Antoinette's use at the Château de Saint-Cloud and now part of the Frick Collection in New York.

EMPIRE SECRETARY WITH A DROP FRONT

Can you tell me anything about this piece of furniture that I inherited? It has a marble top and looks old.

M.N.B. — Nyack, N.Y.

Your drop-front secretary is in the American French Empire style, dating about 1815–1825. This class of writing furniture, which was fashionable in France from about 1750 to 1850, was relatively rare in America, no doubt because we mainly followed English styles. However, for some years after the War of 1812 — from about 1815 to 1830 — French influence was more pronounced.

ROLL-TOP DESK

Our walnut roll-top desk appears to be handmade. Any information concerning its origin would be appreciated.

W.E.D. — Redding, Cal.

Your Victorian Renaissance style roll-top desk was made in America around 1865–1875. This kind of writing furniture with a roll top was introduced in France around the mid-eighteenth century. Probably the most beautiful piece of furniture in the world is the roll-top desk made for Louis XV, known as Le Bureau du Roi Louis XV. This masterpiece was begun in 1760 and completed in 1769, and is now in the Louvre.

VICTORIAN SECRETARY

We would like to know the age of this carved writing cabinet. On the back of one of the small drawers we found this tag: "Thomas Godey (Successor to John Needles), Manufacturer of cabinet furniture, No. 54 Hanover St., Baltimore, Md. Hair, Husk Mattresses."

A.L. — Wilmington, Del.

I would judge that your American Victorian drop-front secretary was made to order in the mid-1800s. The cabinetwork of John Needles (1786–1878), who was working in Baltimore from around 1812 to 1853, was highly esteemed. So it seems reasonable that his successor was also a talented cabinetmaker. Your drop-front secretary showing classical influence probably dates from around the late 1850s or 1860s.

SCHOOLMASTER'S DESK

The father of the former owners of this desk brought it to Arkansas eighty years ago. It is made of walnut, oak and maple, with cast-iron legs. What else can you tell me about it?

R.D.S.—Marianna, Ark.

This is an American schoolmaster's desk with X-shaped cast-iron supports. It was factory made and dates around 1860–1875.

WOOTEN DESK

This desk has been in our family for many years. The flap on the slot on the left is marked "Letters," on the right, "Wooten Desk Manf. Co., Indianapolis, Ind. W. S. Wooten's Patent, October 4, 1874." We will appreciate any additional information you can give us.

J.E.T.—Van Buren, Ind.

The Wooten Company, listed in the Indianapolis directory from 1872 to 1884, made a patented design conceived as a complete office-in-a-desk. Several of these pieces of furniture belonged to prominent people, including Spencer F. Baird, Secretary of the Smithsonian Institution, where his desk is still being used; President Grant, whose desk is now on loan to the Smithsonian; and John D. Rockefeller.

FURNITURE
Continental

BAROQUE BENCH

I picked up this old handcarved hall bench, which was covered with black paint and dilapidated, and restored it. I think it's so ugly it's almost beautiful. How old might it be, and who made it?

D.R. — Aiken, S.C.

Your ornately carved bench, enriched with C-scrolls and other familiar baroque ingredients such as shells and masks, vividly illustrates the Victorian version of the late-seventeenth-century Louis XIV style. It is most likely of German or Austrian origin, probably dating about the third quarter of the nineteenth century.

LOUIS XV STYLE ARMCHAIR

Is my chair in the French Louis XV style? Does the shape of the back have a special name?
                                        J.S. — San José, Cal.

Yes, your upholstered armchair with a cartouche-shaped back and carved wood frame is a fine example of the French Louis XV style, dating around 1740–1750. You can easily recognize the style of your chair by the curving character of all its lines, and especially by its cabriole legs, which were always used. Chairs such as yours were the chief inspiration for the Victorian Louis XV, or revived Louis XV, style chairs.

DRESSING CHAIR

I bought this French Louis XV style dressing-table chair at auction. Were they always caned?
                                        R.V.T. — Miami, Fla.

Yes, this charming and distinctive type of specialized chair intended for use at the dressing table is always caned, as powder would have soon ruined the upholstery. Properly, the loose seat cushion was covered with leather, red and yellow being especially favored. This form of chair is also the typical chair for the writing table, but when it was used for this purpose, instead of being caned it was generally upholstered in leather to make it more durable and perhaps more comfortable.

FRENCH PROVINCIAL SIDE CHAIR

Can you enlighten me as to the age and origin of this chair, which appears to be handcarved? It has been ours for years, but I believe it is of European origin.

W.H.B.—Montclair, N.J.

Your early-nineteenth-century side chair with a lyre-shaped splat shows the influence of the French Directoire style. It appears to be the work of a French provincial chairmaker.

CONVERSATION CHAIR

I recently inherited this French chair from an aunt living in Europe. Does it have a special use?

M.P.T.—Olympia, Wash.

This type of upholstered chair in which the occupant places himself with his back to the front and rests his arms on the padded crest rail became fashionable in France in Louis XV's time. Sheraton refers to this kind of chair in his *Cabinet Dictionary* (1803), in which he writes: "The manner of conversing amongst some of the highest circles of company, on some occasions, is copied from the French, by lounging upon a chair. Hence we have the term conversation chair, which is peculiarly adapted for this kind of idle position." He illustrates a design for one of these chairs and notes that "they are made extraordinary long between back and front, for the purpose of space for the fashionable posture." According to French furniture literature, the chair was particularly used by persons watching card games and games of chance. Your conversation chair is in the Louis XV style.

CONTINENTAL

MEDALLION-BACK CHAIR

Was this type of back much used for Louis XVI style chairs? Are the legs typical?
I.B. — Los Angeles, Cal.

In a general sense Louis XVI style chairs can be divided into two main classes: namely, those with oval medallion backs, and those with rectangular backs; the latter appear in a number of forms. The oval-back chair, when its members are in complete harmony and its back a true oval, was admirable for its refined and graceful elegance. The proportions of your chair are pleasing. A straight tapering leg is typical of the Louis XVI style. It may be turned round, as in your chair, or square in section.

FRENCH DIRECTOIRE STYLE CHAIR

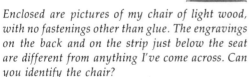

Enclosed are pictures of my chair of light wood, with no fastenings other than glue. The engravings on the back and on the strip just below the seat are different from anything I've come across. Can you identify the chair?
C.O.W. — Sante Fe, N.M.

Your chair, dating from the early nineteenth century, is a charming example of the French Directoire style as interpreted by a chairmaker working in the provinces. The fashionable Parisian motif, the anthemion, or honeysuckle, seen in the openworked splat, is a delightful and unexpected sophisticated touch. Originally these chairs had straw seats, and often flat, loose cushions were placed on them.

FRENCH ARMCHAIR

This chair, one of a pair, is mahogany, joined with mortise and tenon. Can you date it and tell me whether it's American or French?

L.N. — Brooklyn, N.Y.

Your chair is a fine example of the French Charles X style (1824–1830), when furniture design was still dominated by the Napoleonic influence. Some of the best work of this brief period was in chair design.

FRENCH EMPIRE CHAIR

I recently inherited six of these French chairs from my husband's family, who bought them in France around 1900. They are supposed to be much older. What do you think?

F.M. — Riverside, Cal.

Your French Empire style chair with a gondola-shaped back appears to date from around 1815, which is about the time concave front legs, square and slightly tapering, were first used to any appreciable extent in France. This type of leg is known as a saber leg, since it resembles somewhat the shape of a saber. Empire chairs are notable for their broad and simple lines, which were by no means always straight, as your chair clearly shows. The gilt bronze Winged Victory decorating the splat was a favorite Empire motif, and so were the stars.

RENAISSANCE ADAPTATION

I would appreciate any information about this chair that you can give me. The leather back and seat are beautifully tooled. Also, can you recommend anything to preserve the leather?
I.S.S.—Vienna, Austria

Your chair of X-form has been freely adapted from a sixteenth-century Italian Renaissance chair known as a Dantesca. It was probably made either in the late nineteenth or early twentieth century. To preserve old leather many experts recommend Butcher's White Diamond Wax.

ITALIAN RENAISSANCE SGABELLO

I bought this chair at an estate sale. It looks terribly old. I shall appreciate any information about it.
S.M.—San Bernardino, Cal.

This distinctive and popular type of Italian Renaissance carved-wood chair is called a sgabello, or stool, chair. Your fine sgabello probably dates from around 1550 to 1600. Judging from the still-surviving copies, probably trophies from the "grand tour," the sgabello found its way into the entrance halls and libraries of many American houses.

NEO-GOTHIC CHAIRS

Can you please tell us the style, age, and possibly the origin of this pair of chairs?
L.B. — Escondido, Cal.

Your chairs in the Gothic Revival, or Neo-Gothic, style most likely date from about the second quarter of the nineteenth century. The backs are a fantastic Gothic creation and are the work of an accomplished carver. Certain features, such as the intricacy of the carving, suggest European origin.

X-FORM CHAIR

I can find little information about this type of chair except in the encyclopedia, and even that doesn't fully describe it. What can you tell me?
A.C.L. — Rockville, Md.

Your chair is a copy of a distinctive type of sixteenth-century Italian Renaissance folding chair of X-form called a Savonarola. It is probably of European origin, perhaps Italian, and dates from the late nineteenth or early twentieth century, when this style was revived for libraries and entrance halls, and was sold to Americans touring Europe.

The Savonarola chair consists of about seven serpentine X-shaped staves. The lower staves were secured with runner feet while the upper staves or supports were secured by straight arms. It has a flat-arched back rail made of wood, which was joined to the rear ends of the arms. The narrow seat was made of slats and was placed slightly above the intersection of the supports. A loose cushion was usually placed on the seat.

SABER LEG CHAIR

This chair was given to me, and I would like to know more about it. Is it an antique?
P.F. — Chicago, Ill.

Your floral marquetry side chair with rolled-over back and saber legs is in the French Empire style. It is of European, perhaps German, origin dating from around 1850 and is therefore an antique.

DUTCH CANE-BACK CHAIR

This is one of two chairs we acquired recently. We believe they are of Belgian origin. Can you add to our information?
W.E. — Rhinelander, Wis.

This type of tall cane-back chair with spirally turned posts and ornate baroque carving was very popular on the Continent, especially in the Netherlands, during the second half of the seventeenth century. The design was introduced into England after the Restoration in 1660, and is frequently referred to as the Restoration chair. Yours would have to be examined by an expert to determine whether it is an original or a reproduction. If authentic, it is probably from Holland.

VICTORIAN SIDE CHAIR

We would appreciate knowing the approximate date for this chair we recently purchased.

L.J.S. — Charlotte, N.C.

Your interesting parlor chair with an elaborate openworked back is of European, probably German, manufacture, dating around 1860–1870.

BENTWOOD CHAIR

What is the period and style of this chair? The label reads "Jacob & Joseph Kahn, Wien, Austria."

T.B.S. — Kaufman, Tex.

Your bentwood chair dates around 1900. The Rhinelander, Michael Thonet, 1796–1871, perfected a process for bending wood at his factory in Vienna in 1856. His bentwood chairs were an overnight success. Soon other factories were producing their versions of Thonet's bentwood chairs.

VICTORIAN TÊTE-À-TÊTE

My satinwood love seat was purchased in New Orleans, but I believe it was made in France because the name "Poytois & Fix" is on a faded label beneath the seat. Any information would be appreciated.

M.L.W. — Topeka, Kans.

This is a Victorian tête-à-tête, or two-seated chair, dating about 1865–1880. It was probably made in France, but the label may well be that of the upholsterer rather than the maker. The pattern of this S-shaped seat, designed so that two people could sit face-to-face, is reputed to have originated in the 1850s in furniture made to order for the Empress Eugénie of France.

SPANISH RENAISSANCE VARGUEÑO

What can you tell me about my Spanish cabinet, which I inherited from a very close relative who lived in California? What was it used for?
F.P. — Eugene, Ore.

Your cabinet, called a vargueño, was essentially designed as a receptacle for documents and other valuables and could also be used as a desk. It was Spain's most distinctive as well as finest piece of cabinet work. Your vargueño probably dates from the seventeenth century, and the stand on which it rests appears to be original. In the early twentieth century the Florida boom in Spanish architecture resulted in the production of much pseudo-Spanish Renaissance furniture. The vargueño was much used and abused.

FLORENTINE CABINET

Have you any idea of the origin of my cabinet? It is inlaid with ivory and tortoiseshell, has claw-and-ball feet, and at the top center balustrade a brass figure like Ceres. There are brass globes with eagles on them at each end.

P.S.—Lafayette, Cal.

Judging from the snapshot, your inlaid cabinet is of Italian, probably Florentine, origin, most likely dating from the seventeenth century. As this style was popular for a long period, your piece should be examined by an expert to date it accurately.

SPANISH TREASURE CHEST

Where and when was this iron trunk/chest made? I bought it at auction, and on removing the black paint, found it a beautiful piece of craftsmanship. I enclose a picture of the chest open and also a close-up of the lock mechanism.

P.M.—Pennington, N.J.

Your iron strongbox, often romantically called a treasure chest, is sixteenth-century Spanish. It appears to be a very fine piece, similar to one in the Hispanic Museum in New York. You should be proud of your possession, as these chests are quite rare.

EUROPEAN CHEST

This old oak chest with iron lock and hinges is marked "M E L 1782" on the front. Is it American, and is the date accurate?

A.V.—Cleveland, Tenn.

A chest of this kind is probably of European rather than American manufacture and was used to store bedding. The initials are probably those of the original owner; 1782 could well be the year it was made.

LOUIS XV VENETIAN COMMODE

What can you tell me about my chest of drawers with painted decoration? It belonged to my mother's family and is supposed to be an antique made in Venice.

C.E. — *Oakland, Cal.*

Yes, your Louis XV style painted commode with a serpentine front and cabriole legs appears to be Venetian in origin, probably dating around the third quarter of the eighteenth century. Of all painted Venetian furniture the commodes (chests of drawers) are particularly delightful.

FRENCH TALL CHEST OF DRAWERS

Is my French chest of drawers old enough to be an antique? Does it have a special name?

N.T.D. — *Baton Rouge, La.*

Yes, your French chest of drawers is an antique, probably dating around 1760. The valanced base, curving into short cabriole legs, is a marked feature of the Louis XV style. The French name for this piece of furniture is *chiffonnier*. Sometimes it is called a *semainier* (*semaine* — week), as the majority are designed with seven drawers, a drawer for each day of the week. When they only have six drawers — and they sometimes do — it was a short week!

EUROPEAN CHEST OF DRAWERS

This three-drawer chest is 36 inches high, 27 inches deep and 51 inches long. The outside is veneered with various brown and black woods, while the inside is rough and unfinished. Could you date it and tell me where it came from?

C.D.J.—Chico, Cal.

We believe your veneered chest of drawers dates sometime between 1750 and 1775 and is of European provenance (probably from Holland). It is in the Rococo style.

GERMAN CHEST OF DRAWERS

We inherited this German fruitwood chest with black trim. The brasses have flying insects pulling a plow or chariot. When was this chest made?

A.H.F.—Chicago, Ill.

Your chest of drawers is in the early phase of the Biedermeier style, around 1820–1830. As in your chest, this style often displayed a classical simplicity, devoid of decoration, that forecast the clean lines of the modern movement. The oval brasses, with handles of the bail type stamped with popular mythological patterns, are typical and now highly prized.

SECOND EMPIRE CABINET

This cabinet belonged to my husband's grandfather. The legend "Edwards and Robert's, Wardour Street, London" is on the drawer. Can you tell us more about it?

M.F.B.—El Paso, Tex.

CONTINENTAL

Your revived Louis XVI style cabinet and stand, handsomely inset with porcelain plaques, belongs to the French Second Empire (1852–1870). It exemplifies the French taste for richness, brilliance, and striking contrasts, which characterize the best work of this period. Edwards and Robert's was probably the shop where it was sold.

FRENCH PROVINCIAL LOW CUPBOARD

We bought this chest at an auction and want to know something about it.
                    G.E., Jr.— South Kent, Conn.

Judging from the snapshot, your low cupboard was made in a French province early in the nineteenth century. The irregular outline of the arched panels is a charming Rococo touch.

FRENCH SECOND EMPIRE BAS D'ARMOIRE

Would you know the approximate age and style of my cabinet? "Vedder A Paris" is inscribed on the inside of one door.
                    J.R.McB. — New York, N.Y.

Your low cupboard with gilt bronze mounts belongs to the French Second Empire period (1852–1870). It reflects the revival of the earlier Louis XVI style, which was very fashionable then.

BOULLE LOW CUPBOARD

In 1883 this brass-inlaid cupboard was sent to the United States from Europe. We believe the inlay is boulle work. Would you kindly give us your opinion as to age?

F.I.D. — San Leandro, Cal.

Boulle work — a marquetry of brass and tortoiseshell — was named for Charles André Boulle (1642–1732), whose designs are considered the epitome of the Louis XIV style. Furniture with boulle-style marquetry continued to be popular through the Second Empire (1852–1870), which is about the time your low cupboard was made.

LOUIS XV PROVINCIAL DRESSER

What can you tell me about my French dresser, which is a copy of an old one?

N.J.M. — Enumclaw, Wash.

Your French dresser, or *dressoir,* was a favorite and characteristic piece of provincial furniture. In a general sense, it consisted of a lower cupboard section and a deeply recessed superstructure fitted with several rows of narrow open shelves. The majority by far were in the Louis XV style. Marked features of this style, such as the asymmetrically shaped panels and a valanced base curving into cabriole feet, are clearly seen in your example.

PANETIÈRE

I bought this piece in an antique shop. They thought it was some kind of cupboard. Can you identify it?

L.B.C. — Paoli, Pa.

Your hanging cupboard with its decorative turned spindles is one of the most charming pieces of French Provincial furniture. As it is a bread cupboard, its French name is *panetière* (*pain* — bread). Food cupboards are always easy to identify, since the doors are either pierced or spindled for ventilation. It is also easy to recognize at a glance that your cupboard is in the Louis XV style, because the base is valanced and curves into short feet of cabriole form, which is a marked feature of typical Louis XV style furniture. The *panetière* is an original Provençal creation and is often believed to have been first introduced at Arles, which was the great center for Provençal furniture. As these cupboards have retained their popularity, and are therefore much in demand, they are still being skillfully copied. For this reason it would be necessary to have your *panetière* examined in order to determine whether it was made in the eighteenth century.

ART NOUVEAU CUPBOARD

This chest is one of a pair I own and would like identified. They are 29½ inches high, with black-and-white marble tops. The chests are mahogany, with flower inlay in pale yellow and leaf inlays in light and dark green.

B.P.C. — Hickory, N.C.

Your pair of small cupboards are in the Art Nouveau style. They apparently date around 1900–1910, and probably were made in France.

CORNER CUPBOARD

Have you any idea of the origin of this mahogany corner cupboard, which we purchased in Massachusetts? It is in two parts, base and cabinet top, with serpentine front. The piece is extremely heavy and supposedly belonged to a Plymouth sea captain sometime in the eighteenth century.

R.M.C.—*Chicago, Ill.*

Your cupboard is either of Dutch or Portuguese origin. It is not possible to determine from the photograph whether it was made in the late eighteenth or mid-nineteenth century.

LOUIS XV STYLE DAYBED

What can you tell me about my French daybed? Is this the usual form?

R.F.—*Sacramento, Cal.*

Yes, the form of your French daybed is most typical and enjoyed great popularity from about 1740 to 1780. This type of daybed, distinguished by its gondola-shaped back, so called because of its rounded appearance, was made in one piece, such as your example, or in two or three pieces, in both the Louis XV and Louis XVI styles. It is difficult to tell from your snapshot whether your daybed is original Louis XV or a successful reproduction.

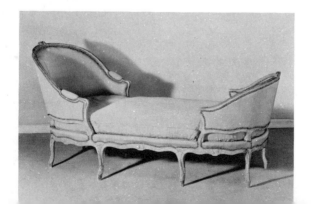

LOUIS XVI STYLE WALL MIRROR

*I bought this Louis XVI style mirror at auction.
Is it a good example?*

S.N. — Bend, Ore.

Yes, your Louis XVI style wall mirror in a carved giltwood rectangular frame surmounted by a pediment is a fine example. Some of these pediments, which display immense variety, are little masterpieces of composition. Among them could be a basket of flowers, an antique vase or, like yours, a trophy of emblems: the quiver, the torch and the bow of love, with the inevitable billing doves. The garlands come fairly well down along the frame and balance with the projections at each bottom corner.

LOUIS XV STYLE SETTEE

*Can you tell me whether my French Louis XV
style settee is truly old or is a copy?*

M.C. — San Clemente, Cal.

Judging from the photograph, your French settee appears to be a period piece dating from around the mid-eighteenth century. However, early in the twentieth century French cabinetmakers and certain American cabinet shops faithfully produced copies of period pieces to the most minute detail for the great houses being built by rich Americans. For this reason we suggest that an expert should examine it. The form of your settee, known as basket-shaped, having a gracefully arched back that continues to curve around the front, forming semicircular ends, was in high fashion in the eighteenth century and is one of the most sought-after types at the present time. It was equally popular in the Louis XVI style.

LOUIS XV DRESSING TABLE

We bought this dressing table from an antique dealer, who said it was French. Can you identify it further?

N.T. — Scarsdale, N.Y.

Your dressing table is a poudreuse — one of the most popular types of furniture turned out by eighteenth-century French cabinetmakers. Its essential features were a hinged lift-up mirror that doubled as a lid for a central cosmetics storage compartment, and hinged side leaves that lifted up and out to provide additional counter space. The cabriole legs of yours identify it with the Louis XV style. Only a firsthand examination by an expert could determine if it is of the period or a later reproduction.

BARBEDIENNE BRONZE TABLE

This is one of two bronze tables I have acquired. The marble tops have deep red insets; the craftsmanship and detail are more than exceptional. Each table is signed "F. Barbedienne." Do you know of this artisan?

J.W. — Coconut Grove, Fla.

F. Barbedienne, who made and signed your tables, was the leading bronze founder of France from about 1860 to 1890. His Paris foundry made bronzes of fine artistic quality, such as your Louis XVI tables. He received many awards for his work, including the French Legion of Honor.

LOUIS-PHILIPPE SOFA

My French sofa is made of rosewood. When it was purchased it had a cane seat and back. To what period does it belong?

H.G., Jr. — Pulaski, Va.

Your triple-back sofa is of the Louis-Philippe period, dating about 1830–1850. It was probably made by a Paris *menuisier*. After the middle of the seventeenth century the word *menuisier* tends to be applied only to those craftsmen who made carved furniture, such as chairs, sofas and console tables.

FRENCH DRESSING TABLE

What is the style and approximate age of this dressing table, which has been in our family as long as I can remember?

C.H.R. — Paoli, Pa.

Your dressing table is in the French Empire style (1804–1814), and is a characteristic piece, with its rectangular marble top, frieze drawer for toilet articles, and curving X-shaped supports. As a rule, the two metal uprights to which the mirror is attached are provided with candle arms. Your table was probably made around 1810–1820.

LOUIS XVI STYLE WRITING TABLE

I shall appreciate any information about my French Louis XVI style writing table, which I bought at auction.

S.S. — Reno, Nev.

This type of Louis XVI style writing table was widely popular in France during the second half of the eighteenth century, until the Revolution. Essentially it was similar to the lower portion of the cylinder desk. The front was designed with five (as in your example) or seven drawers of equal depth. The arrangement in kneehole manner provided ample space for the knees of the writer.

LOUIS XVI STYLE CYLINDER DESK

Was this kind of desk with a roll top "important" in France in the eighteenth century?

R.N. — San Diego, Cal.

The cylinder desk, introduced around the middle of the eighteenth century in France, was a very fashionable and important form of writing furniture. The cylinder top was a happy invention, for at a touch it covered the writing table and concealed from view the clutter of writing paper, notes and writing equipage. The straight tapering legs on your desk tell you that it is in the Louis XVI style.

FRENCH WRITING TABLE

My desk is walnut, inlaid and trimmed in bronze.
The name "J. Pafrat, maître ébéniste" is stamped
on the drawer. I would appreciate any informa-
tion about it.

J.W.C. — Dallas, Tex.

You have a Louis XVI style writing table presumably made by Jean-Jacques Pafrat, who became a *maître ébéniste* in 1785. He made simple, elegant furniture, usually of mahogany. In the mid-eighteenth century the guilds compelled each *maître* to strike his name or initials on every piece he put on sale, and this stamp was the most important means of identifying the maker of French furniture from 1750 to 1800. After the dissolution of the guilds, false signatures occurred frequently. I am not familiar with a stamp that includes the words *maître ébéniste*. It would be well to have your table examined by an expert.

SECOND EMPIRE WRITING TABLE

My desk has Sèvres porcelain medallions. In the
drawer is a porcelain label reading "James School-
bred & Co., Tottenham House, Tottenham Court
Road, London." What can you tell me about it?
B.F. — Williamson, W.Va.

Your writing table with its recessed superstructure is French Second Empire (1852–1870) and in the revived Louis XVI style. Its distinctive richness and brilliance, which we associate with the Second Empire style, offsets its imitative design. The Schoolbred Company is not listed in London directories today.

SECOND EMPIRE ESCRITOIRE

This inlaid and porcelain escritoire belonged to my grandmother. I have been told that the porcelain plaques are Sèvres. The bottom drawer has a velvet-covered tray, which pushes back to reveal a hidden drawer, and double locks. Can you tell me anything further about it?

N.J.M. — Malvern, Pa.

Your writing table, designed for a lady's use, is in the French Second Empire style (1852–1870). Like most nineteenth-century design after 1815, this was an imitative style — the chief inspiration for your desk being eighteenth-century Louis XVI. If your plaques are true Sèvres they will have a manufacturer's mark.

PROVINCIAL SECRETARY

This writing desk — a baroque piece from the Aachen-Luttich area — belonged to my family in Germany for over 150 years. Can you tell me anything about its style?

P.K. — Fresno, Cal.

The upper portion of your slant-front secretary-bookcase with its arched cornice is typically Louis XVI, while the cabriole legs of the lower portion are Louis XV. Perhaps the bookcase was made later and added on. Nevertheless it is a charming example of provincial continental cabinetwork, dating around the last quarter of the eighteenth century.

ROCOCO SECRETARY

This Louis XV salon desk was given to me by some French friends. On the front, back, and sides are oil paintings, one of which is signed "D. E. Boudhy." The name "L. Majorelle" is printed on the bottom of the desk. Can you tell me more about it?

S.B. — Flushing, N.Y.

Louis Majorelle was a well-known French furniture designer. During the 1880s he produced work in the Louis XIV, Louis XV, and Louis XVI styles. He worked mainly in the revived Rococo, or Louis XV, style in the 1890s, which is about the time your desk was made. In the early twentieth century Majorelle achieved renown for his work in the Art Nouveau genre. We have not been able to trace the artist D. E. Boudhy in any of our standard art reference books.

FALL-FRONT SECRETARY

Can you estimate the age and origin of my desk? It is covered with multicolored marquetry motifs.

I.G.S. — Greenwich, Conn.

Judging from the snapshot, your secretary with a fall front, which serves as a writing board when let down, is of early-nineteenth-century Dutch provenance. As in your example, the ample surface of this class of writing furniture was often decorated with marquetry.

FALL-FRONT SECRETARY

I've recently acquired a lady's desk of walnut with ivory inlay. I would appreciate knowing its approximate age and the origin of the inlaid decoration.

C.B. — Seattle, Wash.

Your fall-front secretary is of European manufacture, probably dating from around the second half of the eighteenth century. This distinctive style of ivory inlay of typical Moorish design was in frequent use at Cairo, Damascus and elsewhere in the fourteenth century for the decoration of tables, boxes, and the like. With the growth of Italian trade in the Levant, such articles of "Damascus work" were found in Italy where their influence was clearly evident in Italian Renaissance furniture, notably objects decorated with the so-called certosina work. This style of ivory inlay is especially associated with the Carthusian Monasteries (*certose*) of Lombardy.

DUTCH MARQUETRY DESK

I would like some information about this antique desk with elaborate inlay on lid and drawer fronts.
A.A. — Long Branch, N.Y.

Your slant-front desk is from Holland. The serpentine-shaped façade and the valanced base curving into short cabriole legs are marked features of the Rococo style and indicate a date of manufacture around the mid-eighteenth century. The floral marquetry exemplifies the skill of the Dutch cabinetmaker.

BOMBÉ DESK

What can you tell me about this old desk, which was brought over from Europe by a member of my family?

J.B. — *Riverside, Conn.*

Your slant-front desk with the drawers in the lower, bombé-shaped section is probably Dutch in origin, dating from around the mid-eighteenth century. The French term *bombé* is applied to a vertical, rounded, convex surface and is identified with Rococo style furniture.

GERMAN FALL-FRONT SECRETARY

I recently moved into a house in which there was some furniture left by the former owner. Among the pieces was a cabinet with a label on the back containing writing in German. Can you give me any information about this piece?

N.S. — *Seattle, Wash.*

The prototype of your secretary was introduced in France around 1750, and remained popular for about 100 years. As in the original, your secretary has a fall front, which, when let down, serves as a writing board, and was probably made in Germany around 1850.

REVIVED LOUIS XV STYLE DESK

My mother-in-law left us this boulle type desk. We would greatly appreciate any information concerning its age and origin.

J.F.B. — Bellevue, Wash.

Your slant-front desk in the boulle technique is in the revived Louis XV style, probably dating about 1875–1900. The manner in which the apron continues in an unbroken curve into the cabriole legs is a marked feature of the style. It appears to be European, perhaps French, in origin.

FRENCH PAPIER-MÂCHÉ STAND

Our walnut-veneered, brass-galleried stand has a metal label, "M Alph Giroux, 43 Boul' des Capucines 43, Papeterie Fantaisies." Could you give its approximate age and use?

H.E.G. — Minneapolis, Minn.

Your drop-leaf stand is French, of the late nineteenth century, and was used as a side table. Adolph Giroux made papier-mâché novelties at his Paris address.

ITALIAN GROTESQUES

I bought these figures at an antique shop in Los Angeles. I have had many inquiries about their age and origin. Can you help me?

M.M.C. — Santa Barbara, Cal.

Your grotesque figures are of Italian origin. They derived from the blackamoors that served as candlestands. Figures such as yours were popular about 1880–1900 and were found in entrance halls of private homes. The tray was used for calling cards.

EUROPEAN PLANT STAND

My wire plant stand is made entirely without welding. Thirty years ago I was told it was 100 years old, possibly of French origin. Do you think this is true?

L.R.McC. — Owosso, Mich.

Your plant stand is certainly European, but I don't believe it dates any earlier than the late Victorian period.

FURNITURE

English

ENGLISH GARDEN BENCH

I am interested in knowing the age and origin of my cast-iron settee. In stripping off the paint I found the original coat was gold leaf. I also enclose the foundry mark.

T.E.C. — *Agawam, Mass.*

Your iron garden bench was made in England. The diamond-shaped mark records the fact that the design was registered at the British Patent Office in London on March 8, 1865. The use of iron furniture both for house and garden achieved wide popularity in America in the late 1860s and 1870s.

QUEEN ANNE SPLAT-BACK CHAIR

Is my Queen Anne chair English or American?
How old is it?

S.P. — Eau Gallie, Fla.

Your Queen Anne splat-back chair with a vase-shaped splat and cabriole legs terminating in ball-and-claw feet was made in England, probably around 1715–1725. This chair introduced a new concept of comfort in English chair design and was one of the most graceful chairs ever made.

LIBRARY AND READING CHAIR

I have been told my English chair was used in
cockfighting. Any information will be appreciated.
P.D. — Seattle, Wash.

Your specialized form of chair having an adjustable board and hinged trays below the arms was introduced in England in the early eighteenth century for use in libraries. Such chairs are popularly associated with cockfighting, but though possibly they may have been used on occasion by the judge, their purpose is clearly described by Sheraton in his *Cabinet Dictionary* (1803). He writes, "they are intended to make the exercise of reading easy and for the convenience of taking down a note or quotation from any subject. The reader places himself with his back to the front of the chair and rests his arms on the top yoke." Your chair probably dates around the 1720s.

EARLY GEORGIAN SPLAT-BACK CHAIR

This is one of a pair of old English side chairs that have been in my family for 200 years. I wish to learn their period, style and maker.

S.P.J. — New York, N.Y.

Your chairs are in the English early Georgian style, about 1730–1740. Chairs of this class followed the traditions of the style of Queen Anne, but became more massive in character, and the ornamentation was elaborated. The cabinetwork of this period has always been highly esteemed, but the maker is very seldom known.

CHIPPENDALE SPLAT-BACK CHAIR

I recently inherited this richly carved Chippendale chair, which I think was made in England. What is your opinion?

B.A. — Jackson Hole, Wyo.

Yes, your Chippendale style chair with an openworked splat and cabriole legs terminating in ball-and-claw feet is English in origin and probably dates around 1755–1765. Especially fine is the crest rail in the form of a cupid's bow terminating in turned-up extremities. This bow-shaped crest rail is a marked feature of Chippendale style chairs.

CHIPPENDALE STYLE ARMCHAIR

Is there any special reason why the seat of my English Chippendale chair is so wide?

N.M. — Salt Lake City, Utah

ENGLISH

It is said that this kind of English upholstered chair, with open arms, having a seat of excessive width, was made to accommodate the enormous hoopskirts, which at this time attained their widest dimensions. The pronounced incurving arm supports also contribute to that purpose. The cabriole legs of your chair terminating in French whorl feet show French Rococo influence, suggesting a date around 1750.

LADDER-BACK CHAIR

I bought a pair of ladder-back chairs at auction. The catalogue did not give their age. What is your opinion?

A.M. — *Bellevue, Wash.*

Judging from your photograph, we are inclined to think that your Chippendale style ladder-back chairs are successful twentieth-century reproductions. The seats for this type of chair were either of the "slip in" kind or with the upholstery covering the seat rail. We think the former gives a more finished and therefore more elegant look.

SHERATON STYLE CHAIR

I understand that round legs are associated with the Sheraton style. Does this mean that my chair with square legs is not Sheraton?

P.H. — *Tacoma, Wash.*

No, your chair is in the Sheraton style and was made in England around 1795. The design of the open back, centering between two columns a vase-shaped splat headed with ostrich plumes, is typically Sheraton. Broadly speaking, square and tapering straight legs are associated with the Hepplewhite style, and round and tapering straight legs with the Sheraton style, but this is far from an invariable rule.

LATE SHERATON ARMCHAIR

I recently inherited a set of English dining chairs from my mother. What can you tell me about their style?

F.J.N. — San Francisco, Cal.

Your armchairs belong to the later Sheraton style, dating around 1800–1820. Top rails such as those on your chairs, having an enlarged central portion and on each side a horizontal turning resembling a vase, are a distinctive feature of chair design at this time. Then, too, the backs are generally lower than those of earlier Sheraton designs. There is a noticeable emphasis on horizontal lines, while arms are set high, giving a high-shouldered effect. The front legs are generally straight, turned round, and tapered.

REGENCY STYLE ARMCHAIR

I would appreciate any information you can give me about my new possession. It is inlaid with brass.

M.P.A. — San Luis Obispo, Cal.

Your armchair with brass inlay is in the English Regency style, dating around 1810–1815. A marked feature of this style, and one remaining in fashion until the mid-nineteenth century, is the arms without armposts, which end in huge open volutes resting directly on the tops of the legs. Also characteristic are front legs shaped in bold concave or saber curves; hence the name "saber legs." Finally, inlaid brass was favored as a decorative technique.

REGENCY STYLE CHAIR

Will you help me identify this chair? Because of its webbing, a dealer thought it was probably French. It has brass medallions, and I think it was lacquered originally, but now it looks like ma-hogany.

C.H.D. — Roanoke, Va.

Your chair is not French but is in the English Regency (1800–1820) style. The characteristic curves, derived from the classical Greek chairs, present a very graceful line and are especially pleasing when seen in profile.

VICTORIAN GOTHIC CHAIR

This chair is unlike any other straight-backed Victorian chair I have seen. The design of the legs and lower frame makes me think it might be of American origin. Can you help me classify it?

M.M.B. — Columbus, Ohio

Your side chair is a fine example of the Victorian Gothic style. The open quatrefoil and well-carved crocket finial are important identifying details. The first Victorian furniture incorporating Gothic motifs probably appeared during the second quarter of the nineteenth century. This style was not so well known here as in England, since it was considered too elaborate for American tastes.

VICTORIAN "ELIZABETHAN" CHAIR

Can you tell us the origin and age of this chair, which we got from a Massachusetts house? We were told it is called a "pulpit" chair.

S.E.W. — Port Chester, N.Y.

This type of high-backed, short-legged side chair has been called "devotional," "prie-Dieu," or "vesper." The names describe its intended use — for family prayers — but some were also used in the parlor. The shape and ornamental details are derived from high-backed chairs of the seventeenth century. The Victorians called this style "Elizabethan," and it was popular in England around 1830–1840. Yours is a very typical early Victorian chair.

BALLOON-BACK CHAIR BY GILLOWS

We have six of these chairs. I think they are rosewood. On the frame under the seats are the words "Gillows, Lancaster." Can you tell me more about them?

W.Y.H. — St. Cloud, Minn.

Gillows was the name of a well-known firm of English cabinetmakers who moved to Lancaster in 1695. After 1820 most of their pieces were stamped "Gillows, Lancaster." Your carved rosewood chairs date about 1840. The balloon-back chair was the most popular form of early Victorian drawing-room or dining-room chair. In the earliest versions the front legs were straight, in the classical taste.

BALLOON-BACK CHAIR

I will appreciate any information you can furnish concerning this chair, which we bought at auction in England.
E.E.B.—Winter Haven, Fla.

Balloon-back chairs such as yours were popular during most of the Victorian era, largely because of their comfort—the balloon back supported both the shoulders and the middle of the back. Your chair was most likely made in England around the mid-nineteenth century.

ROCOCO CHAIR

My papier-mâché chair is either English or French. The initials "Rd" inside a painted diamond are on it. Can you identify it further?
G.E.M.—APO, N.Y.

The diamond-shaped device with "Rd" (registered) is probably a registration mark of the London Patent Office. The mark was used to protect the design from piracy by other manufacturers. Since your chair is in the Victorian Rococo style, it was probably made in the mid-nineteenth century.

PAPIER-MÂCHÉ CHAIR

I think this is a papier-mâché chair. On a metal tag underneath the seat is "T. H. Jennens, Patentee, London." What can you tell me about it?
M.C. — *Arlington, Va.*

Jennens and Bettridge of Birmingham pioneered the use of papier-mâché for furniture in the 1820s. Their famous pearl-shell inlay was patented in 1825, and in time they made the bulk of all papier-mâché furniture. However, owing to the limitations of papier-mâché and its unsuitability for legs and frames of furniture, much that survives has a wood or metal frame, and only chairbacks and nonstructural parts are of papier-mâché. Your chair, painted gilt and set with mother-of-pearl, would have to be examined to determine if it is entirely or only partly of papier-mâché. In any case, it is in mid-nineteenth-century revived Rococo style.

REVIVED LOUIS XV CHAIR

I would appreciate information on the period and style of this side chair with oak leaves and acorns carved on the top of the back.
S.A.B. — *Waco, Tex.*

Your chair is in the revived Louis XV style, which is the same as Victorian Rococo. It was made either in England or America around the mid-nineteenth century. The cartouche-shaped back and cabriole legs are marked features of this Rococo style.

ENGLISH VICTORIAN ROCOCO CHAIR

I acquired a set of four of these chairs some years ago. Each bore the customs gold seal as authentic antiques. I would appreciate any information about them.
E.C. — *New Fairfield, Conn.*

ENGLISH

Your balloon-back chairs are English, dating around the mid-nineteenth century. The cabriole legs and sinuous curves show at a glance that they are in the French revived Rococo, or revived Louis XV, style. Also, the balloon back, a hooped or rounded style of chairback with a pronounced "waistline," is especially identified with the Victorian Rococo forms. Chairs like yours were particularly favored for the drawing room.

HALL CHAIR

We would like to have this chair identified. It seems to be rosewood, and the scrollwork is a part of the chairback, not glued on.

W.D.—Cortland, N.Y.

You have a hall chair. Introduced into England in the eighteenth century, these were usually found in halls of the great houses for the use of callers. Your chair seems to be English, dating around the start of this century.

BARBER'S CHAIR

I would appreciate any information you can give me about this chair. It is very crudely made. The seat seems to be fashioned from a slab of wood sawed from a tree trunk.

J.F.—Philadelphia, Pa.

What you have is a barber's chair, or a shaving chair. The additional crest rail served as a headrest. It is probably English, made in the second half of the eighteenth century.

ENGLISH WINDSOR CHAIR

Could you tell me when and where this antique chair was made? A friend bought it in New York.
L.B.McD. — San Juan, P.R.

You have an English hoop-back Windsor chair with pierced central back splat, made about 1850, probably at a High Wycombe, Buckinghamshire, shop. The pierced upright splat extending from the center of the rear of the seat to the center of the top rail is the most noticeable difference between the English Windsors and the American ones.

ENGLISH LOOP- OR BOW-BACK WINDSOR

Can you tell me the age and origin of this Windsor chair?

L.M. — Brooklyn, N.Y.

From such details as pierced back splat and bracing spindles, I would say you have an English Windsor chair. Such chairs were partially handmade and sold in considerable quantities about 1880–1900 by the Windsor chair shops of Daniel Glenister, Walter Skull and Benjamin North at High Wycombe, Buckinghamshire. Many were exported.

ENGLISH REGENCY CHEST OF DRAWERS

My small chest is 12½ inches tall and 6½ inches wide, with five drawers — including the one concealed in the base — 5 inches deep. It has a small marble top, and I believe the veneer is rosewood. Could you possibly estimate the age of the chest?
M.G. — Brooklyn, N.Y.

Your chest of drawers has all the earmarks of an English piece of the latter years of the Regency period—that is, between 1820 and 1830.

BRASS SWING COT

This is a drawing of a brass baby crib that has no dates or markings, and I wonder if you can identify it for us.

M.L.G.—San Marino, Cal.

By the mid-1880s a great amount of brass "sleep" furniture was being made in Birmingham, England. About half of it was exported. English retailers' catalogues of this period were filled with brass beds and swing cots such as yours.

BRASS SWING CRIB

Last summer I bought this brass cradle at an antique shop. The dealer told me it was English. What do you think?

R.A.E.—Laguna Hills, Cal.

Yes, your brass swing crib is English in origin and probably dates around 1885–1895. Contemporary English trade catalogues illustrating these cradles state that they may be japanned (painted) any fancy color and relieved in gilt. The curtain scroll is optional. You were lucky to find a cradle with a curtain scroll and in such good condition.

ELIZABETHAN COURT CUPBOARD

For years my mother promised to give me this piece of antique furniture when I got my own house. Now that it is mine I should appreciate any information you can give me about it.

P.R.T. — *Medford, Ore.*

This distinctive type of Elizabethan richly carved oak cupboard consisting of a simple open superstructure of three shelves is known as a court cupboard. A reference to such a cupboard, which served only for the display of plate, such as gold and silver bowls and pitchers, occurs in *Romeo and Juliet* when the servants are clearing the hall of the Capulets' house for revels—"Away with the joint stools, remove the court cupboard, look to the plate."

VICTORIAN BREAKFRONT CUPBOARD

Is this china cabinet an antique? I know it came from England. The wood looks like cherry, and the drawer pulls and head at the top are hand-carved.

A.S.J. — *Alhambra, Cal.*

Yes, your English breakfront cupboard is an antique. It is in the Victorian Renaissance style, probably dating around 1860–1870. Originally the glazed upper portion probably held books, as it looks like a piece intended for use in the library.

ROSEWOOD ÉTAGÈRE

I bought this handcarved rosewood étagère with interior parts of oak in 1942. It was said to have come from England about 1870. Is this true?
W.W. — Sullivan's Isle, S.C.

The oak interior structure indicates it is English, dating about 1860–1870. The French term *étagère,* meaning to rise tier upon tier (hence a set of shelves), is mentioned in French inventories from the seventeenth century. Thus from early times they were used for the purpose of display. The Victorian predilection for bibelots created a vogue for étagères.

VICTORIAN ÉTAGÈRE

We have wondered about the age and origin of this plant stand. It was called a "brass mantle" by my husband's grandmother, who owned it. The shelves are onyx.
V.R. — Mount Prospect, Ill.

What you have is not a plant stand but an étagère, or whatnot, intended for the display of curios or bric-a-brac. No Victorian parlor was considered properly furnished without one. Your brass étagère dates around the latter part of the nineteenth century.

VICTORIAN FIRE SCREEN

This piece, hanging on a metal rod, is worked in beads and thread, somewhat like needlepoint. The tassels and fringe are thread, and it is fully lined. Can you tell me what it was used for?

C.F. — Galva, Ill.

You have a Victorian fire shield, or screen, used to protect one from the heat of the hearth. It is of English origin, probably made in the mid-1800s.

CELESTIAL GLOBE

Any information you can give me about our Celestial Globe will be appreciated. It is inscribed "Cruchley's (Late Cary's) NEW Celestial Globe." Also inscribed in the metal is "The Gift of Edmund Sexton, Viscount Perry to his Daughter the Honorable Frances Calvert, 1806."

F.V. — Washington, D.C.

Your globe, dating from 1806, the year of its presentation, is mounted in a stand of late-eighteenth-century classical style. Cary was an eminent English globe maker, and Cruchley, his successor, continued Cary's high quality of craftsmanship in his own work. The value of your globe is also enhanced by the fact that it was a presentation piece.

ROCOCO CHIPPENDALE MIRROR

My mother recently gave me this carved and gilt-wood English mirror, which she originally bought at auction. What can you tell me about it?
R.S.F. — Fort Lee, N.J.

The asymmetrical cartouche-shaped frame and fanciful C-scrolls and foliage arranged in a kind of logical disorder tell you that your wall mirror is an example of Rococo, probably dating around the 1760s. Chippendale, through his publication *The Gentleman and Cabinet-Maker's Director* (1754), played an important role in establishing the fashion for Rococo in England.

CHINESE CHIPPENDALE MIRROR

My grandmother has had this mirror in her entrance hall as long as I can remember. What is its style, and approximately how old is it?
J.H.D. — New York, N.Y.

Your grandmother's Chinese Chippendale style wall mirror in a carved gilt-wood frame effectively illustrates how, around 1760, the English designers and carvers of mirror frames skillfully fused Oriental and European motifs. Such fanciful and favorite Chinese motifs as mandarins, pagodas, long-beaked birds and icicles happily mingle with Rococo scrolls and foliage.

ENGLISH SHERATON MIRROR

I bought this English Sheraton style wall mirror with églomisé *decoration at auction. How is this painted decoration on glass done, and why is this term applied to it?*

F.W.A. — *Woodstock, N.Y.*

Sheraton in his *Cabinet Dictionary* (1803) gives considerable space to what he describes as "back painting"—that is, the decoration of mirrors either by painting directly on the back of the glass or by "mezzotint black prints" transferred onto it and colored by hand. He writes that painting may be done directly on glass without a print, but that the "true colors must be laid on first, for they cannot be altered as in the usual way of painting." The French term *églomisé* derives from Jean Glomi (d. 1786), French designer and framer, who is usually given credit for inventing this technique.

CONVEX WALL MIRROR

Can you give me any information about this mirror? It is made of a light wood covered with gold leaf. The eagle and the lion's head are black.

J.W.T. — *Columbia, Mo.*

Your fine English Regency style round convex wall mirror in a carved gilt-wood frame designed with candle arms dates around 1805–1815. This well-known Empire type, introduced from France, became widely popular in England. In fact it was the only variety mentioned in Sheraton's *Cabinet Dictionary* (1803).

REGENCY STYLE MIRROR

The original label still on the back of our convex wall mirror reads "J. Turner, Upholder Cabinet- maker, Appraiser and Undertaker, No. 16 Great Litchfield Street, Cavendish Square, A great variety of paper hanging." What can you tell me about this cabinetmaker?

A.S.N. — Renton, Wash.

The cabinetmaker John Turner, of 16 Great Litchfield Street, appears in Sheraton's list of master cabinetmakers in and around London in 1803. Your handsome Regency style circular convex wall mirror in a carved gilt-wood frame provided with candle arms dates around 1805–1810. The label, which tells so much about the scope of an upholsterer's work in a typical contemporary manner, adds considerably to the value.

QUEEN ANNE DRESSING MIRROR

My lacquered dressing mirror, which I bought at auction, can also be used for writing. Does this make it rare?

E.H. — Snoqualmie Falls, Wash.

In the early examples of the swinging dressing mirror mounted on a box stand — about 1695 — the stand was frequently a miniature version of a desk, the slant front opening to serve as a writing board and to disclose small pigeonholes. The long drawer below was fitted with toilet accessories. During the reign of Queen Anne the desk portion was sometimes omitted. No doubt the examples with writing equipment would be more highly valued.

HEPPLEWHITE DRESSING MIRROR

I recently inherited this dressing mirror. The drawers have small boxes and compartments. Did men use this kind of mirror? Do you think it is an antique?

A.B. — Lee's Summit, Mo.

Yes, your Hepplewhite style shield-shaped dressing mirror having a row of drawers in the stand fitted with compartments for beauty requisites is an antique. It was made in England probably around the 1780s. When men shaved themselves they probably used an ordinary mirror, without the fittings of the type made for ladies. This plain type of dressing glass is not illustrated in the important trade catalogues, but, no doubt, large numbers were made.

VICTORIAN PRINT RACK

When my husband refinished this old piece of furniture, lovely inlaid panels appeared. Is it a music rack? And how old?

J.D.K. — Memphis, Tenn.

You have a print rack that shows classical influence and belongs to the Victorian era. It is probably English, dating in the latter part of the nineteenth century.

SHEET-MUSIC RACK

I have an antique wooden piece with a rounded top. When it is opened, one can see the shield that I've sketched. I would like to know its age and what it was used for.

E.F. — Stockton, Cal.

According to the diamond-shaped registration device, the design for your piece of furniture was registered at the London Patent Office January 10, 1860. It appears to be a stand or rack for holding newspapers or sheet music and is quite unusual.

HOUSEHOLD SAFE

I would appreciate whatever you can tell me about my safe. The four feet are shaped like horses' hooves and just above them are four Egyptian heads.

J.M. — Selden, N.Y.

Your household safe, a very nice example, dates around the 1860s. The best safes were made in England.

ENGLISH JEWEL SAFE

I will appreciate any information as to the age and style of my jewel safe. It is not marked.

G.E.T. — Kansas City, Mo.

Your pedestal-mounted jewel safe appears to be English and in the style of the late years of the Regency. It was most likely made by a cabinetmaker about 1810–1830.

EARLY GEORGIAN SETTEE

Quite a few years ago I bought this English early Georgian settee at auction. Wasn't this kind of back used on Chippendale sofas? Also, the needlework is badly worn. What kind of fabric would you suggest?

B.M.T. — Glendale, Cal.

This kind of arched, serpentine-shaped back with outscrolled arms forming a continuation of the undulating back was the chief feature of Chippendale settees. However, the Chippendale style made no abrupt break with the past, and the same kind of back and arms occurred on Georgian settees around 1750. A rich and strong crimson, gold, or emerald-green silk damask would be appropriate.

HALL RACK

*Any information you can give me about my rose-
wood hall tree will be appreciated.*

G.P. — La Porte, Tex.

The small mirror centered in the openwork back of your hall rack indicates the design is of French inspiration. French hall trees of this
kind are generally of cast iron rather than wood. Yours is probably
English or American. It is in the Renaissance Revival style, dating
around 1860–1885.

CHIPPENDALE DUMBWAITER

*I understand that my dumbwaiter is an antique
and was made in England. Can you tell me why
these were called dumbwaiters and just how they
were used?*

F.T.T. — Pasadena, Cal.

They were used for the service of the dining table. Sheraton defines
it in his *Cabinet Dictionary* (1803) as "a useful piece of furniture to
serve in some respects, the place of the waiter, whence it was so
named." Your type, with three circular trays increasing in diameter
from top to bottom and revolving on a shaft on a tripod base, is
especially characteristic. As a rule the dumbwaiter was placed diag-
onally at the corner of a dining table so that the diners could help
themselves from it when the servants had withdrawn; it held extra
knives, forks and plates, and dessert. It was also useful for after-dinner
drinking.

SHERATON PLATE-AND-CUTLERY STAND

I recently inherited this piece of furniture, but no one knows how it was used or what it is called. Do you?

P.B.A. — Tacoma, Wash.

Yes, your Sheraton stand, dating around 1800–1810, is known as a plate-and-cutlery stand and was one of the numerous accessories introduced in England around the mid-eighteenth century for the service of the dining table. These stands, like dumbwaiters, were particularly used at informal dinner parties. Sheraton writes in his *Cabinet Dictionary* (1803) that this kind of stand was "made to stand by a table at supper, with a circular end and three partitions crosswise to hold knives, forks and plates, at that end, which is made circular on purpose."

ENGLISH CANTERBURY

About one year ago this English stand, or rack, came into my possession. How was it used, and does it have a special name?

M.L.N. — Spanaway, Wash.

In the early nineteenth century, stands such as yours were made to hold bound volumes of music, and the music stand was called a Canterbury. In his *Cabinet Dictionary* (1803) Sheraton writes that the term "Canterbury" was given to "a small music stand with two or three hollowed-topped partitions . . . about three inches apart from each other . . . for holding music books." Sheraton explains that the plain legs are fitted with casters so that the stand can be "run under a pianoforte." Your Canterbury is probably English, of the early nineteenth century.

ENGLISH

HEPPLEWHITE DEMILUNE SIDEBOARD

I bought my mahogany sideboard at a sale in this region. It seems quite old although in perfect condition. Any information about it would be appreciated.

T.W.H. — Swoope, Va.

It is a Hepplewhite demilune (half-moon) sideboard made about 1780–1800. If the drawer sides, bottoms and backboards are of oak, it is English. If they are of pine, it is American.

SHERATON STYLE SIDEBOARD

We inherited this sideboard from my husband's family. What is its approximate age, style, and place of origin?

N.T. — New York, N.Y.

A practical innovation by the English cabinetmakers of the last quarter of the eighteenth century is the sideboard provided with drawers and cupboards. Up until this time the English sideboard (table) was without drawers or cupboards of any sort. "The great utility of this piece of furniture," writes Hepplewhite in his *Cabinet-Maker and Upholsterer's Guide* (1788), "has procured it a very general reception; and the conveniences it affords render a dining room incomplete without a sideboard." Its enduring popularity shows how right Hepplewhite was.

Sideboards showed considerable variation in design, not only in the arrangement and number of drawers and doors but also in the shape of the front. They varied in length from around five to more than nine feet. Square tapering legs were favored, almost always with four in the front, continuing from the stiles, and generally two in the rear. Sheraton's designs for sideboards are similar to those of Hepplewhite's, but they are characterized by a brass rod at the back extending the entire length. It was used, according to Sheraton, to set large dishes against and to support a couple of candlebranches in the middle, which when lighted gave a very brilliant effect to the silverware. Your sideboard with its brass rod, but without a candlebranch in the center, is in the Sheraton style, having been made in England around 1800.

SHERATON STYLE SIDEBOARD

The Somerset County Historical Society of Mary-land has been presented with this sideboard. Could you tell me its age and whether it is an English or American piece?

R.D.B. — Princess Anne, Md.

Your sideboard in the Sheraton style was probably made around 1825, but we cannot tell from the snapshot if it is English or American.

ENGLISH VICTORIAN SIDEBOARD

My sideboard is of solid oak, with doors and drawers covered by mahogany veneer. I have seen similar sideboards, but without the intricate carving and marble top. Is it an English or American piece?

D.J.S. — Falls Church, Va.

From the details, I would say your sideboard is English and made to someone's special order. Such oak sideboards are Victorian, dating about 1860–1870.

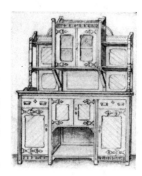

EASTLAKE SIDEBOARD

This English sideboard is solid mahogany and has heavy brass hardware. It was purchased from an estate in Virginia many years ago. Can you help determine its age?

A.K.H.—Plymouth Meeting, Pa.

Your Victorian sideboard, dating around the 1870s, is an interesting example of the so-called Eastlake style. The furniture Eastlake favored was a vaguely traditional rural style based on early English forms somewhat Elizabethan and early Jacobean.

CANDLE TABLE

This small candle table is the only unidentified piece of furniture in a group on loan from Cliveden (the renowned Germantown residence of the Chew family), which is being shown at this year's University Hospital Antiques Show. A friend thought it was made in Philadelphia. What do you think?

S.C.—Philadelphia, Pa.

Legs of the form found on your Chippendale style piecrust table, which dates around 1760, were used occasionally on English furniture of the 1700s. Certain other features—the kind of piecrust molding, the beading—also suggest English provenance. Unless an article of Colonial furniture can be positively authenticated as American, it must be regarded as European.

QUEEN ANNE STYLE CARD TABLE

I would be grateful for any information you can give me about my antique English card table.
S.T.R. — Everett, Wash.

One of the best-known pieces of Queen Anne furniture is the card table having an oblong folding top, four outset rounded corners to hold candlesticks, and four sunken wells for money or counters. The top of your table is covered with the conventional green cloth, which in more costly examples was often replaced by velvet or needlework. The interest in cardplaying and gambling throughout the eighteenth century made card tables indispensable.

PAPIER-MÂCHÉ GAME TABLE

How old is my game table and fire screen? The base is wood, the top mother-of-pearl inlay and some composition material.

P.D.B. — Athens, Ohio

Your table is not a fire screen but a Victorian game table with a papier-mâché top inlaid for playing checkers or chess. It might have been made by the English firm Jennens & Bettridge between 1840 and 1865.

ENGLISH CENTER TABLE

Can you tell the approximate age of my hand-carved table? It was brought from England to Canada many years ago. Is it a Victorian antique?
R.L.K. — The Dalles, Ore.

Your richly carved center table is in the Victorian Louis XV style, dating about 1850–1865. It is called a center table because it was intended to be placed in the center of a room, or at least not against a wall, and was therefore finished on all four sides.

GAME- AND WORKTABLE

I bought my game table in an antique shop and would appreciate anything you can tell me about it.

M.B. — Fredonia, Kans.

Combination game- and worktables such as yours were introduced into England in the early nineteenth century. Yours probably dates in the 1840s. Your table is in the Victorian Classical style of the "pouch" variety. Victorian ladies kept their needlework in these pouches.

GEORGE II CARD TABLE

My grandmother owned this antique table. As you can see, it has a double-hinged extension rather than a swing-out leg. I do hope you can tell me more about it.

E.C.W. — Pittsburgh, Pa.

Your early Georgian hinged-top card table probably dates from around the 1740s. This kind of folding frame supporting the hinged top is called a "concertina movement," and became popular in England after 1715.

GATELEG DINING TABLE

Can you tell me how old my large gateleg table is and where it was made? Was it used for dining?
N.T. — Puyallup, Wash.

Prior to the restoration of the monarchy in England in 1660, meals were served in the great hall, which, in a general sense, was an all-purpose room for dining and entertaining. After 1660, rooms set apart for dining came into general use among the upper classes. At that time gateleg dining tables like yours were the most popular. Sometimes they were very large and had double gates to support the two heavy ends. Your table with baluster-turned supports and single gates probably dates around 1670–1690.

SHERATON DINING TABLE

I bought this English dining table at auction, and I would like to know when such tables were used and if they were popular.
P.B.F. — Boston, Mass.

Dining tables such as yours, made in sections that could be bolted together, were introduced in England around 1800. Sheraton explains this kind in his *Cabinet Dictionary* (1803), where he writes: "The common useful dining tables are upon pillar and claws, generally four claws to each pillar, with brass castors. A dining table of this kind may be made to any size, by having a sufficient number of pillar and claw parts, for between each of them is a loose flap, fixed by means of iron straps and buttons, so that they are easily taken off and put aside." He says that the size may be readily estimated by allowing two feet to each person.

CHIPPENDALE THREE-PART DINING TABLE

Sometime ago my family purchased this English
mahogany dining table at auction, and now it is
mine. I would appreciate any information about it.
                    P.S.N.—New Haven, Conn.

This type of three-part extension dining table came into use in England
around the middle of the eighteenth century and retained its popularity until about 1800. It comprises a central section with two rectangular drop leaves and four cabriole legs ending in ball-and-claw
feet, and a pair of half-round consoles, each on three legs. The whole
or any part could be securely joined together "at pleasure." The two
semicircular ends when detached could be used as side tables. Your
table probably dates around the 1760s or early 1770s.

ENGLISH LIBRARY TABLE

We have a table with a revolving circular top and
drawers all the way around. What kind of a table
is this, and where and when was it made?
                    C.E.R.—Bryn Mawr, Pa.

Your table is described in contemporary catalogues as "a round
mahogany library table." The frieze was fitted with drawers and occasionally divided for books. It is in the late Sheraton style, made in
England around 1800. Many of these tables dating from the early 1800s
were on a turned column with splayed legs. According to contemporary records, the problem of arranging books in a circular space
was surmounted by inserting at regular intervals wedge-shaped blocks
faced with a false book spine.

PEMBROKE TABLE

*We have had this table in our family for genera-
tions. It has drop leaves and a drawer. Has this
type of table a name? How old is it?*

F.H. — Bay Head, N.J.

Your table is called a Pembroke table. These tables always have drop
leaves on both sides, supported on hinged wooden brackets, and are
provided with a frieze drawer. As a rule they are made with four tapering legs. According to Sheraton, they received their name from that
"of the lady who first gave orders for one of them, and who probably
gave the first idea of such a table to the workman" — perhaps the
Countess of Pembroke (1737–1831). "The size of such tables," writes
Sheraton, "is from three feet eight inches to four feet wide, that is
when open; and from two feet ten inches to three feet long when the
flaps are down. The width of the bed should never be less than one
foot nine inches; but in general, they are from one foot ten inches to
two feet one inch, and their height never more than two feet four
inches, including casters."

Though Pembroke tables served different purposes, such as for
having tea or working embroidery, they were mainly used for meals.
According to Sheraton, they were especially appropriate "for a gentleman or lady to breakfast on." The tops of these useful and popular
tables were made in various shapes. However, Hepplewhite writes
in his *Guide* (1788) that oval and square are the most fashionable. Your
Pembroke table with its oval top and square and tapering legs is in the
Hepplewhite style, made in England late in the eighteenth century.

LATE SHERATON SOFA TABLE

*We inherited this table from my great-aunt. It is
6 feet long with the leaves up, but only 2 feet wide,
and about 28 inches high. What is its style and
age?*

M.B.W. — Armonk, N.Y.

ENGLISH

Tables such as yours are called sofa tables, and became popular in England at the close of the eighteenth century. Sheraton writes that they "are used before a sofa" and illustrates an example with a sofa in his *Drawing Book* (1791–1794) so that "a stranger may more clearly see the use of such tables. Ladies [he added] mainly occupy them to draw, write or read upon." The columnar support in conjunction with four inward-curved legs indicates that your table dates from the early 1800s.

PEDESTAL WINE TABLE

We inherited this table from my husband's family, native Bermudians, and were told it is a "gaming" or "hunting" table. The top is a solid piece of mahogany. Any facts about it will be appreciated.
R.H.T. — St. George, Bermuda

Tables such as yours are known as "social" or wine tables and were introduced in England toward the end of the eighteenth century, intended for after-dinner drinking around the fireplace. The two ends of the horseshoe-shaped top faced the fireplace. Some of these tables had folding screens as protection against heat and a network bag stretched across the open portion to hold biscuits. The metal coasters sliding in a well held bottles, to avoid accidents. Judging from the snapshot, your pedestal wine table dates about 1810.

TEA OR CHINA TABLE

I've owned this solid mahogany table for sixteen years. It came from the Chippendale Melody Farms, Lake Forest, Illinois, estate of the late J. Ogden Armour. Could it have been designed by that great cabinetmaker Thomas Chippendale?
E.B.R. — Indianapolis, Ind.

It is not as ornate as the few pieces of known Chippendale workmanship, nor is the design like any table illustrated in his book *The Gentleman and Cabinet-Maker's Director.* Your tea or china table dates about 1750–1770 and was probably the work of some other London craftsman of Chippendale's day.

QUEEN ANNE WRITING OR DRESSING TABLE

Sometime ago I bought this English kneehole desk at auction. Now I am about to give it to my daughter. What can you tell me about it?

Z.E. —Carmel, Cal.

Tables of kneehole form having certain obvious advantages (drawers and a space for the knees) were introduced for writing in England late in the seventeenth century. They were equally popular as dressing tables. Chippendale in *The Director* (1754) gives designs for dressing tables of kneehole form having the top drawer equipped with a mirror and other dressing accessories and calls them "a buroe [desk] dressing table." Your table can serve as a writing or dressing table, and is in the Queen Anne style, early eighteenth century.

DAVENPORT DESK

My mother bought this desk about forty years ago at an auction in British Columbia. She said it is called a "captain's desk," because, compact and solid, it suited a captain's cabin on a rolling ship. I would appreciate anything you can tell me about the history of such desks and where mine comes from.

D.L. —Portland, Ore.

Your small writing table with a sloping top desk above a case of drawers is called a Davenport. Presumably the name derives from one Captain Davenport who ordered a desk of this type from an English cabinetmaking firm in the late eighteenth century. Judging from your snapshot, your Davenport is also of English manufacture, probably dating from around 1870–1880.

FURNITURE

Far Eastern

CHINESE CABINET

Please tell me anything you can about my carved and lacquered Chinese cabinet. It was owned by my mother's family. She said she hated to dust it when she was a child. That would have been in the 1870s in Providence, Rhode Island.

R.E.P. — Livermore, Cal.

Your cabinet is of the early nineteenth century, probably made by native craftsmen in Canton or Shanghai for Americans or Europeans living there or sea captains in the China trade. Providence in the 1870s was the home port of many sailing ships.

CHINESE CABINET

We would appreciate any information about this handcarved teakwood chest that we purchased two years ago.

E.J.S. — *Old Tappan, N.Y.*

Your Chinese cabinet was made by native craftsmen, probably in a seaport city, during the second half of the nineteenth century. Such cabinets were used to display jade, ivory and lacquered objects.

JAPANESE CABINET

I would be grateful for any information you can give me about this chest. It has copper or brass mountings, and the interior is compartmented with seven tiers of drawers. My uncle brought it from the Orient in the early 1900s.

M.T.D. — *Atlanta, Ga.*

Your Oriental cabinet is probably Japanese in origin, dating from about the last quarter of the nineteenth century.

CHINESE MING CHAIR

I inherited this chair from an uncle who lived in Peking, China, for many years. He said that it was a Ming chair. What do you think?
                    L.A.S.—North Bend, Wash.

Judging from the photograph, your splat-back chair could date from the late Ming Dynasty, around 1600–1644. However, in order to be sure, do have an expert examine it. This kind of chair having an arched horseshoe-shaped crest rail continuing to form the arms is one of the two principal types of Ming chairs. Your chair, like all early Chinese furniture, possesses a timeless simplicity in keeping with the finest classical traditions.

CHINESE CHAIR

Can you help us identify this chair? We bought it from a local antique dealer who said it was Chinese Chippendale.

                    E.M.F.—Oakland, N.J.

Your ornately carved chair is an example of Chinese export furniture, probably dating around the late nineteenth century. This is quite different from Chinese Chippendale, in which a medley of Chinese details—pagodas, mandarins, dragons, birds and bells—is grafted onto typical mid-eighteenth-century English furniture forms to create a "Chinese" flavor. During that period, fashionable society was eager for furniture and decorative accessories that suggested the Orient, no matter how remotely.

CHINESE ARMCHAIR

The seat and back of my antique chair are marble inlaid with mother-of-pearl. Can you tell its age and origin?

J.F.L. — Fort Collins, Colo.

Craftsmen made these teakwood chairs in larger Chinese cities during the nineteenth century for well-to-do merchants. Many were also exported to the United States.

KOREAN BRIDE'S CHEST

My husband purchased in Korea this black-lacquered wooden box with mother-of-pearl inlay on three sides and top. It is said to be a bride's dowry chest dating back a hundred years. Can you confirm this?

S.H.O. — Highland Park, N.J.

Yes, it is a Korean bride's chest dating from about the mid-nineteenth century. From earliest times chests were of first importance in all countries, but unlike the situation in other areas, where they were gradually supplanted by more specialized pieces, such as chests of drawers, their popularity has continued in the Far East to the present day.

POTTERY
AND
PORCELAIN

American

WHITE GRANITE JUG

A & M

Can you give me any information as to the age and origin of this old pitcher? I am enclosing a rough sketch of the trademark.

R.H.S.—*New Paltz, N.Y.*

The Empire Pottery was established in 1863 at Trenton, New Jersey. Around 1884 it was taken over by Alpaugh and Magowan, who specialized in semiporcelain ware, chiefly of white granite, which resembles English ironstone china. One of the earliest marks used by this firm was the British Royal Arms with the initials "A&M," such as those you have sketched.

BALTIMORE PITCHER

*I'd like to know the origin of this old pitcher,
which has an owl-and-crescent mark on the bottom and the initials "E.B."*

N.J.DeM. — Portsmouth, Va.

Your pitcher was made around the 1880s at a pottery started at Baltimore in 1846 by the English-born Edwin Bennett. In 1886 the owl-and-
crescent mark was used on chamber sets and jugs.

BELLEEK DISH

*My mother received this Belleek dish as a wedding
present in 1892. Was there more than one factory
making Belleek in America? Is Belleek a rarity?*

J.K.P. — Bloomington, Ind.

Belleek, with its pearly, lustrous glaze, was produced at a number of
American factories around 1880–1900. Perhaps the finest was Lotus
Ware by Knowles, Taylor & Knowles, East Liverpool, Ohio. Examples
of Belleek ware are now collectors' items.

BELLEEK CUP

*My three-handled vase is 7½ inches high, dec-
orated with grapes and vines. My curiosity is
piqued by the mark: a "CAC" monogram in a
circle, with an artist's palette and brushes above
to the left and the word "Belleek" printed below.
This is not the usual Belleek mark.*

J.P.C. — San Francisco, Cal.

When you write of the "usual Belleek mark" you are probably referring to the standard Irish Belleek mark, consisting of a central tower, a dog and a harp above the word "Belleek." However, owing to the almost overnight success of Irish Belleek, a number of American factories, mainly in New Jersey, about the mid-1880s, started to produce their version of Belleek, using a parian porcelain body and the character-istic iridescent pearl-like glaze. It is said that Ott and Brewer, of Trenton, New Jersey, the first factory to produce American Belleek, brought skilled workmen from Ireland to get them started. The Ceramic Art Company (CAC) of Trenton, New Jersey, made your three-handled cup about 1890–1900.

BELLEEK VASE

Enclosed is an exact copy of the mark on my Belleek vase and a snapshot of it. Can you give me more information about it?

L.H. — Carrollton, Tex.

Your vase was made by the Ceramic Art Company, founded in Tren-ton, New Jersey, in 1889 by Jonathan Coxon, Sr., and Walter Scott Lenox. This well-known factory, renamed Lenox, Inc., in 1906, used to excel in Belleek production. Old Belleek is now quite scarce.

CHERUB-AND-GRAPES PATTERN

What information can you give me about this pitcher? The background is a Wedgwood blue, with raised grapes, vines, leaves, and two cupids in white. The pitcher has no identifying trade-mark.

H.W.M. — Hillsborough, N.C.

The cherub-and-grapes pattern on your porcelain pitcher was first made by the United States Pottery Company of Bennington, Vermont (1852–1858). A duplicate of this pattern was made by Wedgwood in England at about the same time. As your pitcher bears no maker's name, it could be either one. This pattern is extremely rare in either blue-and-white porcelain or parian ware.

BENNINGTON PITCHER

A pair of these pitchers has been in our family for over 100 years. They are cream white, unglazed, and stand 10 inches high. The pitchers have no identifying marks, so I would appreciate anything you can tell me about them.

M.L.W. — Rutherford, N.J.

The "Corn Husk" pattern on your parian pitchers is the same design made at the United States Pottery Company, Bennington, Vermont, between 1852 and 1858. Your pitchers were probably produced there during those years, as we do not know of another pottery making this pattern. The pattern is one of the few purely American designs, having no counterpart in English ware, and is considered rare.

BUFFALO POTTERY JUG

What can you tell me about the mark on the bottom of my cream pitcher or jug?

M.G.K. — Weed, Cal.

The mark, dated 1906, was used on Buffalo pottery, made by a company that owed its existence to a brand of soap, Sweet Home Soap, manufactured by the John D. Larkin Company of Buffalo. The practice of giving premiums for the purchase of its soap eventually resulted in the Buffalo Pottery Company, started by Larkin in 1903. Collectors find Buffalo pottery an attractive item.

PORCELAIN CANTEEN

Enclosed is a picture of my husband's great-great-grandfather's porcelain canteen. We are curious to know whether or not he could have carried it into battle during the Civil War.

R.A.D. — Findlay, Ohio

We have never heard of a canteen made of earthenware—much less china—that was used by the soldiers in the American Civil War. A probable explanation is that your canteen was created as a souvenir of the company and regiment in which your husband's ancestor served. As such, it might be a collector's item.

VICTORIAN MAJOLICA

This mark is on the back of my leaf dish—an heirloom. Can you tell me anything about it?
M.K.—South Amboy, N.J.

The American potters, Griffen, Smith & Hill, who operated a pottery at Phoenixville, Pennsylvania, 1879–1890, became widely known for their Etruscan majolica. This kind of Victorian majolica was quite different from true majolica, the tin-glazed earthenware made in Renaissance Italy.

HOUND-HANDLE PITCHER

I bought this pitcher about thirty years ago in a small Nebraska town. We came across an identical copy pictured in a dictionary, which credited it to the Philadelphia Museum. Can you tell me more about it?

W.W.—Omaha, Neb.

Your hound-handle pitcher was probably made by the Vance Faïence Company of Tiltonville, Ohio, started in 1900, which acquired the Bennington hound mold from the pottery at Bennington, Vermont. Your pitcher seems to have the four identifying features of a Bennington hound: the head arched over the paws, with space to insert a finger, the chain collar, ribs that can be felt, and a pointed mold mark down the stomach of the hound.

BALTIMORE POTTERY

My tea set bears this mark. Can you tell me when and where it was made?

R.W.G. — St. Louis, Mo.

Your tea set was made at the pottery J. D. F. Haynes and Company of Baltimore, Maryland, around 1895–1900.

AMERICAN POTTERY MARK

Can you identify this mark, sketched from the back of an old stone china plate my husband dug up in our cellar?

J.R.B. — Addison, Mich.

Knowles, Taylor & Knowles, the pottery that made your plate, was organized in 1870 at East Liverpool, Ohio. In 1890 it became a company and "Co." was added to the name. So your plate dates between 1870 and 1890. Stone china is the same as ironstone china, which is a dense, hard earthenware.

SEMIPORCELAIN PITCHER

This pitcher is part of an eight-piece washstand set, all having the mark of an eagle and the monogram "K. T. & K. Co." on the back. Can you identify the set?

L.C. — Lake Orion, Mich.

Your set was made sometime after 1890 by the firm of Knowles, Taylor & Knowles of East Liverpool, Ohio. Isaac Knowles started the business in 1854 but didn't incorporate it until 1890. Your eagle-and-monogram mark was used on semivitreous porcelain. The firm also made white granite and hotel china.

WEST VIRGINIA POTTERY

I have a washstand set of bowl, pitcher, slop jar, chamber pot, and toothbrush holder with this mark on them. Do you know how old they are?
I.H. — Bumpus Mills, Tenn.

In 1887 the Wheeling Pottery of Wheeling, West Virginia, formed a second company known as La Belle Pottery Company. They called their semiporcelain "La Belle china," and from 1893 they used this name as one of their marks.

LAUGHLIN TEA SERVICE

My tea service bears this mark. Can you tell me where and about when it was made?
F.N. — Ashland, Ore.

Your tea service was made by the still-existing Homer Laughlin China Company, which started in business at East Liverpool, Ohio, in 1874. Yours is one of their early marks and represents the supremacy of the American eagle over the British lion.

OHIO EARTHENWARE

Could you date this pitcher for me? The mark on the bottom reads "D.E. McNicol, East Liverpool, O.," and below that, the number "1118."
R.J. — Memphis, Tenn.

Your earthenware pitcher was made between 1892 and 1900, which were the years when the McNicol Pottery was in business in Ohio. "1118" was the number of the model.

REBEKAH AT THE WELL

I would appreciate anything you can tell me about this teapot. It is honey-brown in color and the printing under the figure reads "Rebekah at the Well."

J.E.B. — Souderton, Pa.

The "Rebekah at the Well" teapot, made in brown, or Rockingham, glaze, was designed in 1852 by Charles Coxon for the E. & W. Bennet Company of Baltimore. Coxon adapted it from an English parian jug. Many American potteries have made copies of this widely popular model.

NEW YORK STATE SEMIPORCELAIN

From these pictures of my white china plate with handpainted gold trim and its mark, can you tell me who made it and how old it is?

A.W.F. — Greenville, Miss.

The plate was made by the Onondaga Pottery Company, Syracuse, New York, which was founded in 1871 and is still in business. From design and decoration of your plate, I believe it dates around 1890. After 1897 the mark "Syracuse China" was used by the company, which had become the Syracuse China Corporation.

ROGERS GROUP

My husband brought home this sculpture group, which is painted and has the words "Neighboring Pews" on the base. Can it be repaired?

A.B.H. — Plainfield, N.J.

Apparently you have one of many groups by the American sculptor John Rogers. Plaster casts of his work were very popular in the 1880s. The record shows yours was cast in 1883. The New-York Historical Society, which has many Rogers groups, might advise you where to have it repaired.

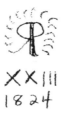

ROOKWOOD VASE

I just read an article describing my vase perfectly. It stated that the vase is Rookwood Pottery, first made in 1880. But the date on my mark is 1824. Can you explain this from my sketch of the mark and a picture of the vase?

A.C. — Chatham, N.J.

In Rookwood, each pattern is identified by a number, which usually appears under the name or the "RP" monogram and date. Thus the "1824" in your marking is the pattern number. The RP monogram was first used in 1886 and became the standard mark. To represent the year 1887, one flame point was placed above the RP; another flame point was added each year, making fourteen by 1900. The RP mark with the fourteen flame points was continued into the new century with the addition of a Roman numeral to denote the year. So the numerals "XXIII" indicate your vase was made in 1923.

OHIO TEA SET

How old is my tea set? The plates are marked with a crown and the name "Sterling China."

M.L.F. — Trenton, N.J.

The Sterling China Company has been active at East Liverpool, Ohio, since 1917. Your tea set decorated with Plymouth Pilgrims appears to be one of their early products.

STONEWARE JUG

Please tell me what you can about my brown-and-cream-colored jug. The only mark is a blue heart with "6" in the center.

A.J.P. — Easton, Pa.

It is an American stoneware jug of the kind widely used for cider, molasses, vinegar, or perhaps for homemade wine. It dates about 1900–1920. The heart may be the maker's mark, and the "6" for six quarts.

OHIO SEMIPORCELAIN

Please tell me what the markings on my white porcelain bowl and pitcher mean.

L.W. — Palo Alto, Cal.

The trademark on your bowl and pitcher is that of Taylor, Smith & Taylor, who began operating at East Liverpool, Ohio, in October 1901. Their principal product was semivitreous porcelain.

AMERICAN MARK

This mark, which looks like an American one, is on a number of plates that I have, Can you interpret it for me?

P.S. — Pasadena, Cal.

The mark is that of the East Liverpool Pottery Company of East Liverpool, Ohio, makers of "Waco" china and other decorated pottery, principally white granite. An earlier mark—a modification of the British coat of arms—was used on the souvenir china the company made for the presidential campaign of 1896.

AMERICAN

AMERICAN POTTERY MARK

The enclosed mark is on a set of china that was a wedding gift to me and now belongs to my daughter. She would like to know where she might obtain missing pieces.

K.M.J. — Washington, D.C.

The helmet and crossed swords was the first mark used by the Warwick China Company, which started a pottery at Wheeling, West Virginia, in 1887. They made semiporcelain wares. Matching pieces might be obtained in antique shops.

SEMIPORCELAIN

Can you estimate the age of this plate? I have a dozen — with four different turkey designs — and a platter. They belonged to my grandmother. I have sketched the mark.

L.M.P. — Philadelphia, Pa.

Your plates were made by the Wheeling Pottery Company, active at Wheeling, West Virginia, 1879–1900. In 1887 a second company was formed under the same management, known as La Belle China Company. They called their semiporcelain "La Belle china," and your mark is one used since 1893. Therefore your plates date after that.

WHISKEY JUG

What sort of jug is this? It is marked "From Park & Tilford, Grocers, 921–923 Broadway, N.Y."

L.P. — Baldwin, N.Y.

It is a stoneware whiskey jug dating between 1865 and 1890, when Park & Tilford was the quality grocery of New York City.

AMERICAN BEER SET

Can you identify my beer set? On the bottom of the mugs and pitcher is a helmet with crossed swords and a sort of scroll with the word "Warwick" on it. I was told that the set came from Germany over a hundred years ago.

M.B.K. — *Grosse Pointe Woods, Mich.*

Your informant was evidently mistaken as to the age and origin of your set. The Warwick China Company began operation in 1887 at Wheeling, West Virginia. The mark you describe was the company's first mark and was adopted about 1892 for making novelties in semi-porcelain.

BELLEEK SALT DISH

I wonder if you can tell from this photograph how old my salt dish is and also explain the marking and the name?

J.M. — *Columbus, Ohio*

The Willets Company of Trenton, New Jersey, was well known for its Belleek wares made during the 1880s and 1890s. Your mark, comprising a snake coiled to form a "W," with "Belleek" above and "Willets" below, is its characteristic mark.

POTTERY
AND
PORCELAIN

Continental

FRENCH PORCELAIN TEAPOT   J12. 597. ℣.

*Can you please tell me when this teapot was made
and by whom? It is very thin china, and the
dragons and flying bird that decorate it are out-
lined in gilt. I could not find the mark in any book.*
V.M.S. — Harrisonburg, Va.

Your teapot was made in the late nineteenth century at the porcelain
factory of A. Sorrel, Ponsas-sur-Rhône. Its mark is recorded in *Handbuch des Europäischen Porzellans,* by Ludwig Danckert, Prestel-Verlag,
München, 1954, and includes the distinguishing initials "AS" in
monogram.

VEILLEUSE

Can you give me some idea of what this floral pink-and-white china piece is called? I have enclosed a copy of the mark on the bottom of the teapot.

V.B. — Bat Cave, N.C.

Your piece of table service is called a *veilleuse;* the name derives from the French *veiller* — to keep a night vigil. It originally referred to any night lamp, but soon came to be given to a warmer for food or drink consisting of a hollow pedestal, containing a small lamp, on which sits a covered bowl or teapot. The bowl or teapot has a projecting bottom that fits into the pedestal so that its contents can be kept nearer to the warming flame of the small lamp. Beginning in the middle of the eighteenth century as food warmers, *veilleuses* were popularized in porcelain by the great German factories at Nymphemburg and Höchst. Soon potteries throughout Europe adapted the form into a tea warmer. Your *veilleuse,* made by W. Guérin & Company at Limoges, France, is of twentieth-century manufacture.

BOHEMIAN PORCELAIN FIGURE

We bought this porcelain piece as one of 500 art objects to be placed in our new bank, but we have been unable to identify it. We would appreciate your help.

T.M. — Lubbock, Tex.

Your ornamental figure was made at the Amphora Porcelain Factory, started by Riessner and Kessel in 1892 at Turn, near Teplitz, Bohemia. It was made most probably in the very early 1900s, when the art of porcelain figure-making was becoming notably effective in the hands of the German and Bohemian artists and manufacturers.

AMPHORA FIGURE

I have traced the markings from the bottom of this piece of pottery. Can you tell me where it came from?

M.B.A. — Wichita, Kans.

Your porcelain figure, depicting a young farm boy scything grain and a hen picking up seeds, was made at the Amphora Porcelain Factory at Turn, near Teplitz, Bohemia. Riessner and Kessel started this firm in 1892, and porcelain figures were its chief concern. This class of ceramic art suggests a popular version of Art Nouveau, which is currently finding interest among collectors.

AUSTRIAN TUREEN

I received this platter and vegetable dish as a gift. Can you tell me anything about them from my sketch of the mark?

L.B. — Union City, Mich.

This mark was used by a porcelain factory started by Oscar and Edgar Gutherz at Altrohlau, Bohemia, in 1899. Your tureen and matching stand were originally part of a table service.

FRENCH FAÏENCE PLATE

How old is this plate? I enclose a photograph of it and a drawing of the mark.

M.K. — Greenwich, Conn.

Your many-colored plate was made in 1887 at the faïence pottery at Blois, France, which was established after 1860.

SPANISH PORCELAIN FIGURE

I am enclosing a photograph and the mark from a china figure I have. The man I bought it from could not tell me its history. Can you?
                    M.A.E. — Chestertown, Md.

Judging from the mark, your figure was made at Buen Retiro, the chief Spanish porcelain factory at Madrid from 1759 to 1808. However, it is best to have it examined by an expert to be certain. Whoever made the mold for the figure was no doubt inspired by Velázquez's "Infanta Margarita," painted about 1659.

CALIFORNIA GOLD RUSH PLATE

Can you help me find out if this set of mining-scene plates is unique? The plates are marked "Mark-Milliet and Co."
                    L.B. — Placerville, Cal.

Your gold-rush plates were made in some quantity in France for American markets.

BOHEMIAN VASE

Can you tell me the make and year of this vase? The mark is "C F" in large capitals and the number "408."
                    A.D.B. — Joliet, Ill.

The vase is Bohemian, made between 1846 and 1857 at the Christian Fischer porcelain factory in Pirkenhammer. The "408" refers to the factory design number.

BISQUE CANDELABRA

The base and candle holders of my candelabra are porcelain, the figures are bisque done in pastel, and some gold leaf still outlines part of the base molding. There are no marks anywhere. Can you identify them?

B.D.P. — Elizabethton, Tenn.

Judging from the snapshots and your description, your candelabra are of Continental — probably French — origin, dating about the third quarter of the nineteenth century, since the practice of painting bisque, or unglazed, porcelain figures dates about mid-century. This medium was to become increasingly popular for less costly figure work in the latter part of the century.

BOHEMIAN VASE

This urn has been in our family for years. It has four parts: top, vase, base, and pedestal. The mark is worn, but you can see a distinct capital "E." What can you tell me about it?

W.O.F. — Great Falls, Mont.

The shape and decoration of your vase is typical of the porcelain for which Vienna was long noted. The capital "E," however, indicates that your piece was made at the porcelain manufactory established at Eichwald, Bohemia, in 1871 by Bloch & Company. The "E" is for Eichwald.

BOHEMIAN FIGURE

I bought this figure from a reputable antique dealer, who could only tell me that it was Bohemian. I have failed to find the mark in any book, and I wonder if you can give me some information about the figure's maker.

A.D.H. — *Westminster, Mass.*

Your figure was made at a porcelain factory started by Ed. Eichler in 1860 at Dux, a town in Bohemia. The factory produced figurines. Judging from the number that survive in the United States, Victorians found them irresistible.

BOHEMIAN FACTORY MARK

This mark appears on some china we own. What can you tell me about the mark?

M.F.A. — *Pomona, Cal.*

The initials "Epiag" are for the Erste [first] Böhmische Porzellan Industrie, A.G., a combine that controls a group of Bohemian factories. These initials appear in a number of twentieth-century Bohemian factory marks. Your mark was used after 1918.

BONN PORCELAIN

I have five dessert dishes bearing this mark. Can you tell me their age and what the 1755 in the mark means?

H.E.W. — *Millheim, Pa.*

Your dishes were made after 1891 at the porcelain factory of F. A. Mehlem, started at Poppelsdorf, near Bonn, Germany. The date 1755 was the year the porcelain and pottery factory was founded here.

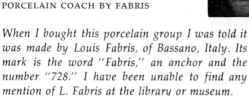

PORCELAIN COACH BY FABRIS

When I bought this porcelain group I was told it was made by Louis Fabris, of Bassano, Italy. Its mark is the word "Fabris," an anchor and the number "728." I have been unable to find any mention of L. Fabris at the library or museum.

C.J.P. — Weston, Mass.

Ludwig Danckert's book on European porcelains, *Handbuch des Europäischen Porzellans,* published in Munich, 1954, mentions Luigi Fabris, who had a porcelain factory in Milan. An expert in New York dates Fabris pieces about 1850 and believes that many of them were similar to eighteenth-century German porcelain groups.

BISQUE FIGURES

I would like to know something about these figures. They were given to a cousin of mine in 1885. She called them bisque, and they are beautifully colored.

L.B.P. — Evansville, Wis.

German and Bohemian porcelain factories made figures like these of bisque — an unglazed porcelain — a little before 1885. At that time pairs of figurines were widely used in this country as parlor mantel ornaments, and they were imported here in considerable quantity.

ATHLETIC YOUNG PEOPLE

My late aunt and uncle left me these 13-inch china statuettes. Could you tell when they were made despite the fact that they bear no mark?

A.F. — Great Neck, N.Y.

Your figurines are of European manufacture — made probably in Germany or Bohemia — and date around the 1880s. Pairs of such statuettes in this genre were exceedingly popular at this time.

LIMOGES PORCELAIN PITCHER

This pitcher was a wedding present many years ago. Can you tell me the name of the maker from the mark "GDA"? I have been unable to trace it in any book of china marks.

W.H.W. — Pound Ridge, N.Y.

The mark "GDA," in script or Roman letters, stands for Gerard & Dufraissiex, who had a porcelain factory at Limoges, France, and their American representative, Abbott. In 1896, with the death of Charles Field Haviland, they acquired his factory, and for a few years some of their porcelain had both the "Ch. Field Haviland" mark and the original "GDA."

RUSSIAN BOWL

My china bowl has an "A," an eagle, St. George and Russian letters on the bottom. I think it's a "Gardner" bowl. Can you tell me about it?

G.K.D. — APO 271, N.Y.

Francis Gardner, an Englishman, established a porcelain factory near Moscow in 1787. Its mark during the reign of Czar Alexander II (1855–1881) was similar to the mark you describe.

GIEN MAJOLICA VASE

I am curious about this bottle-shaped vase. It belonged to my great-grandmother. The mark shows three castles with the word "Gien" below.

M.D.E. — San José, Cal.

The vase is French majolica, made at the pottery in Gien, which was opened in 1864. Majolica is an earthenware with opaque white tin oxide glaze.

FRENCH CHINA CLOCK

*I would like to know something about my por-
celain clock. The mark is a lavender castle with
the word "Gien" below.*

L.T.M. — Florence, Ala.

The classical form and ornament of your French clock case, made at a
ceramic factory in Gien, suggests a date of manufacture around the
1870s. The maker of the works is unknown.

MODERN FRENCH EARTHENWARE

*Would you please tell the approximate age of this
plate, one of a set of twelve I purchased in Aix-en-
Provence. The mark is also enclosed — do you
know whose it is?*

D.C. — APO 401, New York, N.Y.

The plate is modern French earthenware with transfer-printed decoration. It was made after 1900 at the pottery in Gien, France. This pottery
opened in 1864 and first made copies of Italian majolica. After 1900 it
started to produce earthenware with its typical lead glaze.

GOLDSCHEIDER BUST

*Your comments on the age and origin of this re-
cently acquired bust would be most helpful. It is
marked "F. Goldscheider, Wien."*

C.J.B. — Mattapan, Mass.

F. Goldscheider established his pottery in
Vienna in 1882. He made many faïence busts
like yours, marked with his name.

LIMOGES DECORATOR'S MARK

This mark is on my handpainted pitcher. Do you know it?

D.M.S. — Westbury, N.Y.

L. Greaney was one of the independent china painters of Limoges, France, who decorated pieces from the local factories. He decorated your pitcher in 1913.

LIMOGES CUP AND SAUCER

I would appreciate any information about this cup and saucer. The background is a graded series of pastel washes of cerulean blue, pink and yellow. Floral pattern is in darker tones; feet, handle and rim are gold. Mark enclosed.

J.W.R. — Hackettstown, N.J.

The mark as sketched indicates your cup and saucer are French porcelain made at the Limoges factory of Guérin, Pouyat-Elite, Ltd., between 1891 and 1914. Elite was also their trademark.

BAVARIAN FACTORY MARK

Can you tell me the name of the company who made my tea set? Are they still in business?

I.R. — Pittsfield, Mass.

Yes, Heinrich and Company, which made your tea set, is still very much in business. They started to manufacture porcelain at Selb, Bavaria, in 1896. Their wares were popular, and much of their production was exported to the United States in the years prior to World War I.

GERMAN PORCELAIN MARK

Can you identify this mark? It appears on some demitasses of ours which are made of white, very thin china, with gold trim.

G.W.K. — *Winston Salem, N.C.*

Your demitasses and saucers were produced at the porcelain factory of Hermann Ohme, Niedersalzbrunn, Saxony, Germany. The factory opened in 1882, but it did not survive World War II.

HAVILAND CHINA

I would like to know more about my Haviland cups and saucers, which I recently inherited from my husband's family. The saucers have high sides, but no ring to hold the cup.

P.C. — *Pensacola, Fla.*

Haviland porcelain has been made at the famous factory in Limoges, France, since 1842. From the design, I would judge that your cups and saucers were made between 1860 and 1880.

LUNÉVILLE FAÏENCE LION

Is this figurine an antique? The marks are "K&G," with the word "France" below on the back of the base.

O.O'C. — *Schenectady, N.Y.*

It is not an antique but was made after 1891 at the pottery of Keller & Guérin at Lunéville, France. The word "France," was required on all French pottery after 1891. Other Lunéville figurines were post-World War I souvenirs.

BAVARIAN PORCELAIN

Some twenty years ago my husband bought at auction this gilded white dessert service. The pieces are marked "Krautheim — SELB — Bavaria." Can you tell the approximate age of the set?

J.S.G. — Evanston, Ill.

Your set was made at the porcelain factory of Krautheim & Adelberg, Selb, Bavaria, established in 1884. The shape and the gilt decoration would date this service about the 1900-1910 period.

FRENCH INKWELL

Can you identify my china dog inkwell? My great-grandmother, who gave it to me, said it was supposed to have been used by Santa Anna, the president of Mexico. On the underside are the marks "j p."

T.S.C. — Mobile, Ala.

The initials "j p" are probably those of Jacob Petit, a French potter who, with his brother Mardochée, bought a porcelain factory at Fontainebleau in 1830. They later started a branch at Belleville. The models, molds, and marks were used until 1886.

FRENCH INCENSE BURNER

Enclosed are the markings as well as a picture of my Chinese incense burner. It has been in our family for over 100 years. Could you tell its age and origin?

D.P.H. — Berkeley, Cal.

14 74

Your Chinese style incense burner was made at the faïence pottery of Huart de Northomb, Longwy, Lorraine, France, before 1800. Factories producing white earthenware have existed at Longwy from the end of the eighteenth century to the present day.

MONKEY BAND

I have inherited a number of porcelain monkeys, each bearing a musical instrument. The colors are sharp and the glaze is deep. They all have a crossed-swords mark on the bottom. Any information would be greatly appreciated.

M.S.B. — Detroit, Mich.

Your figures bear the mark of Meissen, which first made monkey figurines such as these about 1750. Kaendler, head modeler of the Meissen factory, modeled a band of more than twenty monkeys, including a conductor, to ridicule a personal enemy, Count Bruhl, the leader of the court orchestra of the Elector of Saxony. These figures became widely popular, and numerous copies of them were made at other European factories. For this reason I suggest you have an expert examine your figures, as the Meissen crossed swords — one of the most forged of all marks — may simply indicate on your figures that they were modeled in the Meissen manner.

COACH-AND-FOUR

I would appreciate any information on this piece. My mother bought it years ago and was told that it was quite valuable. The emblem I've drawn is on the bottom in blue.

F.L.B. — Louisville, Ky.

Your coach-and-four dates from about the 1870s or 1880s. It was made at the porcelain factory started in 1850 at Sitzendorf, Thuringia, Germany, by the Voigt Brothers, who specialized in the imitation of Meissen porcelain.

NODDING CRINOLINE GROUP

These three bisque figurines are beautifully colored. The heads are weighted to nod at the slightest touch. There are no identifying marks. Can you tell me anything about them?

C.W.S. — Cincinnati, Ohio

Your crinoline group, modeled in the Meissen manner, is of European origin, probably German, dating from the second half of the nineteenth century. The nodding head originated in China and is known as a *magot*. I have seen single figures with movable heads made at Meissen, but a group such as yours is unusual.

GERMAN CHINA MARK

This mark is on a large set of dishes my father bought for his bride some fifty-three years ago. Can you identify it?

R.D.McW. — Las Vegas, N.M.

Your dishes were made at the German porcelain factory of Paul Müller at Selb, Bavaria. It was in business between 1890 and 1918, when it merged with Lorenz Hutschenreuther, A.G., Selb.

NAPOLEON'S WEDDING COACH

*Can you tell me anything about this porcelain
group? It is marked on each side, "Voiture de
Mariage de Napoleon 2 Avril 1810." On the
bottom of the piece appear the numbers "12731"
and "8" and the word "Germany."*

H.E.T., Jr. — Merchantville, N.J.

Your porcelain piece depicts the wedding coach used by Napoleon
when he married the Archduchess Marie Louise of Austria. The numbers are production symbols. It was made in Germany after 1891.

GERMAN PORCELAIN

*My small handpainted porcelain vase shows a
boy, two donkeys, and some scenery. I have
sketched the mark and hope you can tell me more
about the vase's origin.*

G.C.LaR. — St. Louis, Mo.

Your vase was made by the porcelain factory started in 1794 at Tettau,
Oberfranken, Germany, under royal patronage — hence the "PRIV
1794" in the mark, indicating the royal warrant. The distinguishing
initials "P. T." are for Porzellanfabrik, Tettau. Your vase was made
sometime after 1890, judging from the mark. The factory still exists.

PARIS PORCELAIN

*This sketch of a creamer and its mark are from a
tea set I inherited. Can you tell the age of the set?*
R.K.C. — Washington, D.C.

The Paris porcelain factory of Charles Pillivuyt, Du Puis & Cie., made
your tea set sometime between 1840 and 1860.

DELFT PLATTER

Enclosed is a picture of my Delft platter and the markings on its back. Is it possible to give me any information about it?

V.V. — Rumney, N.H.

The mark is that of the faïence factory De Porceleyne Fles (The Porcelain Bottle) of Delft, founded in 1655 by Wouter van Eenhoorn and Quirinus Aldersz van Cleynoven. Although the oldest Delft pottery in existence, it first used a bottle as its mark in 1795 when Johannes and Dirk Harlees became the owners. Your mark is a modern one, less than 100 years old.

ROSENTHAL MARK

My demitasse and saucer, made by Tilly, have this mark sketched on both pieces. The company no longer exists. Are you acquainted with it?

A.R.I. — Los Angeles, Cal.

The mark is that of Philip Rosenthal, who started this still-existing porcelain factory at Selb, Bavaria, in 1879. It is an early mark. "Tilly" was the name of the pattern.

GERMAN PORCELAIN

I have sketched the mark that appears on the bottom of this statue, which my husband bought at a rummage sale. Can you tell us when and where it was made?

J.M. — Philadelphia, Pa.

The mark indicates that your figurine was made by the porcelain factory of L. Straus & Sons, Rudolstadt, Germany, around 1882–1890. They also made dinner services.

RS PORCELAIN

The mark I have sketched appears on my antique porcelain. Several pieces have "R.S. Germany" instead of "R.S. Prussia." I would like to know something about the origin of the marks, as I cannot find them in any book.

L.T. — Macon, Miss.

Reinhold Schlegelmilch started a porcelain factory at Tillowitz, Silesia, Germany, in 1869. His marks include the initials "RS." An earlier porcelain factory was set up at Suhl, Prussia, by Erdmann Schlegelmilch in 1861. His marks usually include the initials "ES." However, at least one of the marks of this factory bears the initials "RS" and "Prussia," which suggests some relationship between the two factories after 1890.

GERMAN CREAM PITCHER

I made this drawing of my white cream pitcher, originally part of a set belonging to my great-grandmother. It is white, with this mark in green on the bottom. Could you tell me who made it, and where and when?

W.F.H. — Bluffton, Ind.

The initials "C.T." are those of C. Tielsch, who started a porcelain factory at Altwasser, Silesia, Germany, in 1845. Your mark is an early factory mark. Tielsch wares received honorable mention at the Great Exhibition held in London in 1851. The factory was purchased in 1918 by the German firm of Hutschenreuther.

BOHEMIAN PORCELAIN GROUP

How old is this figurine we purchased and where was it made? The marks include a crown and the word "Amphora" in an oval.
                                    L.G.F. — West Roxbury, Mass.

Your porcelain group dates between 1892 and 1918. The mark is that of Riessner and Kessel, who started the Amphora Porcelain Factory in 1892 at Turn, Bohemia, where they specialized in figures. The firm changed its trademark in 1918, when Bohemia became part of Czechoslovakia.

GERMAN VASE

I would like help in finding out about this vase, which was given to me by my grandmother. I've copied the hallmark on the bottom to help you.
                                    L.K.C. III — Jacksonville, Fla.

Your vase was made at the porcelain and faïence factory of F. A. Mehlem, started at Poppelsdorf, near Bonn, Germany, in 1836. From the snapshot, your vase appears to date around the 1880s.

ROYAL SPHINX PLATE

Is the Dutch factory that made my plate still in existence? Who was P. Regout?
                                    F.D.A. — Medina, Wash.

The still-existing Sphinx factory was started by Petrus Regout in 1836 at Maastricht, one of the three important ceramic centers in Holland. Modern marks refer to the wares as Royal Sphinx. Your mark dating after 1891 is listed in current directories.

BOHEMIAN GENRE GROUP

About what year was this group made? It is labeled "Pax et Labour." Inside the base is the triangular mark sketched above.

D.C.—Glen Ridge, N.J.

This genre group was made at the porcelain factory of Edward Eichler in Dux, Bohemia. The style of the modeling dates it about 1890–1910.

ROYAL DUX BUST

Any information you can give me about this piece, known as a Water Lily Lady, will be appreciated. On the bottom, in a triangle, is the letter "E" surrounded by "Royal Dux Bohemia," and above the triangle is the number "621."

R.W.T.—Kansas City, Mo.

Royal Dux was first made in Bohemia in 1860, but the romantic style of your bust is typical of the art of the final years of the nineteenth century. "621" was the model.

DELFT VASE

I recently acquired an urn, or vase, 15 inches high, which I assume to be old German Delft. It is made of pottery, with blue decoration covered with a white glaze. The domed cover is topped by an Oriental-looking foo dog. Can you identify this article for me?

R.F.P. — Shreveport, La.

If your underglaze blue-and-white Delft faïence vase is a period piece, it would have been made at Delft, Holland, around the late seventeenth or early eighteenth century. Because of its continuing popularity, however, old Delft has been notoriously copied and its marks faked countless times. Judged from this snapshot, your vase — from the "vulnerable" finial to the base — looks good, almost too good to be true. Objects that old, especially those made of faïence, will commonly show signs of age. Do have an expert examine it.

MAJOLICA PLATE

My wife and I have two plates and matching cups and saucers, but we have been unable to identify them. The colors include purple, yellow, and orange-red lusters. My wife saw similar plates in the Los Angeles Museum called "Deruta." Can you help us?

D.H.C. — Los Angeles, Cal.

Your pieces are majolica, the name given to Italian tin-glazed earthenware. The art of majolica attained its acme of perfection from about 1505 to 1525. Deruta, Gubbio, Urbino Castel Durante, and Faenza were among the principal centers producing it. In the nineteenth century the Victorians revived interest in Italian majolica. The principal source for much of this work was in Italy, including the Ginori factory at Doccia and the Cantagalli factory at Florence. Judged from the snapshot that you have sent, your plates are nineteenth-century Italian reproductions.

ITALIAN PORCELAIN

In 1954 we went to a moving company auction and purchased a barrel of miscellanea for $5. Among a lot of glassware we found a few pieces of a demitasse set. Could you possibly tell us anything about them from the picture and the sketch of the mark that appears on the bottom of the cups and saucers?

M.W. — Carmichael, Cal.

Your demitasses were produced by the porcelain manufactory of Richard Ginori, which was founded in 1735 by Carlo Ginori at Doccia, near Florence, Italy. In the latter part of the nineteenth century the Ginori manufactory was incorporated with the Società Ceramica Richard of Milan, and became known as Richard Ginori. Your mark dates after this incorporation. The firm has a store at 711 Fifth Avenue in New York City, and you can perhaps obtain more positive identification there.

FRENCH URN

This urn is 17 inches high. I copied the signature and motto from the reverse side. I've been told both that it is Lowestoft Armorial and that it is Samson of Paris, dating about 1900. Can you set me straight?

H.M.J. — Harrisonburg, Va.

Unlike most porcelain, Oriental Lowestoft never has a factory mark or other marks on the back. Any piece with a mark, particularly a square pseudo-Chinese mark in red with a running "S" beside it, such as yours, is china made in France, although it looks like Oriental Lowestoft. Yours is known as Samson — the name of the French manufacturer who copied Lowestoft and also other famous potteries, including Meissen and Chelsea. The consoling feature of a Samson mark is that no one, to the present time, has copied Samson.

SÈVRES VASE

We have an urn decorated with a scene apparently depicting Napoleon's victory at Austerlitz. Can you tell us more about it from its mark?
J.D.H. — Houghton, Mich.

The mark was used from 1804 to 1809 at Sèvres, the government-owned porcelain factory of France. The painters of Sèvres depicted the Napoleonic era with notable skill. The glory of Austerlitz is recalled on large vases of classical form, such as your example.

SÈVRES PLATE MARKS

Here are enlarged copies of the marks on my grandfather's Sèvres plates. What do they mean? The plates were given to him while he headed a Paris publishing house.

J.N.Y. — Easton, Pa.

The marks on your Sèvres plates indicate the following: The "SV. 47" underglaze mark in green is the date of manufacture, 1847. The Sèvres "1848" mark, which may be an overglaze mark in either gold or blue, is the date of decoration. The third mark, "Château des Tuileries" in red, was added to indicate the destination of pieces ordered by the king — at that time Louis-Philippe (1830–1848). It would be a good idea to have the marks examined by an expert and authenticated at first hand, as Sèvres marks have been widely forged.

SÈVRES MARK

Enclosed is a copy of the marks on my richly decorated china plate. Can you give me any details from these marks?
A.L.F.—Norwalk, Conn.

The marks indicate that your plate was made by Sèvres in 1844. It was made for the Château des Tuileries, Paris, the residence of King Louis-Philippe.

RED STONEWARE TEAPOT

My husband's family bought this Chinese-red teapot in 1887, and it was not new then. It is marked "S & G." Thank you for any help you can give me.
H.L.K.—Dallas, Tex.

Your red teapot with designs in relief and in a form somewhat in the style of Wedgwood's stoneware was made at Bodenbach, Bohemia, by Schiller and Gerbing, 1829 onward. (The firm was later separated into F. Gerbing and W. Schiller & Sons.) In England this ware is erroneously attributed to Shore and Goulding of Isleworth.

BOHEMIAN PITCHER

We would appreciate knowing the origin and approximate age of this pitcher. It was given to a member of our family many years ago.
J.M.T.—Tyler, Tex.

Because of the relief decoration on it, your ornamental pitcher is unmistakably a product of the W. Schiller & Sons factory at Bodenbach, Bohemia. It dates approximately between 1850 and 1875.

GERMAN FIGURINES

How old would you consider these figurines to be? Their mark reads "L. Straus & Sons, Rudolstadt, Germany."

B.M.L. — *Brooklyn, N.Y.*

The Straus porcelain factory was in business from 1882 to 1915. Your figurines were probably made around the 1890s.

FRENCH FAÏENCE MARK

Comic drawings of French soldiers are hand-painted on four plates I bought in France this year with this mark on the backs. Can you date them?

B.B. — *Allentown, Pa.*

Your plates were made at a sizable faïence factory started at Sarreguemines, Lorraine, France, around 1770 by Paul Utzschneider and carried on throughout the nineteenth century by his descendants. Your plates were made after 1919, when Alsace-Lorraine was returned to French sovereignty.

DRESDEN LAMP

I have lately fallen heir to what we've always called the "Dresden Lamp." My cousin brought it home from Europe many years ago. My research suggests it might have been made by one Carl Thieme. What can you tell from this picture and the mark copied from the base of the lamp?

C.V.M. — *Mount Airy, N.C.*

Ever since the eighteenth century "Dresden" has been the familiar name given in England and America to Meissen porcelain. Your oil lamp was actually made in the commune of Potschappel (5 miles from Dresden, 25 from Meissen) at a porcelain manufactory started by Carl von Thieme in 1872. Your mark indicates a date after 1890.

CONTINENTAL

VIEUX PARIS TEA SET

This china has been in my family for many years; the original owner died in 1834. The pieces are unmarked. I would appreciate knowing what kind of china it is.

A.R.U.—San Antonio, Tex.

I believe your china is what collectors call Vieux Paris. It was made between 1825 and 1860 by one of the small porcelain manufacturers of Paris, who often decorated their wares with landscape vignettes.

GERMAN STEIN

My father gave this stein to my mother about sixty-five years ago. It is very beautiful, and we would like to know its age.

J.E.F.—Brooklyn, N.Y.

I believe your stein was made by Villeroy & Boch at Mettlach, Germany, about 1885–1900. You might learn more by having the German inscription, illegible in the picture, translated.

GERMAN STEIN

Scenes from Lohengrin *decorate this 33-inch stein. Do you recognize the mark?*

W.L.W.—Fort Worth, Tex.

Your ornamental pottery stein, dating around 1890–1914, was made by the still-existing Villeroy & Boch at their Mettlach factory, Germany. Steins, of which countless thousands were exported to the United States from Germany around the closing decades of the nineteenth century, were a big production item at Mettlach and are highly esteemed by collectors.

GERMAN WILLOWWARE PUNCH BOWL

This gray willowware punch bowl has belonged to Western Kentucky State College for thirty years. We are anxious to learn its origin. A drawing of the mark on the bottom is enclosed.

A.G.A. — Bowling Green, Ky.

The mark shows that your college punch bowl was made by Villeroy & Boch after 1891 in their pottery at Wallerfangen, which is in the Saar Basin. Such bowls were exported to the United States.

DRESDEN FIGURINE

I would appreciate any information on this figurine—a woman in eighteenth-century court dress. It is 23¼ inches tall, expertly molded, with intensive attention to detail. My rough sketch is of the mark.

R.E.S. — Greenfield, Ind.

The oval mark is that of the Villeroy & Boch porcelain and pottery factory at Dresden, Germany, established in 1856. The size of the figurine indicates that it was made between 1870 and 1890.

WALL FOUNTAIN AND LAVABO

What can you tell me about my pottery wall fountain, which my mother bought at auction some years ago? It has no marks.

G.O. — Colorado Springs, Colo.

Judging from the photograph, we believe that your charming wall fountain with matching basin was made in France or Italy and is not significantly old. Through the years the wall fountain, chiefly used in the European dining room, has remained a distinctive decorative accessory. Especially striking are those made of pottery with colorful painted decoration.

GERMAN VASE

What can you tell me about the date and use of this urn? It is 2 feet high, 17 inches wide, and is in three sections bolted together. The portrait of the boy and horse is signed "Wagner."
V.D.G. — Longmeadow, Mass.

Your porcelain vase was made at a German factory, probably Volkstedt, at some time after 1890. The subject of the painting on your vase has been reproduced from "The Milkmaid," by Jean-Baptiste Greuze, French genre and portrait painter (1725–1805), which hangs in the Louvre. The print, taken from an engraving of this subject, which Wagner copied, may have been the one engraved by Levasseur. Your vase was used for ornamental purposes — probably placed on a mantel.

WHITE HOUSE PLATTER

On my White House platter, McKinley is depicted on the border as the latest president. The name "Palm, Fechteller & Co." appears near the house. The back is marked "La Française Porcelain." How old is it?
G.M.S. — Jacksonville, Fla.

The platter was made in France for the American market during McKinley's administration, which began in 1897. Palm Fechteller & Company published the print of the White House that was used on the china. The mark on the back identifies the piece only as a French import.

HUNGARIAN PUZZLE JUG

I was given a yellow-gold puzzle jug with this mark on the bottom: "ZSOLNAY Pécs-057." Where did it come from and how old might it be?

L.A.Y.—Farmingdale, N.Y.

Your jug was made at the Zsolnay pottery at Pécs, Hungary, between 1875 and 1900. A puzzle jug is so called because there is only one, secret way of drinking from it without spilling.

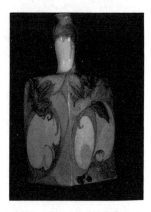

ART NOUVEAU VASE

This vase has been in my husband's family for sixty years. We call it "the potato masher" because of its shape. Can you tell us anything about it?

R.S.W. III—Mountain Lakes, N.J.

The Rozenburg porcelain factory at The Hague is noted for its perfected expression of the Art Nouveau style in ceramics. Collectors of this 1900 period would find your bottle highly desirable.

POTTERY
AND
PORCELAIN
English

ADAMS PLATE

This plate of mine has the inscription "N. Currier"
on the back. What is its origin, and is it rare?
K.A.M.—Camp Hill, Pa.

About 1925 William Adams & Sons, Ltd., of Tunstall, England, made some plates for the American market with the central decoration copied from N. Currier prints. Your plate is of interest, but it is not rare.

ENGLISH AMPHORAE

Can you estimate the age of these Grecian vases?
Inscribed on the base is a statement and the initials
"S.A. & Co."

M.S.G. — Pittsburgh, Pa.

Your pair of vases decorated in the ancient Greek classical style were
made by the potters Samuel Alcock & Company, who were active at
Cobridge and Burslem, Staffordshire, between the years 1823 and 1859.

"ARMS OF THE UNITED STATES" PLATE

The picture does not show this plate well. In the
center is the American emblem — an eagle with an
olive branch in one claw, a bundle of arrows in the
other. The only mark is an "X" on the back. I
would appreciate any information about it.

E.J. — Wichita, Kans.

Plates like yours are called "Arms of the United States" plates. They
are made of Staffordshire earthenware and date about 1810–1825. Since
yours has no mark, we cannot trace it further.

GARDNERS'
EXHIBITION
DINNER SET
LONDON

ENGLISH CHINA FOUND IN JAPAN

What can you tell us about six plates and a small
covered dish that we found in a junk shop in
Japan? The mark is enclosed.

M.V.C. — APO San Francisco, Cal.

ENGLISH

The mark shows these items were made by Bates, Elliott & Company, Burslem, Staffordshire, in business 1870–1875. The pottery was doubtless brought to Japan by an English family stationed there.

STAFFORDSHIRE TUREEN

This blue-and-white tureen, which I bought at an antique shop, is decorated with an Oriental design of birds and flowers with a gold outline. I am enclosing a sketch of the hallmarks. I would like to know more about the piece.

J.L.B. — Oakland, Cal.

The Staffordshire potters Bates, Gildea, and Walker, who operated the Dale Hall Works at Burslem from 1878 to 1881, registered your pattern, "Kioto," at the London Patent Office on November 24, 1880. The pattern was no doubt named for Kyoto, the imperial capital of Japan until 1868.

STAFFORDSHIRE DINNER SET

I recently inherited the remnants of my great-grandmother's dinner set of Oriental design. I have sketched the markings on the bottoms of the pieces. Might this possibly be Chinese export porcelain?

J.E.H. — Middletown, R.I.

Your dinner service bears the mark — a swan over the initials "J.B." — of James Beech, who produced earthenware from 1877 to 1889 at the Swan Bank Works, Tunstall and Burslem, Staffordshire. Chinese export ware, always porcelain, never bears a factory mark.

BELLEEK PITCHERS

Can you tell from the picture and the sketched mark how old these vases are?

M.M.H. — *Birmingham, Mich.*

Your vases are Belleek, a kind of thin, highly translucent porcelain with a lustrous pearly glaze, which was first popularized at the Irish factory of David McBirney & Company, Belleek, County Fermanagh, in 1863. The fact that the mark includes the name of country (Ireland) indicates that your pitchers were made sometime after 1891, probably around the turn of the century.

YORKSHIRE SYRUP JUG

Do you know the origin of this blue-and-white pitcher with either a pewter or tin lid? The mark is a small bell with the initials "JB" inside.

J.M.D. — *Norfolk, Va.*

This is a syrup jug made by the Bellevue Pottery, Hull, Yorkshire, England. It was operated by various owners from about 1802. Your mark was probably introduced by William Bell in 1825–1826, and for nearly twenty years earthenware similar to Staffordshire was made here.

BLACK BASALT JUG

I want to determine the place of origin and the date my black basalt Wedgwood pitcher was made. It has no mark, but has a little widow figure on the lid and pineapple stripes on the sides.

S.H. — *Burlingame, Cal.*

Without a mark it is difficult to determine where or when your jug was made. Several factories were making black basalt in the late eighteenth and early nineteenth centuries, and many of these productions were not marked. Your jug is probably of this period. We cannot say which pottery may have made it, but it does show commendable workmanship.

PARIAN FIGURE

I believe my figure of a woman cutting a lion's claws is parian ware. Can you tell me anything about it? The only marks are "J&TB" on the back.
H.M.—Armonk, N.Y.

The initials "J&TB" were used by Staffordshire potters James and Thomas Bevington, active at Hanley from 1865 to 1878.

STAFFORD KNOT

Can you interpret my sketch of the mark found on the bottom of an old platter belonging to my grandmother?

D.A.H.—District Heights, Md.

The mark indicates that your pattern, "Sandringham," was originally registered at the London Patent Office, November 27, 1863, by Edward F. Bodley & Company of the Scotia Pottery, Burslem, started in 1862. The printed "B & Co." within the Stafford knot was used by this firm only in 1865, so your mark is relatively rare. The Stafford knot was used as a mark by a number of Staffordshire potters in combination with their distinguishing initials.

Legend has it that a local sheriff in medieval times wanted to hang three men at the same time with one rope and that he accomplished his purpose by forming a triple noose, which, because of the county of origin (Staffordshire), became known as the Stafford knot. Such a proceeding is highly improbable. In heraldry this knot was the badge of the Stafford family in the fifteenth century.

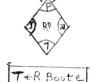

ENGLISH IRONSTONE

Recently at an auction I bought this eight-sided ironstone covered dish. Although I have a number of ironstone pieces, I have never seen one like this. On the bottom is the mark I have copied. What can you tell me about this piece?

R.C.J. — Casper, Wyo.

The diamond-shaped mark states that the design of your English ironstone dish was registered at the British Patent Office, London, July 22, 1851, by T. & R. Boote. Charles Mason of Lane Delph first made and patented ironstone in 1813. The name came from the potter's mixture, which contained iron.

T. & R. BOOTE PLATTER

Can you determine the age of my platter from this mark: English Royal Arms plus the names "T. & R. Boote" and "Lahore"?

J.H. — De Pere, Wis.

Yours is a Staffordshire platter made by T. & R. Boote, Burslem. The design is "Lahore," registered June 7, 1880. The Royal Arms were frequently included in Boote's Victorian marks.

TUREEN AND STAND

This mark is on both my ironstone tureen and its platter. I would like to know where and when they were made.

M.K. — Orefield, Pa.

T. & R. Boote & Co. were potters of Burslem, Staffordshire. The diamond-shaped mark shows that Boote registered the design, "Union Shape," at the British Patent Office on August 22, 1856. You are lucky to have the original stand, as it is often incorrectly used as a platter, which makes its chance of survival more hazardous.

STAFFORDSHIRE TEA SET

The mark on my grandmother's tea set has the initials "GFB" and the words "Dresden Wreath" beneath. Can you tell me anything further about it?

E.M.W. — Wyckoff, N.J.

George F. Bowers & Company, Tunstall, Staffordshire, made your tea set between 1842 and 1868. "Dresden Wreath" was the name of the pattern.

BRIDGWOOD BOWL

Can you tell me anything about my handpainted tea set (the sugar bowl is pictured)? Each piece has a castle, cathedral or landscape scene of England, Ireland or Scotland on it. A few bear the mark "Bridgwood & Son."

M.S.F. — Bennington, Vt.

Your tea service was made by Sampson Bridgwood & Son at their Anchor Pottery, started about 1805 at Longton in the Staffordshire district. Your name-mark suggests a date of manufacture around 1850.

BRISTOL PLATE

We believe this plate, which has been in my family for generations, was brought over on the May-flower. It has no identifying mark. Can you give us any indication of its age?

M.D. — Evanston, Ill.

Your colorful polychrome plate was made in England. It is Bristol Delft and dates from around 1780. Therefore, although it is a collector's item, it could not have been brought over on the *Mayflower*.

POTTER'S MARK

This mark appears on the bottom of my hand-painted wash basin, which has a painting of a woodpecker on a branch with berries and flowers. Can you estimate its age?

L.H. — *Pearl City, Hawaii*

Brown-Westhead, Moore & Company were Staffordshire potters of Cauldon Place, Hanley, from 1862 to 1904. The pattern "Woodpecker" was registered in 1888, probably the year your basin was made.

CHINA MARKS

Here is a copy of the trademarks on the backs of two plates we found in St. Maarten. Can you tell from these how old the plates are and where they came from?

B.K. — *Elizabeth, N.J.*

The "M&B" is for Minton & Boyle (1836–1841). The still-existing Minton Ltd. was started in 1796 at Stoke-on-Trent by Thomas Minton (1765–1836). Your mark covers the years when Boyle was in partnership with Minton. The other plate was made at a still-existing factory started by Petrus Regout at Maastricht, Holland, in 1836. Judged from the mark, it dates before 1890.

STAFFORDSHIRE PLATES

My great-grandmother bought these plates when the English home of the Empress Eugénie was vacated. Were they made for Napoleon III, as I've been led to believe? I've included the design on the side and center of each plate. One stamp on the back says "E. Leveille, 74 Bd. Haussmann, Paris"; another, "B. W. M. & Co., Romeo."

R.C. — *Stowe, Vt.*

The Staffordshire potters Brown-Westhead, Moore & Company, who made your plates, worked at Cauldon Place, Hanley, 1862–1904. They registered the pattern "Romeo" at the London Patent Office, January 25, 1868. Leveille was the Parisian shop where the plates were purchased—which makes it unlikely that they were made specifically for Napoleon III. They might have been owned by him, but to prove that would take considerable research—possibly a hunt through old bills and inventories.

STAFFORDSHIRE PITCHER

Can you tell me which pottery produced this covered pitcher? It was brought to this country from England about 1870 by my paternal great-grandparents. A copy of the raised mark is enclosed.

H.P.C.—Albany, N.Y.

According to the diamond-shaped registration device, the Staffordshire potters William Brownfield & Sons, who were active at Cobridge from 1850 to 1891, registered your pattern at the London Patent Office on November 6, 1859.

CASTLEFORD SUGAR BOWL

Some years ago an elderly cousin gave me this cream-colored sugar bowl of very fine earthenware and told me it had belonged to my great-grandmother. On one side it is decorated with the United States coat of arms, on the other with the head of Liberty. Can you tell its origin? There is no mark.

A.B.—New London, Conn.

Molded white wares of this type with painted blue-enamel lines are traditionally attributed to the Castleford Pottery, operated by David Dunderdale & Company around 1790–1820 at Castleford, near Leeds in Yorkshire, but are seldom marked. Such wares were made by many English potters around 1800–1825. For this reason, in order to be sure, you should have an expert examine it.

CASTLEFORD TEAPOT

My very old teapot is decorated with a raised coat-of-arms eagle and a figure of Liberty. Can you tell when and where it was made?
W.M.W. — St. Cloud, Minn.

The Castleford pottery in Yorkshire, England, made such decorated teapots for the American trade between 1800 and 1820, but few had the pottery mark. Lacking a mark, it remains an attribution, as other potteries also made this type of ware.

COMMEMORATIVE PLATE

The inscription on this old plate says, "Landing of Gen. Lafayette at Castle Garden New York 16 August 1824." The mark states "Clews warranted Staffordshire." Was this plate made 100 years after Lafayette's landing or earlier?
E.H.V. — Charlottesville, Va.

The plate was probably made soon after the landing. James and Ralph Clews operated the Cobridge Works at Cobridge, Staffordshire, England, from 1818 to 1834. They made good-quality blue-printed earthenware, and were proud to mention on their billheads, "Potters to Her Imperial Majesty, the Empress of all the Russias."

TRANSFER-PRINTED PLATE

My mother gave me this plate years ago. I have copied the markings and would like whatever information you can furnish me about its place of origin.
W.E.H. — Charleston, W.Va.

The Staffordshire potter Edward Challinor made your plate with transfer-printed decoration between the years 1842 and 1867. The use of a backstamp like the one you copied from the back of your plate is a feature of great interest associated with transfer-printed pottery. In your case it gives the name of the maker and the title of the fanciful scene on your plate. The device is usually decorative and charming.

LAFAYETTE PLATE

Please tell us anything you can about this plate, which has been in my husband's family over 100 years. On the back is the mark sketched, while on the front is the portrait of Lafayette and the words "Welcome Lafayette, the Nation's Guest and Our Country's Glory."

M.L. — Pomfret Center, Conn.

The plate commemorated Lafayette's return visit to America in 1824. It was made at the pottery of James and Ralph Clews, Cobridge, Staffordshire, shortly before that time.

CHEESE DISH

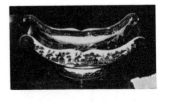

We have been told this dish was made to hold a half circle of cheese. The pattern is "Willow," with the name "Clews" impressed. When and where was it made?

H.T.G. — Culpeper, Va.

James and Ralph Clews made cheese-wheel dishes such as yours at Cobridge, England, between 1818 and 1834. Many attractive serving pieces decorated with the popular "Willow" pattern were made by the Staffordshire potters.

ENGLISH PORCELAIN JEWELRY

This pin-and-earrings set came to me as a present from Montreal. The pieces are marked "Coalport China, Made in England." Do you know anything about this manufacturer of porcelain jewelry?
B.A.T.—New York, N.Y.

Your jewelry was made by Coalport China Ltd., Stoke-on-Trent, Staffordshire, England, and is of recent date. While they are sold widely in Canada and in the English West Indian colonies, such floral pins and earrings are handled by few American shops.

COPELAND PLATTER

From the sketched mark and picture, can you give us any information about our blue-and-white-patterned platter?
C.Z.G.—Buffalo, N.Y.

The Imari-like pattern of your platter, called "Spode's Trophies," was made by W. T. Copeland & Sons, at some time after 1890. It was a revival of a pattern first made by Josiah Spode, who operated the Spode Works at Stoke-on-Trent from about 1784 to 1833. In that year it changed to Copeland and Garrett, and in 1847 to W. T. Copeland & Sons, who have operated the Spode Works at Stoke-on-Trent to the present day. The "& Sons" was added to W. T. Copeland in 1867.

COPELAND WASHBOWL AND PITCHER

I should like to know more about this pitcher and washbasin that I bought recently. There are many markings, but the most prominent are "Copeland," "England," and a crown.
I.O.—Philadelphia, Pa.

Your matching earthenware pitcher and washbowl, important Victorian bedroom accessories, were made by W. T. Copeland & Sons at some time after 1890, probably more or less about 1900.

PARIAN FIGURE

Our little objet d'art was given us by my aunt, who received it fifty years ago. It is a foot high. We'd like to know something about it.
                              M.F.—La Canada, Cal.

Your parian figure made by W. T. Copeland dates around 1847 to 1867 and may have been inspired by Charles Kingsley's book *The Water Babies.* The matte white parian body, originally called "Statuary Porcelain" was probably introduced in England by Copeland and Garrett, Stoke-on-Trent, who showed examples at the Manchester Exhibition, 1845–1846. Parian busts, figures and groups were produced in quantity from the late 1840s to the 1890s.

PARIAN BUST

This bust I recently acquired is titled "Hop Queen." Can you trace it from these markings: "Ceramic and Crystal Palace Art Union, Pub. January, 1873, Copeland, J. Durham, A.R.A."?
                              M.R.—Columbus, Ohio

Your parian bust, "Hop Queen," made by W. T. Copeland & Sons in 1873, often was distributed to subscribers of the Ceramic and Crystal Palace Art Union. The sculptor Joseph Durham (1814–1877) was an associate member of the Royal Academy where his sculpture "Leander and the Syren" was exhibited.

ROYAL CROWN DERBY VASE

Could you give me any information about my vase from its picture and sketched mark?
L.P. — Dorval, Can.

The mark is one used by the Royal Crown Derby Porcelain Company Ltd., Derby, England, from about 1878 to 1890. Properly, year ciphers occur below this mark.

ENGLISH IRONSTONE MARK

The enclosed tracing is the mark on the back of a decorated platter that belonged to my great-grandmother. Can you identify it for me?
N.H.J. — San Angelo, Tex.

You have an ironstone platter made by Davenport of Longport, Staffordshire. It probably dates between 1850 and 1870. "Friburg" was the pattern name.

ROYAL DOULTON JUG

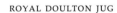

From these sketches can you identify my small pottery jug in the form of a soldier or a peddler? There is another figure under the glaze on the side of the jug.

K.Q. — Geneva, Switz.

Your jug was made by the Royal Doulton Pottery, Burslem, Staffordshire. "Rd No. 436948" indicates the design was recorded in January 1904. King Edward VII authorized Doulton in 1901 to use the word "royal" in describing its products.

DOULTON PUNCH BOWL

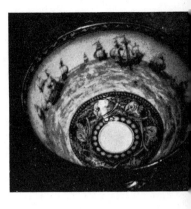

Our punch bowl has a blue transfer pattern of several galleons, all sailing on collision courses. The galleons are repeated inside the bowl, and there are several borders, one of which is of dolphins. When was the Doulton plant operating at Burslem, and is it still there?

I.W. — Washington, D.C.

In 1877 Doulton acquired a pottery in Burslem previously owned by Pinder, Bourne & Company. Your punch bowl has one of the early printed or impressed marks and was made between 1891 and 1901. In 1955 the company was renamed Doulton Fine China Ltd. It is still at the same address.

"EAR OF CORN" PITCHER

My English aunt gave me a set of corn pitchers, one slightly smaller than the other. This marking is found on the bottom of each of them. Can you identify the pitchers for me?

R.B. — Lincolnwood, Ill.

The "Ear of Corn" pattern was one of the most popular of all Victorian patterns both in England and America. It was found on useful as well as ornamental wares, the former generally in Victorian majolica, the latter in parian porcelain. The "Ear of Corn" pattern was especially suitable for vases and pitchers. Your pitchers were registered by a Staffordshire potter at the London Patent Office on October 26, 1869.

EDGE, MALKIN MARK

I have a set of willowware that has been in the family for years. Can you tell me anything about it from the enclosed mark that appears on each piece?

J.H.D. — *Long Island City, N.Y.*

Your pottery was made by Edge, Malkin & Company, Burslem, Staffordshire, England. The firm used this mark from 1873 to 1903. After 1891 "England" was added to the mark. "Mysore" was the pattern.

STAFFORDSHIRE PLATE

The dinner plate shown in the two photographs has been in the possession of my family for years. Can you give me the history and origin of it?

J.C.R., Sr. — *Greenwood, S.C.*

Your plate was made by Edge, Malkin & Company, Burslem, Staffordshire, England, about 1880, when Oriental decoration was very popular. "Chang" was the pattern name.

STAFFORDSHIRE BOWL

This bowl is about 8 inches in diameter. The people who gave it to me said it is over 100 years old. Do you know anything at all about its maker?

J.K. — *Friendship, Wis.*

James Edwards, a Staffordshire potter, operated the Dale Hall pottery at Burslem from 1842 to 1851. According to the mark, the pattern for your bowl was registered on September 30, 1847.

ENGLISH EARTHENWARE

This tureen, with the mark pictured, belongs to a supper set that includes six matching soup dishes. I think it is English ironstone. Can you tell its age?
L.D.R. — Pomona, Cal.

Your tureen was made by Thomas Elsmore & Son at their Clayhills Pottery in Staffordshire, established in 1872. According to the registry mark, the set is earthenware, and the pattern was registered at the British Patent Office on May 14, 1878.

STAFFORDSHIRE PLATTER

Can you identify this platter, which belonged to a set of dishes owned by my great-grandmother? And, from the mark, can you tell approximately when it was made?

R.T.L. — Columbus, Ohio

The initials "J&TF" are those of Jacob and Thomas Furnival, who started a pottery at Miles Bank, Shelton, Hanley, around 1843. About a year later the firm name was changed to Thomas Furnival & Company. Your transfer-printed platter is a relatively rare piece of Staffordshire earthenware since the original pottery was active only that one year.

ENGLISH IRONSTONE

*The enclosed sketch is of markings on plates be-
longing to my grandmother. Can you decode them?*
L.McL. — Durbin, W.Va.

Jacob Furnival & Company was active between 1845 and 1870 at
Cobridge, Staffordshire, England. Although its mark usually consisted
of the initials "JF & Co.," not "Furnival & Co.," it seems reasonable to
assume that your plates were made at the Furnival pottery.

ENGLISH POTTERY MARK

*Two earthenware plates I have show this mark.
When were they made?*
L.W. — San Francisco, Cal.

The plates were made about 1880–1890 by W. H. Grindley & Company,
who still operate the Woodland Pottery, Tunstall, England.

RICHARD JORDAN PLATTER

*I would like information about this antique plat-
ter. The mark on the back states "The Residence
of the late Richard Jordan New Jersey," and under
that the initials "JH & Co."*
F.W.C. — Frankfort, Ind.

Richard Jordan was a prominent Quaker minister at Newton, New Jersey. After his death in 1826 his friends sent an engraving of his residence to the Joseph Heath Company of Tunstall, Staffordshire. Heath used the picture as a pattern to decorate entire dinner services; your platter must have come from one of them—they were popular with American Quakers. The pottery was active from 1828 to 1841.

ENGLISH TEAPOT

This teapot was given to my mother forty years ago by her great-aunt, who said it was then over 100 years old. The colors are rich and beautiful. There are no identifying marks. Can you give me any information about it?

E.P.V.—Black Mountain, N.C.

Your English teapot belongs to a class of Leeds pottery, dating from after 1790, painted with designs in high-temperature mineral colors. It is one of the so-called "Gaudy" patterns that enjoy great popularity in America.

MINISTER JUG

I bought this white Apostle pitcher with pewter lid in Germany. We found there is one like it in the Metropolitan Museum. Can you identify ours by "Registered March 17, 1842—Chas. Meigh—Hanley"?

E.L.O.—Ft. Rucker, Ala.

The stoneware jug with relief figures in eight Gothic niches was registered by Charles Meigh, who operated the Old Hall Works at Hanley from 1835 to 1849. This jug is often referred to as the "minister jug" in English books.

QUEEN VICTORIA MINTON PLATE

This plate made by Minton was given to my husband's grandfather when he was American consul at Stoke-on-Trent in about 1890. It was said to be from Queen Victoria's china set. It has the medallions of the thistle, shamrock and rose, signifying the three sections of Great Britain. Could it be an authentic piece of Victoria's china?

B.C.T. — Maple Valley, Wash.

Yes, Minton has identified your plate as being part of a dessert service that was produced by them and used by Queen Victoria at Balmoral Castle, Scotland. This particular service was first produced in December 1878 and supplied through John Mortlock of London, who were Minton's London agents at that time. Minton kindly sent us one of their old brochures with this caption under a picture of your plate: Dessert service used by her late Majesty Queen Victoria at Balmoral Castle, Scotland, showing emblems of England, Ireland and Scotland.

STAFFORDSHIRE PLATTER

I hope that you can read the mark on the back of our old platter from the picture. It says: "PW & Co British manufrs. Kingston, Lake Ontario." Family history suggests that it dates back to Colonial times. Is there any truth in this supposition?

H.S.L. — Romulus, Mich.

"PW & Co." stands for the pottery Podmore, Walker & Company, Tunstall, Staffordshire, England, in business 1834–1853. Since the scene on your platter is of Kingston, Ontario, we believe that it was made when Kingston was the capital of Canada (1841–1844).

STAFFORDSHIRE BOWL

I photographed my brown luster bowl so you can see the inside design of Roman soldiers, a dog, and a horse in two different poses. Can you tell from this mark when and where the bowl was made?
P.P.K. — Roanoke, Va.

Your pattern, "Trajan," was registered April 28, 1873. Although made by Powell & Bishop, who were active at Hanley only from 1876 to 1878, the design was registered by their predecessor, Livesley Powell & Company. Since Powell & Bishop were in business so short a time, their mark is rare, which enhances its value.

PORTLAND VASE

This vase has been in my family for many years. It is green with white cameolike decorations on its sides and bottom. There are no identifying marks. What can you tell me about it?
J.J.C. — Lebanon, Ore.

Your vase is a copy of the celebrated Portland Vase, now in the British Museum. The original is of glass, with an almost black ground, and is considered one of the masterpieces of the glass cutter's art. It is believed that the vase may have served as a receptacle for the funerary ashes of Alexander the Great. Discovered in an excavation in Rome late in the sixteenth century, it was called the Portland Vase because it was purchased in 1786 by the Duke of Portland. Many copies of this vase have been made over the centuries, the most renowned being those by Josiah Wedgwood. We would have to have more specific information about your copy to date it.

ENGLISH CANDLESTICKS

I recently purchased these candlesticks from an antique dealer who knew nothing of their history. They are 9 inches high, colored Wedgwood black, with gray figures and gold-and-white trim. I am also enclosing a copy of the manufacturer's stamp. Anything you can tell me about them will be appreciated.

C.F.M., Jr. — Williamsport, Pa.

The Staffordshire potters F. & R. Pratt & Company Ltd. were established about 1818 in Fenton, England. Cauldon Potteries Ltd. took over in the 1920s but still used the Pratt name. Your printed mark, used between 1847 and 1869, is rare. It was imprinted only on fine-quality Etruscan-pattern vases and articles such as your candlesticks.

NEW HALL TEA SET BY WILLIAM RATCLIFFE

Our family in England says that this china tea set is between 150 and 200 years old. From these pictures of the mark and a few of the pieces could you give me some idea of the period when this china was manufactured?

R.K.D. — Piqua, Ohio

A circle enclosing an "R" and surrounded by sunrays is the mark of William Ratcliffe, who operated the New Hall Pottery at Shelton, Staffordshire, between 1831 and 1840. Your set was made for export, the design copied from Chinese porcelain.

EARLY STAFFORDSHIRE

Can you tell from the sketch of its mark how old my stone china is?

E.R.M. — *Loudonville, N.Y.*

The Staffordshire potters John and William Ridgway operated the Cauldon Place and Bell Works, Shelton, Hanley, from 1814 to about 1830. Your sketch, including the pattern name "India Temple," is one of their accepted marks. Stone china is the same as ironstone china and was first patented by Charles Mason in 1813. The Ridgway family of Shelton potters made many fine pieces of earthenware and porcelain in the nineteenth century. Their family history is rather involved. The initials "JWR" predate 1830, for in this year the two brothers, John and William, separated.

RIDGWAY STONEWARE

From this picture of a platter and its mark, can you tell me anything about the ironstone china that I have acquired from several antique shops? I am interested in its origin, and would also like to know if the factory is still operating.

V.A.R. — *Dothan, Ala.*

The Staffordshire potters John and William Ridgway, who used the distinguishing initials "JWR" in their backstamps, were active at Shelton, Hanley, between 1814 and 1830 — so your stoneware platter is truly antique. The Ridgways were a well-known family of potters. At the present time Ridgway Potteries Ltd. is active at Shelton, Hanley. One of their marks states: "Est. 1792."

RIDGWAY CHINA

I have owned a set of dishes for about twenty-five years and have never been able to find out their origin. They are white, rather heavy — like ironstone china — with a small bluish-green flowerlike design. On the back of each piece is this crest and embedded in the china is the name "John Ridgway." Please help identify them for me.

F.E.McG. — Owings Mill, Md.

The Staffordshire potter John Ridgway was active at Cauldon Place, Shelton, Hanley, around 1830 to 1855. He produced porcelains and earthenwares, and registered the design "Coterie" on November 19, 1839. The mark on your plates is the full royal arms mark — a popular Ridgway mark. The supporters of the royal arms are a lion and a unicorn, a fabulous beast that has as its chief feature a long, sharp, twisted horn set in the middle of its forehead.

STAFFORDSHIRE MARK

My sketch is of the mark on my oval blue-and-white platter. The scene depicted on the platter is of the Alps, a lake, a couple of peasants with a goat in the foreground. The mark shows an anchor leaning against a Medici urn filled with and surrounded by flowers. Below the urn is "WR & Co," and under the initials the word "Tyrolean." Can you trace the pattern?

M.A.R. — Honolulu, Hawaii

"WR & Co" denotes the Staffordshire potters William Ridgway (& Co.), who operated the Bell Works in Shelton and the Church Works in Hanley, England, from 1830 to 1854. The "& Co." first occurs in the records for 1834. "Tyrolean" is the pattern name.

NINETEENTH-CENTURY SCENIC PLATTER

My old turkey platter is marked "View of the Capitol at Washington, W.R." and "Opaque Granite China, W.R. & Co." Can you give its age and maker?

M.H.W. — *Evansville, Ind.*

William Ridgway & Company, Shelton and Hanley, Staffordshire, made your opaque granite china platter between 1830 and 1854. The view was copied from a London print; the original drawing is by William H. Bartlett, an English artist who visited the United States four times to make sketches of American scenes.

STONEWARE JUG

This pitcher of heavy pottery belonged to my husband's family in England. Each side depicts a jousting knight. In script on the bottom is "Published by W. Ridgway, Son & Co., Hanley, September 1, 1840." I will appreciate anything you can tell me about it.

B.T. — *New York, N.Y.*

The impressed "Published by" marks indicate the date and by whom the design was registered. William Ridgway, Son & Company was active from 1838 to 1848. Many molded stoneware jugs of this type were produced in the 1830s and 1840s. Your design of the jousting knight is illustrated in Geoffrey A. Godden's book *British Pottery and Porcelain*.

STAFFORDSHIRE PITCHER

What can you tell me about this pitcher? Stamped on the bottom is "Published by W. Ridgway & Co., Hanley, September 1, 1840."

B.S. — Hoboken, N.J.

The Staffordshire pottery of William Ridgway & Company was active at Hanley from 1838 to 1848. Hunt scenes, such as the one on your pitcher, were common during this period in England and inspired similar scenes on American pitchers. Many early jugs and other relief-decorated wares bear the legend "Published by" followed by the maker's name and an exact date, which indicates that a representation of human or animal forms has been entered for protection at Stationers' Hall under the legislation dating from the reign of George III.

STAFFORDSHIRE STONEWARE

This is part of an incomplete set of china. On the large plate is an oval enclosing "Stone Ware JR" with the word "Bentick" underneath. Can you help me to identify the set?

G.K. — San Francisco, Cal.

Your set of dishes was made by John Ridgway & Company of Cauldon Place, Shelton, Hanley, active 1830–1855. The pattern "Bentick," illustrated in Staffordshire reference books, was used on stoneware made from about 1830 to 1841. About 1841 "& Co." was added to Ridgway's mark. Wares made by John Ridgway were of the highest quality, and he was appointed potter to Queen Victoria.

RIDGWAY PLATTER AND MARK

I am enclosing a picture of a blue-and-white platter and its mark. It has been in our family for a great many years. Can you possibly tell me how old it is?

L.R.W.—North Hollywood, Cal.

John Ridgway made your platter at the Cauldon Place pottery, Shelton, Hanley, Staffordshire, which he operated between 1830 and 1855. Sometimes Ridgway included the pattern name and the number as part of the mark—in this case "Palestine, No. 1754."

REGISTRATION MARK

What does the diamond-shaped mark on my platter mean?

J.P.U.—Lemmon, Ariz.

This diamond-shaped device is found on English Victorian ceramics from 1842 to 1883. The purpose of the mark was to show that the pattern or shape had been registered at the London Patent Office and was therefore protected from being copied by other manufacturers for the first three years. When this mark is complete it is possible to tell the exact year, month, and day that the manufacturer registered the pattern or shape at the London Patent Office. For example, in your case the Staffordshire potters Ridgway registered the pattern name "Indus" at the London Patent Office on June 18, 1877. This does not mean that your platter was made that year, as these patterns continued in use for a number of years, depending upon their popularity.

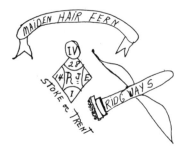

EARTHENWARE TRADEMARK

This mark is on a set of children's dishes that we purchased at an auction. Any information about them would be welcome.

G.S. — Wausau, Wis.

The Ridgways operated the Bedford Works at Shelton and Hanley, Staffordshire, from 1879 until 1920. The bow-and-arrow trademark on your dishes was registered in 1880. According to the diamond-shaped registry mark, your dishes are earthenware, and this particular pattern was registered at the British Patent Office on July 28, 1881. Ridgway became Ridgway Ltd. from 1920–1952. After several changes in name it became Ridgway Potteries Ltd. in 1955.

STAFFORDSHIRE PLATTER

Can you give me any information about this large blue platter? "Riley" is the name on the back.

B.A. — Watervliet, N.Y.

Your decorated earthenware platter was made by the brothers J. & R. Riley at their pottery in Burslem, Staffordshire, England, between 1802 and 1828. The Rileys exported decorative "Gaudy Dutch" pottery to America.

IRONSTONE MARK

These markings appear on my grandmother's set of china. Would it be possible for you to trace the age and origin of the set?

H.B.S., Sr. — Gallatin, Tenn.

The mark on your ironstone is that of Anthony Shaw, who was active at Tunstall, Staffordshire, England, from about 1851 to 1856.

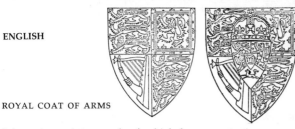

ROYAL COAT OF ARMS

I have two plates, each of which has a coat of arms on the back. One plate bears the inscription "Hicks, Meigh and Johnson." Can you tell me approximately when the plates were made and identify the two coats of arms?

R.E.C. — New York, N.Y.

The British Royal Arms appear in the trademarks of many nineteenth- and twentieth-century British manufacturers, as well as some foreign ones. Your plates illustrate the two basic forms of royal arms that serve as a guide to the date: All arms engraved prior to the accession of Queen Victoria in 1837 have a small shield in the center of the quartered shield; after 1837 they have a simple quartered shield only. Your plate with double shield was made between 1822 and 1835 by the Staffordshire potters, Hicks, Meigh and Johnson. Your other plate, because of its single shield, was made sometime after 1837.

STEVENSON MARK

This mark appears on a decorated plate with matching sugar bowl. Can you tell their age and make?

C.A.G. — Buffalo, N.Y.

The Staffordshire potter Ralph Stevenson was working at Cobridge from about 1810 to 1832. The printed marks included "& Son" from 1832 to 1835. The name of the individual pattern is often included in the mark — in your case "Swiss."

JOSEPH HEATH MARK

This mark is on the back of a twelve-sided plate with Oriental design. It has been in the family for seventy-five years. Where was it made?

H.S. — Poland, Ohio

Your plate was made by the Staffordshire potter Joseph Heath, who operated a pottery at Tunstall from 1845 to 1853.

LIVERPOOL PITCHER

This pitcher has been in our family for years. Can you tell where it was made and about what period?
M.F.F. — Clayton, Mo.

Pitchers of this sort were produced by several Liverpool potters around 1800–1820. American sea captains brought them home as presents. They are now highly prized.

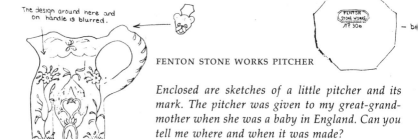

FENTON STONE WORKS PITCHER

Enclosed are sketches of a little pitcher and its mark. The pitcher was given to my great-grandmother when she was a baby in England. Can you tell me where and when it was made?
R.M.R. — Athens, Ga.

"Fenton Stone Works" was one of the printed marks used by the Staffordshire potter Charles James Mason of Lane Delph from about 1825 on. "No. 306" refers to the pattern. In 1813 Charles James Mason patented ironstone china, which is supposed to have pulverized slag of iron as an ingredient in its clay composition.

ENGLISH MATCH POT

An elderly friend gave me this figurine. It is sort of taffy tan in color. I have always wondered what it is for and where it came from.
S.C. — Long Beach, Cal.

Your figure, probably intended as a match pot, was made at an English Staffordshire pottery sometime around the 1860s. It has a charming simplicity, and lots of collectors of Staffordshire would like to have it in their collections.

NINETEENTH-CENTURY PLATTER

My great-aunt gave me this platter years ago. On the back is the mark "T. J. & J. Mayer Florentine." Where does the platter come from?
                    A.K.S. — Long Beach, Cal.

It was made in England. Thomas, John & Joseph Mayer operated the Furlong Works and Dale Hall Pottery at Burslem from 1843 to 1855. Their work was varied and highly regarded. The name of the pattern, in your case "Florentine," was often included in the company's identifying mark.

ENGLISH EARTHENWARE

The mark on my china has a small tigerlike animal and the words "Etruscan Vases" and "J. & J. Mayer." Could you give me more information?
                    M.P. — Chelmsford, Mass.

Your table service was made by the Staffordshire potters J. & J. Mayer around 1843–1855. The Victorians, whose desire to imitate the past created a fashion for forms and decoration directly inspired by ancient classical examples, still described as "Etruscan" the artwork normally associated with ancient Greece and Rome. Hence your printed pattern, "Etruscan Vases."

ROYAL ARMS MARK

A friend gave me a china creamer and sugar bowl on a little platter. They are white and gold, with this mark. Can you date them?
                    R.G. — San Antonio, Tex.

The Staffordshire potters J. & G. Meakin made your ironstone pieces sometime after 1891, the year English firms were required to add "England" to their marks on wares made for the American market. You may recognize the seal as the royal arms, used by many firms.

ENGLISH POTTERY MARK

I have a set of dishes I would like to know more about. I have sketched markings that are on the back of each. Can you help me identify them?
F.W. — Utica, N.Y.

Thomas, John & Joseph Mayer operated the Furlong Works and Dale Hall Pottery at Burslem from 1843 to 1855. According to your mark, they won a prize medal at the Great Exhibition held in London in 1851 — the first world's fair. Your dishes date about 1852–1855.

STAFFORDSHIRE MARK

I have sketched the mark on the bottom of a very beautiful old vase. Could you tell me who made it?
A.W.H. — Columbus, Ohio

Old Hall was a pottery built in 1790 at Hanley, Staffordshire, by Job Meigh, a leading English potter. He and his sons continued making pottery there until 1834.

VICTORIAN GOTHIC PITCHER

My pitcher is a light mustard yellow, with this mark in pale blue on the bottom. I would appreciate any information you can give me about its age and origin.

R.H. — New Rochelle, N.Y.

Your eight-sided pitcher with Gothic arched panels is an example of English pottery done in the Victorian Gothic style. The Staffordshire potter Charles Meigh, who operated the Old Hall Works at Hanley, 1835 to 1849, registered the design at the London Patent Office on March 17, 1842.

BACCHUS-ADORNED MUG

I recently purchased this 8-inch-deep mug. What does the seal on the bottom denote?

B.H.—Parsippany, N.J.

Charles Meigh, a Staffordshire potter, operated the Old Hall Pottery at Hanley from 1835 to 1849. The seal denotes an award for this mug by the Society of Arts. The mug's decoration shows Bacchus, a bit tipsy, being escorted from a feast.

ENGLISH MOCHA WARE

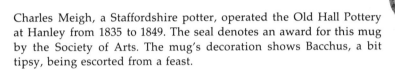

This bowl has belonged to my family since ante-bellum days. It has no identifying marks. I have seen a similar pattern in North Carolina museums. Can you identify it?

H.S.W.—Greensboro, N.C.

Your bowl is an example of English Mocha ware, which enjoyed a great vogue in the first four decades of the nineteenth century. It was produced by many Staffordshire potters and made mainly into bowls, jugs, and mugs that were often exported to America.

STAFFORDSHIRE PLATTER

These sketches are of a portion of the design on the border and center of an eight-sided platter and also of the marks on the back of it. Can you identify the platter?

C.H.—Waverly, N.Y.

Staffordshire potters Francis Morley & Company were active at Shelton, Hanley, England, from 1845 to 1858. Your platter bears one of their accepted printed marks. "Aurora" is the pattern name.

NODDING FIGURINES

These nodding-head figurines are English. Can you trace their origin more specifically?
                                    B.C.L. — Woodbury, N.J.

They were made by some Staffordshire pottery between 1830 and 1850. Their origin derives from the amusing small grotesque Chinese figures, generally having movable heads and hands, and modeled in a sitting position.

PARIAN VASE

From the enclosed picture can you tell the age and origin of my 6¼-inch-high vase?
                                    M.B. — Kittery, Maine

Your parian vase with applied flower-and-leaf work appears to be English in origin, probably dating around 1855. Their popularity was short-lived, as such dust-catching and fragile pieces could only be kept under glass domes.

STAFFORDSHIRE COVERED DISH

Any comments on this covered dish will be appreciated. There is no trademark, but as you can see, there is some sort of coat of arms. Mottoes on banners read "Firm as an Oak; Sobriety; Domestic Comfort; Health, Wealth, Wisdom; Be Thou Faithful Unto Death."
                                    G.L. — Elmira, N.Y.

The dish with the quaint mottoes appears to be Staffordshire earthenware, dating about 1870–1880. Since it bears no maker's mark, we cannot identify it further.

STAFFORDSHIRE TEA SET

Was this English pottery part of a larger set? At one time I had twelve cups and saucers. It has been in my family for over 100 years. The only mark is the number "503."

G.D.V.N. — *Arcadia, Cal.*

Originally this set may have included twelve tea plates and two cake plates. The mark "503" is merely the pattern number. From the shape and floral decoration of your pieces, I would say they are Staffordshire, made between 1820 and 1840.

HEIRLOOM SPANIELS

What is the history and origin of these ceramic dogs? They were brought from England to my grandmother over sixty-five years ago.

J.F. — *Belleville, Ill.*

From 1830 to 1860 various potters in Staffordshire made such white glazed earthenware dogs in pairs. They are now considered collectible antiques. Beware, however, as ingenious copies are still being made today.

STAFFORDSHIRE SPANIELS

My husband's grandfather played with these china dogs as a child. They have no marks. Where are they from?

M.M.R. — *Chicago, Ill.*

They are typical English Staffordshire earthenware dogs, made between 1830 and 1860, of the kind often used as mantel decorations.

WALLEY POTTERY

These marks are on my heirloom china, the cups of which have no handles. What do the marks mean?

W.A.G. — Chattanooga, Tenn.

According to the marks, your china was made by Edward Walley at his Villa Pottery, Cobridge, which was active between 1845 and 1856. The registry marks indicate that your pattern, "Palissy," was registered at the London Patent Office on November 29, 1856.

SUMMERLY'S FIGURINES

These rubbings are from two female figures holding shields and helmets. They are 14 inches high, probably parian. Can you tell their age and rarity?

M.B.H. — Woodmere, N.Y.

The mark shows that the figurines were registered in October, 1847, for the Summerly's Art Manufacturers (1847–1851), founded by Sir Henry Cole to improve English taste. Sculptor John Bell designed your figurines, and they are relatively rare.

WEDGWOOD GROUP

What information can you furnish about this Cupid and Psyche — 8¼ inches high and marked "Wedgwood"?

O.H. — Glasco, Kans.

Your parian group was made by the Josiah Wedgwood pottery about one hundred years ago. Cupid and Psyche were a favorite Victorian theme.

WEDGWOOD MAJOLICA

My great-grandmother brought this green plate with her when she came from England many years ago. The name "Wedgwood" is stamped on the back. Can you tell me how old it is?
J.A.C.—Lincoln, Neb.

Majolica plates with the sunflower pattern, such as yours, were made by Wedgwood around 1840–1860. This kind of lead-glazed Victorian majolica is quite different from the original tin-glazed Renaissance majolica.

WEDGWOOD BLACK BASALT

We recently acquired this black, ribbed cream pitcher and sugar bowl. Both are marked "Wedgwood." What can you tell me about them?
H.B.F.—Indianapolis, Ind.

They are black basalt, made by Josiah Wedgwood & Sons, Eturia, Staffordshire. In 1769 the famous English potter perfected a kind of pottery he named "black basalt." It was considered one of his major achievements. The popularity of black basalt waned, but was revived by the company in 1900. Your table pieces date around 1918.

THE OTHER WEDGE WOOD

My grandmother brought a twelve-sided blue plate with her when she emigrated from Germany. I have copied the imprint on the back of the plate. Can you identify it?

S.K. — *Kalamazoo, Mich.*

The mark on your plate, showing the name "J. Wedgwood," was used by Staffordshire potter John Wedge Wood, who was active from 1841 to 1860. This mark has often been mistaken for that of Josiah Wedgwood, the most famous of English potters, whose firm used only the mark "Wedgwood," without any initial.

IRONSTONE TEAPOT

I have made a drawing of the mark on my light-cream marbleized teapot and bowl, as the antique dealers here are unfamiliar with it. Can you identify and date the pieces?

N.C. — *Albuquerque, N.M.*

Your ironstone china with marbled surface was made by the Staffordshire potter John Wedge Wood, who was active from 1841 to 1860. The technique of blending together different colored clays to produce a ware resembling marble or agate dates back to ancient Roman times and was successfully used by Staffordshire potters, as is evident in your teapot.

STAFFORDSHIRE MARK

I am trying to identify the enclosed mark, which is on an old tureen and plate I own that is blue underglaze on an off-white plate. I have looked through many books but have not been able to find this mark.

R.M.H. — *Chicago, Ill.*

"EW&S" are the initials for the Staffordshire potters Enoch Wood & Sons, who operated at the Fountain Place, Burslem, from 1818 to 1846 and exported vast amounts of pottery to North America. (A single shipment to their Philadelphia agent totaled 262,000 pieces.) "Toyoda," the name of your pattern, is a Japanese surname: *toyo* meaning abundance, *da* or *ta,* a rice paddy. In Japan, abundance of rice is equivalent to good luck.

SWALLOW PLATTER

Enclosed is a photograph and an attempt to copy the markings on the back of my Swallow platter. I hope you will be able to tell me from these how old it is.

W.C.M. — Olympia, Wash.

The Staffordshire potter James F. Wileman operated the Foley China Works at Fenton from 1869 to 1892. According to the diamond-shaped registration mark, your pattern, "Swallow," was registered at the London Patent Office on April 23, 1881.

ENGLISH MARK

The design copied here is on the back of a platter that my mother's family has had for years. Could you tell its age and maker?

M.N.G. — Phoenix, Ariz.

The mark is that of Enoch Wood & Sons, Burslem, Staffordshire, who were in business from 1818 to 1846. "Pagoda" is the name of the pattern, which no doubt made use of roofs of spreading canopy form typical of Oriental architecture.

STAFFORDSHIRE EARTHENWARE TEAPOT

My teapot is in two shades of blue and has the mark I've copied on the bottom. How old is it?
P.H. — Fairfield, Iowa

The teapot is typical Staffordshire earthenware, made about 1820–1830. The mark is that of Enoch Wood & Sons of Burslem. This firm dates from 1818 to 1846. They were large producers of decorated earthenware, and exported it to the United States.

STAFFORDSHIRE MARK

This mark appears on the back of some blue china I purchased. If it is not old, could you tell me where I could buy missing pieces of the set?
M.K. — Evanston, Ill.

Wood & Son Ltd., Burslem, Staffordshire, England, made your blue china after 1891. Herman C. Kupper, Inc., 11 East 26 Street, New York City, are the American distributors for this company. "Wincanton" is the pattern name. The registration number indicates a date around 1911. The "& Son" in the mark was changed to "& Sons" about 1907; "Ltd" was added about 1910.

PARIAN BUST

Although I have made an intensive effort, I have not been able to learn anything about the background of this parian bust that I acquired in Maine some years ago. The inscription reads "W. H. Kerr & Company," followed by an insignia of the crown, and below that "Worcester." I would like to know the bust's age, background, and, if possible, of whom it is a portrait.
E.R.L. — Mineola, N.Y.

In the nineteenth century the Worcester Porcelain Company of Worcester, England, added earthenware and parian ware to their production. The mark on your bust was used during the period of 1856–1862. If you write directly to the company, now the Worcester Royal Porcelain Company Ltd., they will perhaps be able to identify the subject.

WORCESTER PARIAN FIGURE

I recently acquired this figure. Could you identify it from the picture and the sketch of the mark?
                                    N.L. — Kearny, N.J.

We do not know whom the figure represents, but the mark indicates it is parian by Worcester Royal Porcelain, about 1852–1862.

WORCESTER BONE CHINA

Enclosed is a photograph and marking of a Royal Worcester demitasse set. Could you tell me its approximate age?

W.B.M. — Lawton, Okla.

According to the registration number, the Worcester Royal Porcelain Company registered your pattern at the London Patent Office in 1893.

POTTERY AND PORCELAIN

Far Eastern

CHINESE FIGURINE

My wife was given this glazed porcelain Chinese statue thirty-five years ago. We heard that during the Ming dynasty women used the hollow centers of these statues to transport valuables and carried the statues in the long sleeves of their kimonos. Is the statue really Ming?

J.A.K. — Tucson, Ariz.

Your Chinese figurine is of late-eighteenth- or nineteenth-century manufacture, not Ming. If it were, the modeling of the figure would be quite different. Ceramic figurines are of necessity hollow, to allow for shrinkage when they are fired in the kiln, but the material is too fragile to permit them to be used for any but ornamental purposes.

MING DYNASTY PLATE

My Chinese porcelain dish is supposed to be from the Ming dynasty. Could you tell me if this is correct?

J.A. — Newark, N.J.

Judged from your snapshots, your porcelain dish, painted in underglaze blue, was made in China during the Chia Ching reign of the Ming dynasty (1522–1566).

"TOBACCO LEAF" TUREEN

This tureen with a tobacco-leaf design will be on display at our antiques show. Can you give me its approximate date and tell me something about the pattern?

B.A.R. — Atlanta, Ga.

The "Tobacco Leaf" pattern is an over-all design chiefly of tobacco leaves and flowers in combinations of shades of brown, blue, green, pink, rust, and gold. There are about eight or ten variations of this popular pattern in various shades. Quite often, as in your tureen, the design includes a pair of interlinked circles and a larger circle containing four flowers. Your Oriental Lowestoft piece probably dates about 1780. This type of ware is also called "Chinese export porcelain," because it was made in China for export only and is a true porcelain.

TAO KUANG VASE

A Chinese general presented this vase to my cousin and said it had been in his family for over 400 years. Is this possible?

H.E.R. — Meadville, Pa.

Although your Chinese porcelain vase does bear the Ch'êng-hua (1465–1487) mark, the form of the vase indicates that it was made later, probably during the reign of Tao Kuang (1821–1850). Chinese potters, out of admiration for the designs of earlier periods, often stamped the names of former reigns on their ware, and this is probably what happened with your vase.

CH'ING DYNASTY VASES

I purchased this pair of vases in 1945 at Chungking, China, where I was stationed when the war ended, and was told they were quite old. Many families sold such heirloom pieces to obtain money for passage back to the coast. The scenes painted on them are exquisite workmanship, even under magnification. I've copied the six marks that appear on each vase. Can you identify them?

S.A.M. — North Olmstead, Ohio

This is a beautiful pair of antique Chinese vases of the Ch'ing dynasty, Ch'ien Lung reign (1736–1796). As you probably know, Chinese is read from right to left, generally in columns running downwards. As a rule the "six character" mark is written in two columns, composed of two characters signifying the name of the dynasty prefaced by the word great (*ta*), two the reign name, and two more meaning "period" (*nien*) and "make" (*chih*).

IMARI VASE

Anything you can tell me about my decorated covered jar will be appreciated. The jar has no identifying marks.

J.I.M., Jr. — Farmville, N.C.

Vases such as yours are frequently referred to as Victorian Imari. They were made at Arita, Hizen province, Japan, in the 1800s. Arita ware is popularly called Imari ware, because in the Edo period (1615–1867) it was shipped from the port of Imari, near Arita.

ROSE MEDALLION PORCELAIN

What can you tell me about my porcelain vases and bowl? They are vividly enameled with flowers and figures.

V.E.S. — Hampton, Va.

Your Rose Medallion enameled porcelain, which was a popular Chinese export ware, is probably of nineteenth-century Chinese manufacture. Much of it was decorated at Canton and shipped from that port.

JAPANESE BOWL

I would appreciate any information on this bowl I acquired recently. It is porcelain over copper; most of the figures hold bottles, one holds a fish.
L.M.R. — Corona Del Mar, Cal.

Your shallow bowl with surrounding figures is Japanese. I have seen others like it that were imported around 1900 in considerable quantity for Oriental shops. Whatever was placed in the bowl, such as plant life, the contents remained well below the bowl's rim.

SILVER
American

MATCHING TEA SERVICE

This coffee and tea service has been in my family for many years. It has a flower and leaf pattern, with small birds as finials. The mark is that of R. & W. Wilson, Philadelphia. Can you give me any information about this set. Should I have a matching teakettle made?

E.B. — Danville, Va.

Your tea service was made by Robert and William Wilson, active in Philadelphia from 1825 to 1846. You could always have a matching teakettle made, but a true lover of old silver will never find fault with a service that does not match exactly. In fact, the complete matching tea service as a product of one workshop made at the same time — that is, not assembled over a number of years — first began to appear about 1790. Especially favored was the six-piece tea service, consisting of a teapot, coffeepot, sugar bowl, cream jug, slop bowl, and teakettle on stand.

AMERICAN COIN-SILVER SERVICE

Can you give me any information concerning this silver set, which has been in my husband's family for years? The only mark is "C. Aldis" on the bottom of each piece.

J.J.S. — Westmont, N.J.

Your tea service was made of coin silver by Charles Aldis, who worked in New York around 1814.

COIN-SILVER SPOON

The sketched dessert spoon is made of a very soft metal with the name "C. Bard & Son" on the back. I saw one recently in a Jacksonville, Oregon, museum. What can you tell me about it?

B.V.P. — Grants Pass, Ore.

Your American coin-silver teaspoon was made by C. Bard & Son, who were active in Philadelphia in 1850.

SILVER LADLE

These sketches are of my ladle and its hallmarks. Can you identify the ladle further?

M.S. — Austin, Tex.

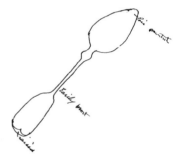

Your ladle is coin silver, made by Bailey & Company of Philadelphia between 1846 and 1850. The firm eventually became one of the leading Philadelphia jewelers, Bailey, Banks & Biddle.

COIN-SILVER SPOON

I would appreciate an estimate of the age of my coin-silver spoon. The initials "BB" and a sheaf of wheat are on its handle.

E.B. — *Glendale, Cal.*

The initials "BB" were used by several American silversmiths. Yours may possibly be those of Barzillai Benjamin, who was working in New York in 1825. The sheaf-of-wheat pattern was widely popular in the late 1820s and 1830s.

AMERICAN COIN-SILVER MARKS

Can you identify my spoon from my rather crude drawings of the marks? The piece is a berry spoon, 9½ inches long.

S.M. — *New York, N.Y.*

Your spoon is a coin-silver tablespoon made by S. Douglas Brower, who worked in Troy, New York, from 1832 to 1836 and in Albany, New York, from 1837 to 1850. Many American silversmiths used such marks, which resemble English hallmarks.

COIN-SILVER SPOON

I have my great-grandmother's wedding silver: 12 teaspoons and 6 dessert spoons, marked "B. M. Bailey." When and where were they made?

M.T.J. — *Warren, Ohio*

Bradbury M. Bailey made coin-silver spoons and other items in Rutland, Vermont, from 1852 until 1870.

SILVER FOOTED BOWL

I just inherited this silver footed bowl. It has the markings of "Wm. Gale & Son 1852" and, on the front, the inscription "M. H. Lord 1854." Can you identify it further?
                    H.M. — Massapequa, N.Y.

The silversmiths William Gale & Son were active in New York City from 1850 to 1866. Their address "116 Fulton St." is included in one of their marks.

COIN-SILVER SPOON

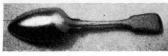

This spoon, which belonged to my husband's great-grandmother, is marked "Gelston & Treadwell–JC–NY." Can you tell us its age?
                    J.C.H. — Atlanta, Ga.

Gelston & Treadwell were active in New York City about 1840. It is interesting to note that in 1837 the United States Mint raised the silver standard for coins from 892 parts pure silver per 1000, which they had fixed in 1792, to 900 parts pure silver. So your coin silver spoon may have the higher standard.

COFFIN-END SERVING SPOON

My coin-silver serving spoon has the initials "I.G." on the back. It has been in my family for generations, and I have not been able to identify the silversmith mark.
                    R.D. — New York, N.Y.

The distinguishing initials "I.G." were used by several American silversmiths. However, as the coffin-end spoon was not introduced until about 1800, your spoon dates between 1800 and 1810. It was made by Philadelphia silversmith John D. Germon, who was active in Philadelphia from 1782 until at least 1816. Apparently the coffin-end was the only innovative American spoon pattern, as the other patterns had been borrowed from the English spoon.

AMERICAN SILVER CUP

I would like to know the age and maker of my silver cup.

H.F.M. — Atlanta, Ga.

Your cup was made by the Gorham Company, Providence, Rhode Island, who adopted your familiar trademark—a lion, an anchor and a capital "G"—in 1868, the year they abandoned the coin-silver standard (900/1000) and adopted the sterling standard (925/1000) for fine silver. The engraving dates your cup from around 1880–1890.

GORHAM PUNCH LADLE

I have a beautiful silver punch ladle with gold bowl and sculptured handle. The sketched mark includes a lion, an anchor and an Old English "G." My great-uncle's name is also engraved on it: "Frederic E. Smith, 1894." Can you tell me who made it?

W.E.F., Jr. — Alice, Tex.

Your sterling silver punch ladle was made by Gorham Company, Providence, Rhode Island. This firm dates back to Jabez Gorham, who began working as a silversmith in 1818. The engraved year dates it.

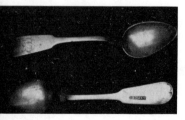

AMERICAN SILVER SPOONS

Can you identify these two teaspoons that are of some very soft metal and marked "D.B.H. & Co."? My mother's family has owned them for many, many years.

A.A.S. — Camarillo, Cal.

The mark "D.B.H. & Co." was used by D. B. Hindman & Company, an American silversmith active in Philadelphia around 1833.

AMERICAN

AMERICAN SILVER SPOONS

These spoons were given to my father-in-law by his grandmother. He thinks she told him that one — or all of them — was brought over on the May-flower. Could this be true? The two largest are marked "W. Moulton" on the back stem, the next two "J. Moulton," and the smallest spoon has an "AS" on the handle. Can you identify them further?

R.R.R. — Buffalo, N.Y.

Your fiddleback type American silver spoons suggest a date about 1830–1835. They were probably made by William Moulton (1772–1861) and his son Joseph (1814–1903), members of the well-known family of silversmiths who were active at Newburyport, Massachusetts, for no less than two hundred years. The initials "AS" on the small straight-style spoon may be those of Anthony Simmons, who was working at Philadelphia, Pennsylvania, in 1797.

COIN-SILVER SPOON

From the outline and marks I sketched, can you tell me when and where my heirloom spoons were made?

H.D. — Valentine, Neb.

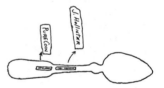

Your spoons quite probably date between 1840 and 1850. They were made by Julius Hollister (1818–1905), who worked in Oswego, New York, in 1846. Early American silver was generally made from coin. Although there was no official regulation to control the actual fine silver content, as a whole it was of a high quality. During the early nineteenth century the word "coin" was stamped on silverware to indicate that its fineness was equal to that of silver money — being 900 parts fine silver and 100 parts alloy in each 1000 parts.

PHILADELPHIA SPOON

Can you tell the age of my silver spoons from this drawing of their mark?

M.E.B. — Selma, Cal.

Your spoons are of coin silver, made by Nicholas LeHuray, who was working in Philadelphia from about 1809 to 1831.

INDIAN TRADE SILVER GORGET

This silver gorget was made by the noted silversmith Joseph Richardson (1711–1784). It was one of the highlights of the loan exhibit of eighteenth-century Philadelphia silver at the 1969 University Hospital Antiques Show in Philadelphia. We would like to know just how these pieces were used.

B.D.—Gwynedd Valley, Pa.

Originally the gorget was part of a knight's suit of armor, used to protect the throat. Yours, however, belongs to a later era, when a gorget or a crescent-shaped ornament was worn on a chain around the neck by an officer as a badge of rank. Your gorget engraved with a seated Indian, sun, fire and a Quaker with a pipe of peace, tree at right, is a superb example of Indian Trade Silver. It was made for "The Friendly Society for Propagating Peace with the Indians by Pacific Measures" of which Joseph Richardson was a member. The Indian chief who was given this piece of silver coveted it as personal adornment.

AUGUSTUS ROGERS TEAKETTLE

The mark on the bottom of my teakettle is enclosed. Can you give me further information?

M.T.W.—Annapolis, Md.

Your coin-silver teakettle-on-stand of *chinoiserie* design was made by Augustus Rogers, who was listed in the New York City Directory, 1831 to 1832, and in the Boston City Directory, 1840 to 1850.

KENTUCKY SILVER SPOON

Can you tell from the sketched mark when and where my heirloom silver spoons were made?

V.I.D.—Houston, Tex.

Your spoons were made by Richard Erving Smith (1800–1849), who was working at Louisville, Kentucky, from about 1821 to 1849.

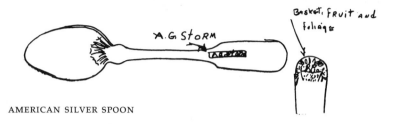

AMERICAN SILVER SPOON

When and where was this old silver spoon made?
It is not like any old silver I have seen. The decora-
tion at the tip of the handle, although worn almost
flat is exquisitely done.

H.D. — Valentine, Neb.

The silversmith Abraham Storm (1779–1836) advertised at Poughkeepsie, New York, from 1818 to 1830, when he moved to Albany.
From 1823 to 1826 he was in partnership with his son, John Adriance
Storm (1801–c. 1863), under the firm name of A. G. Storm & Son, at
Poughkeepsie, New York. Your fiddleback coin-silver spoon, decorated
at the end of the handle with a basket of fruit, probably dates about the
1820s.

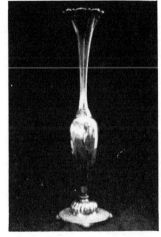

SILVER VASE

I inherited this silver vase from my grandmother.
It is 23 inches high, with a bell-like top and heavy
grapelike clusters for decoration. The marks on the
base are "Tiffany and Company, Sterling Silver,
925–1000, C." Anything you can tell me about it
will be appreciated.

J.C.S. — Richmond, Va.

Until recently it was the tradition of Tiffany and Company to use the
initial of their current president on their silver during his tenure. Thus
the "C" on your vase stands for Charles T. Cook, president from 1902
to 1907.

COIN-SILVER SPOON

I have a dozen silver spoons in three patterns. The ones whose picture I enclosed are marked "R&W.W." The others are marked "Hall & Elton," and "Butler & McCarty." When and where were they made?

B.D. — *Miami Springs, Fla.*

The spoon marked "R&W.W." was made by the R & W. Wilson silversmiths, active in Philadelphia around 1825–1846. The silversmiths Hall & Elton flourished at Geneva, New York, in the early 1840s, and the silversmiths Butler & McCarty were listed in the Philadelphia directory in 1850.

SILVER SUGAR BOWL

This sugar bowl, on loan from the Philadelphia Museum of Art, will be on display at our Antiques Show. It was made by Bancroft Woodcock and was owned by James Smith of Pennsylvania, a signer of the Declaration of Independence. Can you pinpoint its date?

B.D. — *Philadelphia, Pa.*

The inverted pear-shaped form of the body suggests a date around 1770. Woodcock, the silversmith who made the piece, selected a shape that was introduced in England around 1760 — about the usual time lapse before it became fashionable here. Bancroft of Woodstock (1732–1817) was working at Wilmington, Delaware, from around 1754 to at least 1772 and was the best known of any of Delaware's silversmiths.

SILVER
American plated

ICE-WATER PITCHER

Is this a coffee server, as I think it is? "Aurora Triple Plate" is marked on the bottom. I would appreciate anything you can tell me about the piece.

H.L.G. — Hillsdale, Mich.

You have an ice-water pitcher. The Aurora Silver Plate Co., Aurora, Illinois, was active from 1869 to about 1915. These pitchers, especially your tilting type, sat on a tray with a matching goblet, and date around the 1860s into the 1890s. Pitchers such as yours are collectors' items today.

QUADRUPLE PLATED SILVER

Can you estimate the age of this silver bowl that has belonged to my family for many years?
D.J.K. — Harper Woods, Mich.

Your bowl was made by the Barbour Silver Company of Hartford, Connecticut (1892–1898). The word "quadruple" in the mark means that the base metal (usually nickel) was coated with silver four times. Quadruple is the best quality of plated silver made in America.

PLATED SILVER MARK

My silver-plate bowl has the mark I have sketched. Where and by whom was it made?
J.D.H. — Jacksonville, Fla.

This mark depicting an American Indian replete with bow and arrow was used by R. Gleason & Sons of Dorchester, Massachusetts, and has been attributed (perhaps erroneously) to the Manhattan Silver Plate Company of Lyons, New York. Both companies were manufacturers of plated silverware and were active at sometime in the second half of the nineteenth century.

VICTORIAN HOLDER AND SPOONS

Can you date this spoon holder and spoons? Each spoon is 7 inches long, marked "Forbes Silver Co."
W.S.M. — Greer, S.C.

The Forbes Silver Company of Meriden, Connecticut, made your plated silver spoon holder and spoons probably about the later 1890s. The Victorian spoon-holder often housed a call-bell in the base. Yours rather looks like it might also serve this purpose.

AMERICAN PLATED

PICKLE CASTER

I inherited this cube-sugar holder and tongs, made, I think, of pewter and glass. I've sketched the mark on it. Can you date it?

                R.W.M. — Dillingham, Alaska

You have a plated-silver pickle caster — not a sugar holder — made by the Meriden Britannia Company of Meriden, Connecticut, around the 1870s. The pickle caster was a fashionable piece of Victorian tableware, and it is now very popular with collectors.

PLATED SILVER BOAT

What was this silver boat-shaped bowl used for? It is marked "Middletown Plate Co. Triple Plate."

                R.L.K. — Sacramento, Cal.

Bowls like this were used as dining-table centerpieces, usually to hold fruit. The manufacturer was in business at Middletown, Connecticut, between 1864 and 1898. Triple plate is the second-best quality of plated silver made in America.

TILTING ICE-WATER SET

What was this set for? The mark on the porcelain-lined urn is "No 87 Quadruple Silver Plate. Pat. appl. for July 13, 1868. Meriden B Company."

                H.P. — Fontana, Cal.

You have an American Victorian plated silver ice-water set, and the patent date establishes its age. It seems the ice-water pitcher dates from a patent of 1854 issued to the Meriden Britannia Company. Later, in 1886, Meriden Britannia offered no fewer than fifty-seven different patterns of ice-water pitchers.

245

VICTORIAN BOTTLE HOLDER

I would like to know what this metal container was used for and how old it is. It's about 21½ inches high and has 6 doors. The bottom has a raised round emblem of an Indian with bow and arrow and a 5-pointed star.

D.C.—Appleton, Wis.

You have a portable silverplated Victorian wine bottle holder, mid-nineteenth century. It's also equipped for storage of wine glasses. The mark (see page 244) on the bottom is that of R. Gleason & Sons, Dorchester, Massachusetts, whose work was highly esteemed.

REPRODUCTION OF EARLY SILVER

Our tea set is marked "Pairpont Mfg. Co., New Bedford, Mass." Do you know the age of the set or its history?

J.C.A.—Kansas City, Mo.

Your tea set was made sometime between 1880, when Pairpont was established, and 1900, when it became the Pairpont Corporation. The company made reproductions in plated silver of early sterling silver designs.

PLATED-SILVER CASTER

Can you date my handsome caster? I've sketched the mark on its bottom. Where was it used?

R.A.—Rockford, Ill.

Your silver-plated caster was made by the Meriden Britannia Company, active at Meriden, Connecticut, from 1852 to 1898, when they merged with the International Silver Company. However, they operated as a division and made silver plate with their own trademark until about 1934 or 1935. Your caster appears to be quite an early one, made in the 1860s or 1870s. The caster was one of the most widely used pieces of Victorian electroplate. According to directions for setting the table in nineteenth-century cookbooks, the caster was placed in the center of the table.

PLATED SILVER PITCHER

My silver pitcher with grapevine design has the mark "Reed & Barton 1794" on the separate bottom piece. Can you tell when it was made?
D.C. — Tarrytown, N.Y.

Reed & Barton silversmiths, of Taunton, Massachusetts, made your plated silver pitcher between 1880 and 1890 ("1794" was the style number).

PLATED SILVER COFFEEPOT

About how old is our family's silver coffeepot with the mark "Rogers Brothers Plate, Hartford, Conn."?
D.S.M. — Charlotte, N.C.

Rogers Brothers started manufacturing plated silver in 1847. The design of your coffeepot dates it about 1855–1860.

VICTORIAN BUTTER DISH

This silver butter dish was a wedding present to my mother-in-law from her grandmother. It is marked "Rogers, Smith & Co., New Haven, Ct." The lower compartment is for shaved ice to keep butter firm. Can you tell me how old it is?

P.D. — Glendale, Cal.

Your plated silver butter dish was made by Rogers, Smith & Company between the years 1862–1877, when their factory was located at New Haven.

AMERICAN TEA SERVICE

Four pieces of my old tea set are marked "Rogers, Smith & Co., Hartford, Conn., No. 1919"; the mark on the other two is "Design Patented Jan. 12, 1855. 1919." Can you give me any further information?

C.F. — Pacific Grove, Cal.

Rogers, Smith & Company made plated silver at Hartford from 1857 to 1862, when they moved to New Haven. Since most of the pieces are marked "Hartford," the set was probably made during the firm's stay there; "1919" is the style number.

AMERICAN "SHEFFIELD"

The mark sketched is on the bottom of my silver-plated sugar and creamer. The Sheffield name is on both pieces although they were made in the United States. Was any genuine Sheffield plate made here?

G.M.M. — Mojave, Cal.

AMERICAN PLATED

Genuine Sheffield plate (the name comes from Sheffield, England) was apparently not made in America. The making of this plate practically ended when manufacturers began to use the electroplate process, which was less costly. The word "Sheffield" simply means that the manufacturer tried to achieve the look of the original. Your pieces were made by the Knickerbocker Silver Company, Port Jervis, New York (1900–1935).

RICHMOND BLUES CANTEEN

I would appreciate your comments on the age and function of the flask sketched here. It appears to be plated silver, as the edges are quite worn.
C.G.L. — Farmington, Mich.

It is a Richmond Light Blue Infantry Regiment canteen made by the Van Bergh Silver Plate Company, Rochester, New York, after 1892. The regiment was established in 1789 and is now in the National Guard.

AMERICAN SETTING

My mother received these table settings as a wedding present in 1895. The marks are: a boar's head, "Waldo," initials "HE." It appears to be gold. Any information will be appreciated.
G.N.M. — Xenia, Ohio

Your flatware was made by the Waldo Foundry of Bridgeport, Connecticut, which was founded in 1894 and closed in 1905. According to their trademark, their specialty was "aluminum-gold flat and tableware."

AMERICAN TEA SERVICE

Please tell me, if you can, the date this silver was made. The maker was Simpson, Hall, Miller & Company, of Wallingford, Connecticut.
E.A.W.—Providence, R.I.

The firm that made your plated silver tea service was in business from 1866 to 1898 and made your service about 1880–1890.

PLATED SILVER SET

My silver-plated washbowl, pitcher, covered soap dish, waste bowl, toothbrush, and razor holders have "Made & plated by Wallace Bros. Silver Co." marked on each. I wrote the present company, but they could not give me any information about the set. Perhaps you can trace it somehow.
H.D.N.—Longview, Tex.

The Wallace Brothers Silver Company, of Wallingford, Connecticut, was started in 1875 for the manufacture of plated silverware. In 1879 R. Wallace & Sons Manufacturing Company bought the business, so your washstand set was made prior to this date. The washstand set was an important accessory in the Victorian bedroom. Since the majority of them were made of ironstone or semiporcelain, your set is most unusual.

SILVER
Continental

FRENCH SILVER COFFEEPOT

With the aid of a magnifying glass I can distinguish the following marks on my solid silver coffeepot: a salamander at the top, a plumed fleur-de-lis, and below that the initials "A.L." I inherited it from my French grandfather. How old might it be?

S.H. — Oak Park, Ill.

According to the hallmark, your coffeepot was made in Paris in the eighteenth century, possibly by Alexis Loir, a silversmith who was active around 1733.

FRENCH TEA SET

I bought this silver tea service in Victoria, British Columbia. It enchanted me because it was so unusual, and I hope it will become a family heirloom. We had the set appraised, but the appraisers could not tell us its country of origin. What is your opinion?

C.B.B. — Seattle, Wash.

Your tea service is French. It dates from the Second Empire period, 1852–1870, and was probably made around 1860. The form and ornament of the set have been borrowed mainly from the Louis XV and Louis XVI styles.

GERMAN BAND

We recently inherited this set of silver figurines, whose heads are mounted on springs and separate at the shoulder line, so the bodies, which were once gold-washed, can be used as cups. I hope you can identify the figures.

P.A.K. — Meadville, Pa.

Your set of silver figures representing band musicians is of German origin, most likely dating around 1880–1890. The medley of marks that you sketched are mainly fake marks, put on to make the figures seem even older than they are.

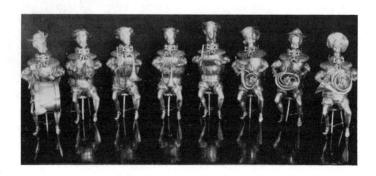

SEVENTEENTH-CENTURY BEAKER

Can you tell me the approximate age of this cup, the country in which it was made, and the individual who might have made it?
I.R.W. — Dallas, Tex.

The hallmark indicates your beaker was made at Augsberg, Germany, in 1693, but the maker's mark, "DB," is not recorded in books on seventeenth-century German silver. The bishop's miter surmounting the engraved coat of arms indicates the beaker was probably made for a clergyman of some importance.

GERMAN ÉPERGNE

Please tell me something about the origin of my épergne. The figurines are marked "sterling," and the initials "WMF" are on the base. A jeweler suggested that a dagger belongs in the hand of the figurine holding only part of a handle.
C.G. — San Francisco, Cal.

The initials "WMF" belong to the still-existing German metalwork factory, Wüerttembergische Metallwarenfabrik. Your centerpiece was advertised in their catalogue of 1888 and was described as a fruit bowl with a special vase attachment. The figure on the right side held a heavy sword. The sterling mark was added later.

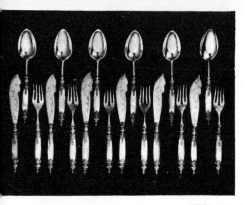

800🌙

VERMEIL FLATWARE

Enclosed is a photograph of my set of pearl-handled vermeil flatware and a close-up of the hallmarks on a fork. Curiously, some pieces in the set are unmarked. I would like to know the age of the set, the quality, where it was made, and the purpose for which it was intended.

B.B.B. — San Antonio, Tex.

Your flatware is gold-plated silver of German origin. The quarter moon and crown are the Reich silver mark, which came into use in 1888 — so your pieces date after that time. The mark was stamped only on pieces that had a silver content of 800/1000 parts — the standard for German silver (which is somewhat less than the English standard for sterling of 925/1000 parts silver). Sets such as yours were used for the dessert course.

DUTCH SERVERS

We purchased this silver fork and spoon at a recent sale. The unusual design makes us wonder if you could throw some light on their origin.

F.Q. — Hamilton, Ohio

Serving pieces such as these, with pierced handles terminating in a ship design, are characteristically Dutch. They were made in Holland around 1870–1890.

GERMAN SILVER

I bought this silver tureen and mirror plateau in Germany some years ago. They are marked "Strube & Sohn" and bear the number "800." The tureen has a separate liner of plate silver on copper. Some of the baroque trimming and handles are fastened with small silver bolts. Can you give me any further information?

E.A. — Atlanta, Ga.

Strube & Son made your serving silver piece and plateau in Berlin between 1860 and 1880. The number 800 indicates that the silver alloy contains 800 parts fine silver out of every 1000 parts. Copper has always been the most effective alloying metal with silver. Thus it is always used. The best known silver copper alloy is sterling silver which contains 925 parts of silver and 75 parts of copper per thousand.

DUTCH MINIATURE CHAIR

I have a sterling silver miniature chair, 2 inches high. The marks on its back are, from the top, "S.B.I.," "F," crown, lion, and, I think, an "L." On the bottom is a sailing boat, "930," and a sign of a bell. What does it all mean? How old is it and where was it made?

E.L. — Atlantic City, N.J.

Your miniature silver chair is Dutch in origin. The marks under the seat are more or less meaningless; "930" is probably the standard of silver. The full set of Sheffield marks on the front of the back panel was put on at the time the chair entered England, its foreign origin being shown by the "F." The date letter is not entirely legible. It may be "C" (1895–96) or "R" (1909–10). The mark centered in the crest rail is probably a Dutch control mark.

SWEDISH SPIRIT CUP

My silver "skol" is a family heirloom from Sweden. It is 1¼ inches high. On the bottom are "ET," a number "03," three circles, and a mark that looks like a castle. Can you tell me where, when, and by whom it was made?

T.H.P. — Everett, Wash.

Your silver cup was made by the Swedish silversmith Ernst Tengvall, who worked at Hälsingborg from 1803 to 1823.

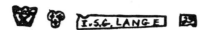

SWEDISH SILVER BOX

My small solid-silver box has the enclosed marks on the underside of its lid. The inside is gilt, and the box was perhaps used for snuff. Is Lange a silversmith's name?

C.E.A. — Raleigh, N.C.

Your silver box, the work of the Swedish silversmith Johan Samuel Gottfrid Lange, who worked at Växjö, dates from around 1815. The three crowns are the symbol for Sweden.

SCANDINAVIAN SPOONS

My husband is a disc jockey, and one of his fans sent me these spoons. The bowls are gold and the handles silver. Can you tell me anything about them?

W.R.P. — Northbrook, Ill.

I believe your silver spoons with filigree handles are of Norwegian or Swedish provenance, dating about 1880–1900. Since you mention no mark, they cannot be traced further.

RUSSIAN SILVER WITH NIELLO INLAY

Enclosed is a photograph and my best attempt to copy the markings on what I believe to be a Russian vermeil enameled tea service. I hope that you may be able to identify the service in more detail.

J.H.W. — *Villanova, Pa.*

"MA" is the maker's identification mark, "BC" the assayer's mark, "1863," the year of manufacture, "84" the silver content. The final mark seems to be St. George and the dragon, which denotes Moscow. The inlay work, with black designs incised on silver, is called niello. This type of decoration was popular as far back as the Roman Empire and is still extensively used in Russia and India.

FRENCH PLATED SILVER

I inherited my silver service from an aunt who told me it was French. The name "Christofle" appears in the hallmark. Model numbers on the individual pieces include "410864" on the teapot and "411129" on the tray. I would like to know how old the set is.

M.H.M. — *Palo Alto, Cal.*

Your plated silver tea set was made in 1880 by Christofle Silver, Inc., established in Paris in 1837 and still flourishing. Charles H. Christofle introduced a silver-plating process that produced an especially bright finish. Although the firm also made sterling, it is known for plated silver.

SILVER
English

ENGLISH SILVER TEA CADDY

Enclosed is a picture of a small silver box and its marks. It was described as an old English tea caddy when I purchased it at a country shop. I should like to know whether it is sterling and when it was made.

R.E.W. — *Manhasset, N.Y.*

The hallmarks on your tea caddy—"HA" in a rectangle, crown, lion passant, and capital "Z"—indicate that it was made in Sheffield, England, by Henry Atkin or Hy. Archer & Company (1892–1893) and is of sterling quality; that is, 925 parts fine silver per 1000.

258

GEORGE III TEAPOT

The loan exhibit at the 1968 University Hospital Antiques Show in Philadelphia will consist of some exceptionally fine pieces handed down by several generations of the family of Joseph Wharton, the eminent Philadelphian, who lived from 1707 to 1776. One of the highlights will be this teapot, a wedding present to one of Mr. Wharton's descendants. Inadvertently its date tag was lost, and family members cannot agree on its age. Our committee would like to know the date of the teapot, if possible, from the photograph and the inexpertly sketched marks.

B.D. — Gwynedd Valley, Pa.

The London silversmiths Anne and Peter Bateman made the Wharton silver teapot in 1794–95. The bright cutting that decorates the piece first began to appear around 1790. The Bateman family — Anne, Hester, Jonathan, Peter, and William — were all well-known silversmiths in the George III era, and among the most brilliant and popular craftsmen of their time.

GEORGIAN SILVER TEAPOT

I bought this silver teapot in London as an antique some time ago. It has marks on the bottom, which I have sketched side by side — "HC," a crowned leopard's head, lion passant, the small letter "i," and the king's head. From this information, can you tell me anything about its origin and if it is an antique?

M.E.R. — Royal Oak, Mich.

Yes, your oval-shaped silver teapot with a straight spout in the Neo-Classical style is an antique. "HC" are the initials of Henry Chawner, a London silversmith, who entered his mark in 1786. The hallmarks tell you that it dates from 1787–1788.

259

ENGLISH SILVER DESK SET

Please explain these hallmarks I have sketched. They belong to this old silver desk set I recently purchased.

I.W. — San Diego, Cal.

The desk set is of English sterling silver and was made in London 1845–1846 by E. E. and J. W. Barnard, silversmiths.

SILVER-MOUNTED CLARET JUG

This claret jug was brought from England. Anything you can tell me about it will be most welcome.

P.K. — Tacoma, Wash.

From the hallmark we can determine that the silver mounts on your jug were made in London in 1900–1901.

ENGLISH SPOON MARKS

Can you help us identify our silver coffee spoons by the marks we have copied?

L.S.T. — Toms River, N.J.

These hallmarks indicate the spoons are sterling and were made by Elkington & Company, Birmingham, England. The design was registered on March 8, 1865.

ENGLISH SILVER CANDLESTICKS

My candlesticks have these markings. Are they antiques?

P.D. — Gary, Ind.

"M.S." is the maker's mark, not traceable. The lion passant stands for English sterling; the leopard's head for London; the date letter "r" for 1932–1933. To be classified as an antique an article must be no less than one hundred years old.

ENGLISH MUG HALLMARKS

These crude drawings are of the hallmarks on a beautiful silver mug that was given my husband by his British godfather over thirty years ago. We believe the mug is quite old. The marks seem similar to those on the Bateman teapot shown in your April column. Any information you can give me will be appreciated.

W.C.T. — Richmond, Va.

The hallmarks, although of British origin, differ considerably from those on the Bateman teapot. Both the silversmith's initials and the date mark are different. According to the London hallmarks on your mug, it was made by silversmith Crespin Fuller between 1819 and 1820.

SILVER CAKE BASKET

The marks on my silver cake basket, I am told, indicate that it was made in 1791–1792, the makers' mark, "SG-EW," standing for the London silversmiths Samuel Godbehere and Edward Wigan. What does the crown on the upper rim represent?

D.W. — Portland, Ore.

The crown is a family crest mark. It was almost standard for English silversmiths to put their marks on the upper rim of a basket.

ENGLISH STUFFING SPOON

Recently I received a gift of a stuffing spoon, presumably an antique. I am enclosing pictures of the front and back. Could you identify the hallmarks and give me an approximate date?

M.C.B. — Waterbury, Conn.

The makers, Samuel Godbehere, Ed. Wigan and J. Bult, registered their mark at Goldsmiths' Hall, London, 1800. These spoons make marvelous casserole serving pieces.

VICTORIAN SILVER

From the hallmarks and the photograph of my serving pieces, please tell me what you can about them. The only information I have is that they are early eighteenth-century.

F.K. — Rumson, N.J.

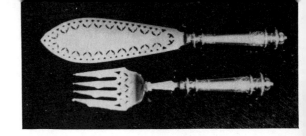

Your silver fish slice and fork were made by the Sheffield silversmiths Martin Hall & Company, Ltd. in 1872–1873, and are therefore Victorian, not eighteenth-century.

ENGLISH SILVER INKSTAND

I bought this piece in England and would like to know its age and maker. The tray, candlestand and mountings of the inkwells all bear the same hallmarks.

V.H.K. — Dover, Mass.

Your sterling silver inkstand was made by the Sheffield silversmiths Martin Hall & Company, Ltd. in 1885–1886. Your inkstand is fitted with two pots and a taper stick—a miniature candlestick used for melting wax to seal letters. Until about the middle of the nineteenth century the second pot contained sand commonly used as a dusting powder for drying ink before the invention of blotting paper.

LATE GEORGIAN SPOON

Enclosed are enlarged copies of the front and back of one of my antique silver spoons. I look forward to any identification of it you can give me.

H.U.T., Jr. — Morgantown, W.Va.

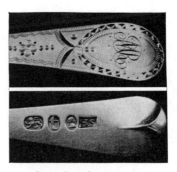

According to the hallmarks on your spoon it was made in London in 1794–1795, possibly by silversmith Henry Sardet.

THOMAS SATCHWELL'S ENGLISH HALLMARKS

Last summer at an estate sale we bought a small silver pitcher with the enclosed marks. We know the family came from England about 125 years ago. Can you help us find out who may have made it?

C.H. — *Minneapolis, Minn.*

From your sketch of the hallmarks we believe you have an English sterling cream jug. It was made in London by Thomas Satchwell, who worked there from 1773 to 1789. The date letter "M" indicates that your pitcher was made in 1787–1788.

EARLY GEORGIAN MARROW SCOOP

I received this interesting silver spoon as a gift. The marks reading from the spoon head are: "JS," a lion rampant, a crown and the letter "Q." What was it used for, and when was it made?

M.C.B. — *New York, N.Y.*

You have a sterling silver, handwrought marrow scoop. It was made in 1731–1732 by a London silversmith with the distinguishing initials JS, which may be those of Joseph Smith, John Sanders, James Savage and others who entered their marks in the 1720s.

ENGLISH SILVER TEA CADDY

I bought this tea caddy in England and wish to know its age.

V.H.K. — *Dover, Mass.*

Your tea caddy is English sterling, made in Birmingham in 1912–1913. "H & Co.," the maker's mark, cannot be traced.

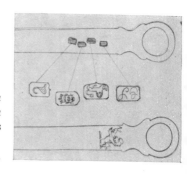

GEORGIAN SILVER SKEWER

Some time ago I noticed a charcoal gray tool in our toolbox. On polishing it, I found it to be a silver letter opener. Can you explain the marks sketched?

J.A., Jr. — New York, N.Y.

You have a silver skewer. The hallmarks indicate it was made by London silversmith George Smith in 1776–77. Originally used to hold meat firmly on the platter while it was being carved, the skewers are popular today as letter openers.

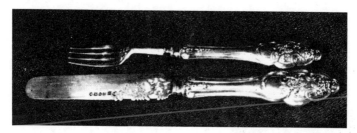

VICTORIAN SILVER DESSERT SERVICE

Here are two pieces of my antique dessert service that I purchased in London in 1941. Can you tell by the marks on the knife when and where it was made?

E.M. — Arco, Idaho

The five hallmarks indicate that your sterling silver flatware was made by the English Sheffield silversmiths Hy. Wilkinson & Company in 1856–1857. The punches are a crown for Sheffield; "N," the date letter; lion passant, the quality mark; sovereign's head, the excise tax; the maker's mark, a shield enclosing the initials H W & Co.

265

SILVER
English plated

VICTORIAN PLATED SILVER COFFEEPOT

The photographs are of my coffeepot (and its mark) from a silver service that I believe is English Sheffield plate. I would appreciate learning what you can tell about it.

M.T.G. — Schenectady, N.Y.

The mark tells that your service is English plated silver, dating about 1860–1880. The maker, A G & Company, cannot be traced; the mark is not recorded. "A1" indicates the best grade of plated silver; "1730" is the style number; and "7" means a seven-piece service.

PLATED SILVER BISCUIT BOX

I bought this piece in England. From these photographs of it and its marks, can you tell me about it?

V.H.K. — Dover, Mass.

You have a biscuit box of plated silver ("EPNS" means electroplate on nickel silver). The initials indicate it was made by Atkin Brothers, Truro Works, Sheffield, which is still in business. Plated pieces are never dated, but from the design it appears to be a reproduction of an early Sheffield box.

VICTORIAN JUG

I'd appreciate any information you can give me about this pitcher I inherited, or about its mark. The design is chocolate brown on white, and the pewter snap-up lid is stamped: "Atkin Brothers — Sheffield."

S.L.S. — Bloomington, Minn.

The snap lid is not pewter but English plated silver, and the jug was made by Atkin Brothers. The diamond-shaped mark shows that the design was registered at the British Patent Office on April 25, 1863.

SHEFFIELD CANDELABRUM

My late grandmother's silver-plate-over-copper candelabrum has a mark like a double sunburst. Can you tell who made it and when?
M.J.P. — Hartsdale, N.Y.

Your candelabrum is genuine antique Sheffield plate. Matthew Boulton of Birmingham made Sheffield plate with this mark from 1784 to 1809.

ENGLISH CANDLESTICK

Could you give me any idea of the age of this candlestick and snuffer? A tiny bird imprint is nearly worn off the handle.
J.L.B., Jr. — Harvey, Ill.

Since the maker's mark is so worn, we can only say that your English plated silver bedroom candlestick and snuffer probably date around 1850–1875.

ENGLISH PUNCH LADLE

This ladle came from a secondhand shop in Edinburgh, Scotland. The bottom of the bowl is marked "JC & S" and "EP." I am interested in knowing its origin, age and usage.
D.E.M. — Tacoma, Wash.

ENGLISH PLATED

You have an English punch ladle dating about 1900 and made by John Chatterly and Son, London and Birmingham. Electroplating (EP in your mark) is a method of silver-plating by electrolysis in which the silver is decomposed in a bath of potassium cyanide and deposited on a base metal, such as German nickel or white metal.

SELF-POURING TEAPOT

In Canada we bought a teapot that works by suction to pour an exact cup of tea. We would like to know its history, if possible.
M.S. — *Dearborn, Mich.*

The Hovles self-pouring teapot was patented in 1886. Your plated silver one was made as a novelty by James Dixon & Sons, Sheffield, England.

PLATED SILVER EGG CASTER

How old is this silver-plated egg caster, brought from England over sixty years ago? It has no identifying marks.
J.K.S. — *Hammond, Ind.*

Your egg caster is Victorian and dates between 1860 and 1880. It was probably made in either Birmingham or Sheffield, the chief English centers for the manufacture of plated silver. A caster was used to serve boiled eggs at breakfast in well-appointed homes.

ENGLISH PLATTER WITH COVER

The mark on the bottom of my covered server is a crown and the name "E & Co." A knight's helmet is engraved on the cover. How old is it?
J.R.H. — Cordele, Ga.

Your platter with dome-shaped cover is English plated silver, made by Elkington & Co., Birmingham, about 1870–1890. Hot water was put in the base of the platter to keep roasts warm.

PLATED SILVER SUGAR BOWL

Attached is the picture of a sugar bowl I own. The mark is "W & H" with pennant. Do you know where it was made?
T.L.L. — Cleveland, Ohio

The piece is English plated silver, made by Walker & Hall Ltd., Howard Street, Sheffield, after 1900. The firm still operates.

ENGLISH MUFFINEER

What was this silver dish used for, and where was it made? On the bottom are the initials "JR & S."
W.M.B. — San Diego, Cal.

Silver pieces like this are English and called rolltop muffineers — they are used to keep muffins hot. Yours is plated silver, made by Joseph Rodgers & Sons, Sheffield, between 1880 and 1910.

VICTORIAN FISH KNIFE

I would like to know the age of my large knife with decorated silver blade and bone-color handle. There is a matching fork with a little less detail.
                    A.V. — Wilton, Conn.

Your knife and fork are plated silver from an English fish set, made about 1880–1890 by E. Howard & Son of Sheffield, England. The firm is still in business.

VICTORIAN HOT-WATER KETTLE

My grandfather's silver tea kettle is marked: "Walker, Knowles & Co., Sheffield." How old is it?

                    E.B.T. — Clifton, N.J.

This company recorded their mark in 1840, so your English Sheffield-plate kettle was probably made in the 1840s, when electroplating supplanted Sheffield plate, as it was cheaper and more adaptable to the ornate decorative treatment favored by the Victorians.

PEWTER

AMERICAN PEWTER

These pewter pieces were found recently among my mother's effects. The mark, which I have sketched, says "Boardman & Co., New York, N.Y.," and has an American eagle with outspread wings in the center. The cover is interchangeable, fitting both pieces equally well. What can you tell me about them?

T.M.B. — Grand Rapids, Mich.

The mark you have sketched was used by the American pewterers Thomas Danforth Boardman and Sherman Boardman sometime between 1825 and 1827.

DANFORTH PEWTER MARK

This mark is on a pewter plate, one of six my
great-great-grandmother received in 1809. Are
they American pieces?
                    F.J.H. — Silver Spring, Md.

Your plates were made by the American pewterer Samuel Danforth,
who worked in Hartford, Connecticut, from 1795 to 1815.

BRITANNIA WARE

I inherited four pieces of Britannia ware. They
are marked: "James Dixon and Son 1782." Can
you tell me their history?
                    M.W.H. — La Jolla, Cal.

Your Britannia-ware vessels were made by the still-existing firm of
James Dixon & Sons Ltd., Sheffield, England. They were made about
1830, as the firm was called James Dixon and Son for only three years.
"1782" is the stock number, not the date.

ENGLISH GEORGIAN PEWTER

Please advise me as to the age and origin of this
pewter plate, one of several I possess. I am also
enclosing a photograph of their mark.
                    T.W. — Brooklyn, N.Y.

The mark is that of Samuel Ellis, a tinsmith who worked in London
between the years 1771 and 1773.

ENGLISH PEWTER PLATTER

These badly worn marks are on the back of my large pewter platter. Are they clear enough for you to identify it?

P.M.E. — Adrian, Mich.

Richard Goeing (note the "e") of Bristol, England, used the Lamb-and-Flag mark with his name from about 1715. He died in 1764, so your platter was made sometime within this fifty-year span.

AMERICAN PEWTER COFFEEPOT

My pewter coffeepot is about one foot high and is marked "Roswell Gleason" on the bottom. We saw a similar one in a restored historic house in Maine. Can you give me some information about the maker?

G.A.Y. — Simsbury, Conn.

Roswell Gleason, who made your coffeepot, was first listed as a pewterer about 1830 at Dorchester, Massachusetts. He was noted for the fine quality of his work. Your coffeepot dates between 1830 and 1850. In time the business started by Gleason became one of the largest and most important in Dorchester. After 1850 its products were mostly plated-silver. The firm closed in 1871.

VICTORIAN PEWTER COFFEEPOT

This pewter coffee server was brought from England and had a pedigree, which was lost before we received it. Would you know its age or anything else of interest? Enclosed is a picture and a sketch of the mark on the bottom of the server.

R.J.W. — Napa, Cal.

274

Your coffeepot was made by Shaw and Fisher, Sheffield, England. The diamond-shaped mark records the fact that this firm registered its design at the British Patent Office in London on May 2, 1845. This registry date is the earliest that your pot could have been made. The design was probably in use for another five or ten years.

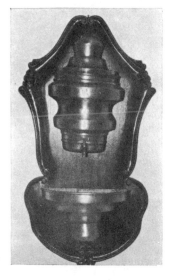

PEWTER WALL FOUNTAIN AND LAVABO

I bought this lavabo in Switzerland. The shop-keeper could give me no clue to its origin or approximate age. It is pewter and in excellent condition. The pencil rubbings are of the stampings on the back of the water tank. I will appreciate any information.

M.G. — APO, New York

The marks indicate your wall fountain and lavabo (or wash basin) are nineteenth-century German. The wall fountain with lavabo beneath was always a distinctive decorative accessory, found chiefly in the dining room and used for washing cutlery during dinner—a practice that persisted well into the nineteenth century.

My pewter jug is six-sided, with a screw-top ring handle. Each side is engraved with flowers, and the date "1705" appears on one panel. Can you tell me what the jug was used for?

L.M.W. — Mahwah, N.J.

This is one of two heavy pewter tankards I bought several years ago. It has a screw-top ring handle, a crest, but no identifying marks. Can you give me any information about it?

E.H. — Glens Falls, N.Y.

Both of these artifacts are *pots de viande* (literally "pots for meat"). They were used to store the essence of cooked meat in jellied form, to be melted down later and added to sauces. The larger one is probably French, and dates, as it is marked, from 1705. The spouted *pot de viande* is nineteenth-century Dutch or German, most likely the latter.

GLASS
American

*I would like to know something about this glass
bowl. Satiny white inside, with shades from light
to darker pink outside, it has a handetched design of eagles with a banner interspersed with
sprays of flowers and leaves. There are no identifying marks.*

T.R. — Waterford, Mich.

Your cameo-glass bowl is American art glass, the name given to a
ware produced by glassworks around 1880–1910. It was made, probably in the 1880s, by the Mt. Washington Glass Company, active at
South Boston and New Bedford, Massachusetts, 1837–1894. Originally
the bowl was inserted in a silver-plated frame called a "cameo bride's
basket" — a traditional wedding gift.

SPATTER-GLASS VASE

Any information you can give us about our glass vase will be appreciated. It has a lot of markings of different colors, especially rosy red and pink.
C.E., Jr. — Jackson, Ohio

Your variegated glass vase is a pleasing example of spatter glass, a popular kind of American art glass, dating from 1880 to 1900. During the past ten years or so there has been a noticeable growth of interest in American art glass, most of which, unfortunately, was seldom marked.

AMBER PATTERN-GLASS MUG

We rediscovered in an old trunk this cup that belonged to my mother. Can you tell when or where it was made?
E.B. — Bowie, Tex.

Your amber pattern-glass mug was made after 1900 in an American glass factory — but it is hard to say in what part of the country. Possibly it was Vineland, New Jersey.

AMERICAN ART GLASS

We would appreciate anything you can tell us about this very thin glass vase with handpainted floral decorations. I tried to draw it in scale; 13¼ inches tall, 6⅛ inches wide at top.
A.S.M. — Washington, D.C.

AMERICAN

You have an American art-glass vase dating about 1890–1910. The floral decorations were put on with colored enamel after the vase was blown; then the whole piece was refired in a furnace.

AMERICAN GLASS BREAD PLATTER

Would you be able to tell from the enclosed drawing anything about this glass dish, which I presume was used for bread?
M.M.R. — *Santa Fe, N.M.*

Pressed-glass bread platters such as yours were a popular commemorative item for the Centennial Exposition year. The design patented July 6, 1875, depicts in the center Carpenters' Hall, where the First Continental Congress met. It was probably made at the Philadelphia glassworks of Gillinder & Sons, who made many pattern-glass dishes for the exposition.

COMMEMORATIVE PLATTER

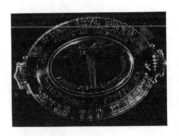

I believe I have a commemorative glass platter marking the hundredth anniversary of our country's freedom. I would like to know who made it and anything else you can tell me about it.
A.R. — *Stamford, Conn.*

Platters such as yours were made for the Philadelphia Centennial Exposition of 1876 and continued to be made up through the Columbian Exposition of 1893. Most were made by the firm of Gillinder & Sons of Philadelphia. The names William Prescott, Israel Putnam, John Stark, and Joseph Warren on your platter identify officers who distinguished themselves at the Battle of Bunker Hill. These American commemorative platters with American historical significance are very popular with collectors of pressed glass.

COMMEMORATIVE PITCHER

I would be interested in anything you can tell me concerning my clear glass pitcher, which I have tried to sketch. The front depicts a spread eagle with these words underneath: "Gridley, you may fire when ready." On the other side, the following words and date are listed: "Olympia, Petrel, Concord, Raleigh, Boston, Baltimore, McCullough, May 1, 1898."

B.J. — Belleville, Pa.

Your pressed-glass pitcher commemorates the Battle of Manila, which occurred on May 1, 1898, during the Spanish-American War. The names on the side list the American ships on the scene: four cruisers (the flagship *Olympia, Baltimore, Raleigh,* and *Boston*), two gunboats (*Concord* and *Petrel*), and a revenue cutter, the *Hugh M'Culloch* (not McCullough). The quotation (which has been variously reported) was Admiral Dewey's famous command to the captain of the flagship.

GLASS CANE

My clear glass cane has a red streak running inside the complete length of its 35 inches. It is one inch across at the top, tapering to a half inch at bottom. Can you tell when and where this cane was made?

B.M.W. — Saratoga, Wyo.

It is generally believed that glass canes such as yours, made in New England and other American glasshouses around 1840–1865, were not definitely production items, but were "exercises" of glass blowers, who often gave them to friends as gifts. Their origin must remain uncertain.

CRANBERRY CRYSTAL

Our cranberry crystal goblets, champagne, and wine glasses are, we have been told, Steuben's "Swirled Cerise Ruby." Is this a fact?
J.V.L. — St. Claire Shores, Mich.

From what I can tell by your photograph, I do not believe you have Steuben "Cerise Ruby," since the shape is not characteristic of that glass. But I do think your crystal dates from about the same period — that is, the early years of the twentieth century, 1910–1930.

WASHINGTON-EAGLE FLASK

I found this bottle in the shallows of Gasparilla Sound, Florida, full of sand but unbroken. It has a sketch of George Washington on the other side. Do you think it has any history?
M.S.B. — Placida, Fla.

Some thirteen early American glass factories around Pittsburgh made slightly varying versions of this Washington-Eagle flask, beginning as early as 1820. The type you have is rated as scarce by collectors.

CUT-GLASS MARK

Last summer I bought a small bottle of cut glass with this mark on the stopper. Can you tell where it was made?
J.C. — Moravia, N.Y.

HAWKES

This is the trademark of T. G. Hawkes, Corning, New York, a firm that was in business from 1890 to 1962 making quality cut glass.

CARNIVAL PUNCH BOWL

Can you tell me how old my punch bowl and cups are? They are Carnival glass, with the letter "n" on them.

L.J.S. — Garden Grove, Cal.

Your pressed iridescent glass punch bowl set was made around 1910–1920 by the Northwood Glass Company of Wheeling, West Virginia, one of the outstanding producers of Carnival glass. It derives its name from the fact that it was a giveaway at carnivals and fairs. An imitation of Tiffany art glass, it is also called Poor Man's Tiffany Glass. It should be remembered that the luster finish was applied only to the surface of the glass, and for this reason can be washed away or badly faded by the effects of the sun's rays.

"LOG CABIN" GLASS

My grandmother's lidded glass dish shaped like a log cabin is now mine. Could you estimate its age and origin?

A.E.W. — Kingston, Ont., Can.

Molded glass in this "Log Cabin" pattern was made by a Pittsburgh glass factory around 1880–1890. They also made creamers, spoon holders, and a compote in the same design.

MARY GREGORY GLASS

I have a pair of vases that were given to my grandmother about 1890. They are a deep opaque blue, handblown, with a handpainted figure of a boy on one and girl in a swing on the other. They are signed "Mary Gregory" — is that what this kind of vase is called?

S.DeL. — Sulphur, Okla.

Your vases were made at the Boston & Sandwich Factory, Sandwich, Massachusetts, where Mary Gregory was one of the staff decorators. This glass was made between about 1875 and the date the factory closed — January 1, 1888.

MILK GLASS PITCHER

From the picture and mark, can you please identify my twelve-panel blue milk glass pitcher?

C.B. — *Plainville, Kan.*

Harry Northwood, an English glass specialist, established the Northwood Glass Company in 1888, located first at Martin's Ferry, Ohio. The pitcher dates around 1900.

IRIDESCENT QUEZAL GLASS

The word "Quezal" is printed on the bottom of this candy dish, which belonged to my mother. What can you tell me about it?
J.S.C. — *Washington, D.C.*

The short-lived Quezal Art Glass and Decorating Company, active in Brooklyn, New York, from 1916 to 1918, turned out lovely pieces of iridescent glass. The name came from the quezal bird of Central America, noted for its long feathers of iridescent golden green. The popularity of quezal glass reached its peak in America between 1910 and 1920.

GOTHIC PICKLE BOTTLE

The bottle sketched here is light blue-green glass with large bubbles through it. The marks "IG Co" are on the bottom. What was it used for?
                              F.M.C. — Tuscumbia, Ala.

You have a pickle bottle of Gothic design made between 1870 and 1900 by the Illinois Glass Company. These bottles were packed with pickles and used in window displays at luxury grocers.

VICTORIAN NOVELTY GLASS

My parents received this goblet as a wedding present. It appears to be silver over glass and has a cork in the bottom. The cup has a delicate design etched around the bowl. We would like to know more about this kind of piece.
                              R.W.K. — La Habra, Cal.

Silver glass, a curious Victorian novelty, was introduced in America in the 1850s and enjoyed great popularity in its day. It was made in two layers. The clear glass was blown first, then nitrate of silver was blown into the hollow space between the layers through a hole in the base, which was then sealed.

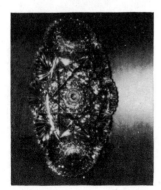

CUT-GLASS CELERY DISH

The cut-glass dish I inherited has an engraved "S" in a circle on its center. Do you know who made it?
                              F.M.C. — Columbia Falls, Mont.

Your cut-glass celery dish was made by H. P. Sinclaire and Company, which was active at Corning, New York, from 1905 to 1929. Sinclaire cut glass was of fine quality and included many original patterns. The "S" in a wreath was their trademark.

"WESTWARD HO" COMPOTE

What can you tell me about the "Westward Ho" glass compote that I recently inherited? It bears the name "Gillinder."

G.W. — *Claremont, Cal.*

Your pressed-glass pattern "Westward Ho" is just about as American as cherry pie. Especially choice is the compote with a frosted finial in the form of an Indian, and a decorative band including scenes of a log cabin in the mountains, bison running on the plains, and deer. The well-known Philadelphia glass house Gillinder & Sons introduced this pattern soon after the Philadelphia Centennial Exposition of 1876.

TUTHILL CUT GLASS

I inherited this piece of crystal recently. It is signed "Tuthill," and the grapes, pears, and leaves are translucent intaglio. Is it a valuable piece?

A.F. — *Racine, Wis.*

Your compote was made by the Tuthill Cut Glass Company, Middletown, New York, which was active from 1900 to 1923. The firm specialized in intaglio carving. Almost any piece of Tuthill glass is now a collectors' item.

TIFFANY FAVRILE BOWL

My iridescent glass bowl is slightly irregular around the rim. Scratched on the bottom is "L. C. Tiffany Favrile 7754." What is the origin of this bowl?

R.C.K. — Kenansville, N.C.

Your glass bowl was made by Louis Comfort Tiffany (1844–1933), who was the outstanding producer of iridescent glass in America between about 1894 and 1920. "Favrile" was Tiffany's trade name for his distinctive handmade glass created by a complicated and expensive process. He registered it in 1894. More than one explanation has been given for the origin of the word favrile, which was to become a household word. Robert Koch in his book on Louis C. Tiffany, *Rebel in Glass,* published by Crown, New York, 1964, writes: "An 1896 brochure stated that the word (favrile) was derived from the Old English 'fabrile' meaning 'belonging to a craftsman or his craft.'" Briefly, handmade.

MEXICAN PITCHERS

We wish your opinion as to whether these pitchers are handblown glass of Early American vintage or Mexican pitchers.

M.P. — Scranton, Pa.

These are Mexican handblown pitchers from small Mexican glassworks and date about 1910–1930.

GLASS

European

ENGLISH BRISTOL VASE

Enclosed is a photograph of one of my two almost identical vases. There are no marks on either of them but I do know they are about 100 years old. Can you tell me anything more about them?
R.J.B. — Old Lyme, Conn.

Your vases are a type that was very popular during the mid-nineteenth century. They were usually made in pairs, and are generally identified as English Bristol.

GEORGIAN GLASS CELERY HOLDER

This cut-glass vase has been in my family since before the Civil War. It has no marks. Would it be a celery glass even though it is 9 inches high?
M.S.McL. — Bath, N.C.

Yes, you have a fine example of an English Georgian celery holder dating from around the early nineteenth century. Nine inches is a proper height. In fact, this type is often 10 inches tall. Celery holders retained their popularity throughout the nineteenth century. Now they are favored as flower holders.

ENGLISH EPERGNE

What is the approximate age, nationality, and original use of this epergne?
M.R. — Scarsdale, N.Y.

Your epergne appears to be of English manufacture, probably dating from the 1840s. It should be examined at first hand to be sure, because the framework looks older than the glass. "Epergne" comes from the French *épargner,* meaning "to save." Waste of costly fruits and nuts was avoided, as each person used the glass dish in front of him — part of the elaborate centerpiece — and took only as much as he wanted to eat.

NAILSEA GLASS

This handsome brown-and-white bottle is unevenly shaped, and the stripes continue on the bottom. How old do you think it is, and where did it come from?

B.C.L. — Woodbury, N.J.

Your bottle looks like Nailsea glass, and therefore may date from the late eighteenth century. Although Nailsea, England, is the home of this glass, it was imitated elsewhere, so you should have an expert examine the bottle to authenticate it.

·

OPALINE GLASS PITCHER

We would appreciate any help you can give us in identifying this pitcher. There are no words or numbers anywhere on it.
D.F.O. — Kingsport, Tenn.

Judging from your snapshot, your pitcher is opaline glass of English manufacture, probably dating between 1870 and 1880.

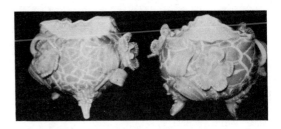

SATIN-GLASS BOWLS

I inherited this pair of old vases. The outside is a deep pink with white lines, the glass flowers and leaves are lemon color, as is the lining. There is no mark on either vase. What can you tell me about them?
H.M.C. — Duluth, Minn.

Your bowls are fine examples of English satin glass with applied glass flowers and feet. They probably date around 1880.

FRENCH "NESTING HEN"

I bought this hen dish at a sale in this area. Is it a fake, a foreign piece, or an American antique?
M.B.R.—Petoskey, Mich.

A glass expert considers your "nesting hen" to have been made by the well-known and still-existing French glassworks called Verrerie de Vallerysthal. Of all the pressed-glass dishes with covers made in animal forms, generally of the domestic or barnyard variety, the "nesting hen" is probably the most popular.

MIDDLE EUROPEAN VASES

I would appreciate information about my glass vases. Are there reference books I can consult on such pieces?
J.D.—Larchmont, N.Y.

Your glass vases appear to be in the overlay, or case-glass, technique, of Middle European manufacture, perhaps Bohemian, dating from about 1860 to 1870. Unfortunately, there is no single reference book on this class of glass, but librarians can direct you to books and antique magazines in their library where examples may be shown.

NINETEENTH-CENTURY VASES

Our Rusk County Heritage Association was recently presented with these two blue vases, but we have no information about them and would be very grateful for whatever you can tell us about their place and date of origin.
E.H.L.—Henderson, Tex.

EUROPEAN

Your dark-blue glass vases with white enameled decoration appear to be of mid-nineteenth-century continental manufacture. The light and graceful, almost lacelike, decoration shows Grecian influence and is the work of a talented artisan.

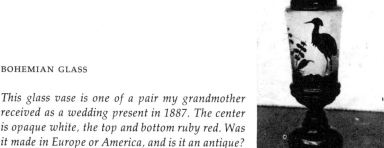

BOHEMIAN GLASS

This glass vase is one of a pair my grandmother received as a wedding present in 1887. The center is opaque white, the top and bottom ruby red. Was it made in Europe or America, and is it an antique?
J.G.H. — Vancouver, Wash.

Vases like yours were made by the Bohemian glass factories between 1860 and 1880. They were imported as mantel decorations and are now considered antiques.

ART-GLASS VASE

My small glass vase has color decorations and is rather irregularly shaped. Do you think it an American piece?
C.S.P. — Batesville, Ark.

It could be either European or American; I would date it about 1900 or a little later. Such art-glass vases were decorated in enamel colors fused by a second annealing in a gloss kiln.

CLOCKS
AND WATCHES
American

CONNECTICUT SHELF CLOCK

Inside this rosewood clock there is a printed circular of directions with the maker's name, Ansonia Brass and Copper Co. I purchased it a year ago and would like to know more about it.

D.S.S. — Dallas, Tex.

The Ansonia Brass and Copper Company of Ansonia, Connecticut, started the Ansonia Clock Company in 1851 as a subsidiary, to increase the use of brass. The clock company was successful and became a separate company about 1859. Your shelf clock was probably made from about 1851 to 1859.

NEW ENGLAND MANTEL CLOCK

We bought this old timepiece in New England. In metal, inside the clock, is engraved: "Ansonia Clock Co., Ansonia, Conn., U.S.A." Can you tell us something of the clock's history?

S.T.M. — New York, N.Y.

This mantel clock was made by the Ansonia Clock Company of Ansonia, Connecticut, active there from 1851 to 1878, when they moved to Brooklyn, New York. The case, in Victorian Renaissance style, suggests it was made between 1860 and 1875. It was surely made before 1878, as it bears the original address.

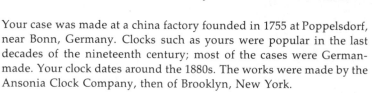

NINETEENTH-CENTURY CLOCK

I would appreciate any information about the origin of my table clock. On the interior pendulum mechanism is "Ansonia Clock Co., Patented June 14, 81, N.Y., U.S.A." On the back of the porcelain case: "Royal, 1755, Bonn, La Loire."

V.K. — Brooklyn, N.Y.

Your case was made at a china factory founded in 1755 at Poppelsdorf, near Bonn, Germany. Clocks such as yours were popular in the last decades of the nineteenth century; most of the cases were German-made. Your clock dates around the 1880s. The works were made by the Ansonia Clock Company, then of Brooklyn, New York.

CONNECTICUT SHELF CLOCK

The poster inside my shelf clock states: "Extra, eight day; Rolling pinion steel pivot; Brass clocks manufactured by Birge, Peck & Co., Bristol, Conn." Can you tell me how old the clock is?

L.M. — Vandalia, Ill.

John Birge, Ambrose Peck & Company were active at Bristol from 1849 to 1859. The firm finally became part of the Sessions Clock Company. Many Birge clocks of the shelf type are still in use. The flat molded cornice, columns and scroll supports reflect the influence of the Empire style.

CONNECTICUT BANJO CLOCK

The antique dealer from whom I bought this American mahogany clock called it a Connecticut banjo. Is this correct?

K.V. — Walla Walla, Wash.

Brooks Palmer in his book entitled *The Book of American Clocks* calls this type a Connecticut banjo. However, some sources list it as a shelf clock. In any case, it is an unusual form. Your fine timepiece probably dates around 1820.

AMERICAN FIGURAL MANTEL CLOCK

My grandparents received this clock as a wedding gift in 1895. We think the figures and case are bronze. The face is marked: "Mfg. by the Ansonia Clock Co., N.Y., U.S.A." Could it be much older than 1895?

B.B.R. — Shreveport, La.

You have a fine example of an American metal figural clock case, probably dating around the 1880s. It was made after 1878, as this was the year the Ansonia Clock Company moved from Ansonia, Connecticut, to Brooklyn, New York.

STEEPLE SHELF CLOCK

We don't know the history of this old clock found in my husband's family attic. A yellowed paper behind the brass pendulum states: "Made and sold by Brewster and Ingrahams, Bristol, Connecticut." Perhaps you could tell its age.

V.G. — Mason, Mich.

Brewster (Elisha) & Ingrahams (Elias and Andrew) were active at Bristol, Connecticut, from 1844 to 1852 and were one of the most prolific producers of clocks of the period. Elias Ingraham's design of the Sharp Gothic, now called Steeple, introduced about 1845, became extremely popular and was extensively copied.

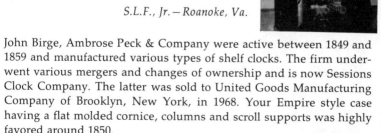

AMERICAN SHELF CLOCK

This clock belonged to my grandfather. On the inside is printed: "Manufactured and sold wholesale and retail by Birge, Peck & Company, Bristol, Connecticut." Have you any idea how old it may be?

S.L.F., Jr. — Roanoke, Va.

John Birge, Ambrose Peck & Company were active between 1849 and 1859 and manufactured various types of shelf clocks. The firm underwent various mergers and changes of ownership and is now Sessions Clock Company. The latter was sold to United Goods Manufacturing Company of Brooklyn, New York, in 1968. Your Empire style case having a flat molded cornice, columns and scroll supports was highly favored around 1850.

EPHRAIM DOWNS SHELF CLOCK

I purchased this clock from an American family in Tokyo. The label inside reads: "Made and Sold by Ephraim Downs, Bristol, Conn." I am interested in further facts.

W.W.E. — San Francisco, Cal.

Ephraim Downs worked in Bristol from 1810 to 1842. Many of his clocks had wooden movements. Judging from the case, I would say yours is a typical Connecticut shelf clock dating 1815–1835.

MOUSE CLOCK

How old is this Dickory Dickory Dock clock, which is still in good working order? It was made by Dungan and Klump, Philadelphia, Pennsylvania.

J.M.W. — Billings, Mont.

Your nursery-rhyme wall clock, which tells time by the figure of a mouse instead of the usual hands, was the invention of Elmer Ellsworth Dungan. It was first patented on February 16, 1909, by Dungan and Klump. Other models and patents followed. Though it is not an antique, it is eagerly sought by collectors interested in novelty clocks. Over the years many replicas of Dungan mouse clocks have been made.

GILBERT REGULATOR CLOCK

Can you tell the age of my clock? It has an all-brass eight-day movement.

E.G. — Bridgeport, Conn.

The circular pendulum indicates it is a regulator clock, a precise time-keeper used by people to regulate their watches. It was made by the Gilbert Clock Company of Winsted, Connecticut, and dates between 1890–1910. Clocks of this type were generally found in offices and stores.

SCROLLED CLOCK

On the face of my oak seven-day clock is "E. Ingraham Co." The clock strikes each hour and half hour. Can you tell me its style and age?
J.B.B. — Everett, Wash.

From around 1880 to 1900, kitchen clocks, many of them charmingly carved and scrolled, were made of oak or walnut by E. Ingraham Company and by E. N. Welch. The style has no particular name.

ITHACA CALENDAR CLOCK

My husband was given this clock several years ago. At one time it hung on the wall of the City Hall entrance in Richmond, Virginia. Can you identify the clock?
A.C. — Sharpsburg, N.C.

Yours is a calendar clock, made by the Ithaca Clock Company, Ithaca, New York, in business from 1865 to 1914. It dates about 1880–1900.

NINETEENTH-CENTURY CLOCK

This clock was purchased twenty-five years ago from an antique dealer in Palo Alto, who got it from a family that claimed it was brought west in covered-wagon days. Most of its works are of wood. The makers' certificate reads, "Jeromes & Darrow." Any information about the makers will be greatly appreciated.

J.G. — Los Altos, Cal.

The firm of Jeromes & Darrow of Bristol, Connecticut, produced your shelf clock sometime between 1824 and 1833. They had factories on both sides of Main Street, near the Requabuck River.

"FASHION" CALENDAR CLOCK

Could you trace the maker of this clock? It is a family heirloom.

B.P. — Fort Lauderdale, Fla.

This "Fashion" calendar clock was made by the Southern Calendar Clock Company, located at 802 Washington Avenue, St. Louis, Missouri. It was operated by the three Culver brothers from 1875 to 1889. The mechanisms were made by the Seth Thomas Clock Company.

SHELF CLOCK

Could you identify this clock? On the back it is marked: "Manufactured and sold by William S. Johnson, Courtlandt St., New York, N.Y."

R.B.R. — Charleston, S.C.

William S. Johnson is listed in the New York City Directory at 16 Cortlandt Street from 1841 to 1848. It is not known if he made clocks; he may have only assembled or perhaps purchased them.

JEROMES AND DARROW CLOCK

I would appreciate your opinion on the age of this clock. On the inside, behind the door and below the wooden works, are the words: "Improved clocks made and sold by Jeromes & Darrow, Bristol, Conn. Warrented if well used. P. Canfield printers."

C.D. — *Miami, Fla.*

The American clockmakers Jeromes and Darrow made wooden-movement clocks, thirty-hour, eight-day, from 1824 to 1833 at Bristol, Connecticut. Chauncey Jerome made the cases, Nobel Jerome the movements, and Elijah Darrow the tablets, or labels.

ELI TERRY CLOCK

I'd like information on my antique shelf clock with wooden works. The maker was Eli Terry. In the door is a Currier & Ives print, "Daniel in the Lions' Den."

D.P.K. — *Paducah, Ky.*

Eli Terry (1772–1852) was a Connecticut clockmaker from 1800 to 1835. The case style indicates this clock dates about 1820–1830. But the print, published shortly after 1856, replaced an earlier painting on glass that was part of the original case.

NEW HAMPSHIRE MIRROR CLOCK

We wonder if this clock, with mirror and table all rosewood, is German. It is an eight-day, weight-driven clock, with paintings on glass around the face.

I.P. — Blandford, Mass.

This clock is not German. Your timepiece appears to be a New Hampshire mirror clock, dating around 1830, which is attached to a stand and table in the American Empire style. This unusual type of wall clock, indigenous to New Hampshire, is an effective combination of good timepiece and attractive mirror.

SETH THOMAS CLOCK

My Seth Thomas clock was handed down to me by my grandfather. Any information about its age and rarity would be appreciated.

C.R. — Saginaw, Mich.

Seth Thomas made shelf clocks like yours between 1825 and 1850. These clocks are now collectible antiques, but were made in quantity, so they are not rare.

AMERICAN CLOCK

This grandfather clock belonged to my grandparents, and I know it is over 100 years old. It is 8 feet tall, and the name "Joseph Rothrock" is on the face. What can you tell me about it?

D.R.M. — San Francisco, Cal.

Joseph Rothrock, clockmaker, was active at York, Pennsylvania, about 1783–1790. The scrolled broken pediment and arched dial are characteristic of a type popular among American clockmakers in the late eighteenth century.

GRANDFATHER CLOCK

My grandfather clock is rather unusual, with glass on three sides and metal-filigree face. How old would it be?

W.H.N. — *Decatur, Ga.*

From the style of the case, with the long glass door showing pendulum and weights, I would say your grandfather clock is American and was made after 1900. It might well be from the Seth Thomas Clock Company of Connecticut.

RILEY WHITING CLOCK

Can you estimate the age of this old shelf clock? It was made by Riley Whiting of Winchester, Connecticut, with wooden works, a pendulum, and two large iron weights.

H.A.D. — *Spokane, Wash.*

Riley Whiting started his clock shop in 1813. He died in 1835. Your shelf clock, judging from the style of the case, dates about 1830.

WILLARD BANJO CLOCK

I have been told that my clock is a museum piece. "A. Willard, Jr., Boston" is printed on its face. The clock is wound once a week and keeps perfect time. Can you add to my information about it?
E.T.A. — Coos Bay, Ore.

Aaron Willard, Jr., made your banjo clock sometime between 1823 and 1850, the years he was in business. Simon Willard (1753–1848) was the inventor of this popular form of wall clock, which he patented in 1802.

ALARM-BELL CLOCK

Is the wheel in the center of the clock used for setting the alarm? The name of the manufacturer is "E N Wel—" (could not make out the rest of the last name), and the address is Forestville, Connecticut. When did clocks first have alarm bells? I certainly will appreciate any information you may be able to provide.
P.C.M. — Baltimore, Md.

You are correct, the alarm was set by the wheel in the center of the dial. E. N. Welch made your shelf clock during the 1860s. The principle of utilizing a bell to tell time is of very early origin. Originally, the striking of a clock was the all-important consideration, and probably many early medieval clocks had neither dials nor hands, but told the time only by striking the hour on a bell or gong. Thus the word "clock" is derived from the French *cloche*, German *Glocke*, a bell. After time was indicated by means of a single pointer, or hand, the hours were struck on the bell above the case, which in other instances was utilized merely as an alarm.

AMERICAN

HENRY WISMER CLOCK

*The name "Henry Wismer" is faintly discernible
on the face of our grandfather clock, which has
been in my husband's family as long as we can
remember. We'd like to know more about it.*
F.T.M. — Kirkwood, Mo.

Henry Wismer worked in Plumsted township, Pennsylvania, from
1798–1827 and made brass eight-day clock movements.

BIRD-CAGE CLOCK

*I hope you can tell me the date when my small
clock was made. It is marked: "The National
Clock Company, Made in Japan."*
R.F.K. — Kankakee, Ill.

Your bird-cage clock was made in Japan for the National Clock Company of Brooklyn, New York, between 1900 and 1930. The company is
no longer in business.

CLOCKS AND WATCHES

Continental

SWISS CLOCK

I have always been curious about the origin of this clock that my husband bought at an antique shop. On the face is the name "J. G. Bachler" and under it "St. Gall."

M.G. — *St. James, N.Y.*

Your clock has a French type porcelain case dating about 1800. The movement by Johann G. Bachler, a German clockmaker, was made during the years he worked at St. Gall, Switzerland.

GERMAN MANTEL CLOCK

Enclosed are a picture of my clock and a sketch of the mark on the back of the movement. Can you tell me something about it, possibly its vintage?

M.G.B. — *Glenview, Ill.*

Gustav Becker of Freiburg, Saxony, Germany, made excellent mantel clocks like yours between 1870 and 1890. The quality of his workmanship was rewarded by a number of gold medals that he received from various European expositions.

GERMAN MANTEL CLOCK

I have copied the mark from my antique clock and would appreciate learning its history and where it was made.

F.L. — *Cincinnati, Ohio*

Gustav Becker made clocks at Freiburg, Saxony, Germany, from 1870 to 1890. The serial number, "1424172," would indicate that your clock was made toward the end of that period.

FRENCH CLOCK

How old is this clock? On brass, behind the bell, is "A. Brocot, Paris" and "Médaille d'Argent."

C.P. — *North Haven, Conn.*

Your clock dates about 1850 and is in the classical style. Achille Brocot (1817–1878) was an eminent French clockmaker. He developed a type of escapement known by his name and widely used by his contemporaries. Brocot received a silver medal (Médaille d'Argent) for the original model of your clock.

FRENCH GRANDFATHER

Was my grandfather clock made during the reign of Louis XIV? It is decorated with boulle work.
T.H. — New York, N.Y.

No, your grandfather clock was made much later, probably around the time of the French Second Empire, 1852–1870, or even later, as the fashion for boulle work continued throughout the nineteenth century. You are fortunate that Father Time still graces your tall case clock, a charming but typically Victorian decorative detail that is often lost from these clocks.

NAPOLEONIC MANTEL CLOCK

The inscription on the face of our clock reads: "Champion br. du Génie, Rue de Feuillade, Paris." It is bronze or brass covered with gold and is 20 inches high. How old do you think it is?
H.A. — Toronto, Can.

Your clock is a typical timepiece of the Napoleonic period. The maker, Champion, worked in Paris between 1807 and 1825.

FRENCH EMPIRE CLOCK

This clock has been in my family for several generations. It was made by Collard. Could you please tell me its approximate age?

P.F. — Brooklyn, N.Y.

Your clock dates from the Napoleonic period. Collard worked in Paris between 1805 and 1815.

COPY OF A CLOCK IN THE LOUVRE

Is this clock an antique? I would appreciate any information you can give me about it.

E.M. — Bronx, N.Y.

Your Louis XVI style veneered and inlaid tall case clock, enriched with gilt bronze, is a fine copy of a famous tall case clock in the Louvre, attributed to the great French cabinetmaker Martin Carlin between 1775 and 1785. Your copy is not an antique. It was made in France in the early years of this century, when many period pieces were faithfully reproduced for use in mansions being built by wealthy Americans. In this example the cabinetmaker and not the clockmaker receives the attention.

LOUIS XVI GILT-BRONZE CARTEL CLOCK

I acquired this heavy brass wall clock with a porcelain face about a year ago. The inscription on it reads: "Delarue, à Paris, 8 Rue Vielle de T." A number preceding the "8" and letters after the "T" are chipped off. When was it made?

B.S. — Buffalo, N.Y.

Your French wall clock is eighteenth-century and is probably gilt bronze, not brass. Nicoles Delarue worked as a master clockmaker in Paris, starting in 1770. He must have made the movement of your clock between that date and 1793. The case is in the Louis XVI style.

FRENCH MANTEL CLOCK

What can you tell me about my inherited French clock made by Dubuc (the Elder), with a statue of George Washington?

H.P.W. — Panama City, Fla.

Dubuc, who was working in Paris about 1780–1819, was an important supplier of French clocks for the American market. A clock like yours is in the White House collection that Mrs. Kennedy assembled. Such clocks were made shortly after Washington's death, in 1799. You are fortunate to have the glass dome.

FRENCH FIGURAL MANTEL CLOCK

Could you tell me the age of this French clock? The label, "Barbedien—Paris," is on the dial, and "F. Barbedienne—Fondeur" is recorded on the base of the statue.

J.L.C. — Newman, Ga.

The figure of the classic huntress Diana on your clock is the work of François Barbedienne, a leading French founder, who was awarded several medals and the Legion of Honor for the quality of his bronzes. Some of his signed bronzes are in museum collections. Your clock probably dates between 1870 and 1890.

JAPY FRÈRES MANTEL CLOCK

I purchased this clock in the Netherlands. Its works are marked "Japy Frères." Can you tell me its age?

Z.N. — Alice, Tex.

The well-known and still-existing French firm Japy Frères & Cie made your figural mantel clock, probably during the 1870s. Frédéric Japy (1749–1813), who was the first to manufacture watch *ébauches* (partial watch movements) by machine tools in 1776, founded the watch factory of Japy Frères and designed its machines. In 1810 he started a factory for clock *ébauches* at Baderel.

EIGHTEENTH-CENTURY FRENCH CLOCK

I recently purchased this gilded clock in Paris, where we were stationed with the Air Force. On the face it has the name "Jarossay & Cie á Paris." Can you tell me when it was made?

J.R.S. — APO 55, New York, N.Y.

The inscription indicates that your clock was made by Urban Jarossay, master clockmaker of Paris in the latter half of the eighteenth century. From 1784 to 1789 he worked under the patronage of Charles Philippe, Count d'Artois, who was the brother of King Louis XVI.

FRENCH MANTEL GARNITURE

Could you give us any idea of the approximate age and style of this marble-and-ormolu clock and matching candlesticks? The clock is unmarked.

A.D.G. — York, Pa.

The style of your clock and matching candlesticks mounted in gilt bronze is unmistakably French. They were made either during the reign of Louis-Philippe (1830–1848) or that of his successor, Napoleon III, who reigned from 1852 to 1870.

FRENCH MANTEL OR BRACKET CLOCK

We would like to know the approximate age of this clock. It is marked: "Duverdrey & Blognei, France."

K.M. — South Kent, Conn.

We are unable to identify Duverdrey & Blognei. However, the fact that your clock bears the name of the country of origin, France, indicates that it was made for export to America after 1890. The McKinley Tariff Act of 1890 established the requirement that imported goods bear legible indication of the country of origin, and that requirement has continued to this day to be applied to all articles of foreign manufacture. The act became law on the first day of March, 1891.

FRENCH TABLE CLOCK

What style is this clock? On the brass filigree underneath the dial of the clock there is a porcelain plaque reading: "A. Martinot, Paris."

G.R.D. — Des Moines, Iowa

You have a fine French Louis XVI style table clock richly mounted in gilt bronze. A. Martinot was a Paris clockmaker of the late eighteenth century.

PRIZE-WINNING CLOCK BY MARTI & CIE

Could you date this clock, which has a marble case with gold-and-silver inlay? The mark stamped inside is "Médaille de Bronze—L. Marti & Cie."

R.K. — *Taunton, Mass.*

Your French clock dates between 1870 and 1890. The design evidently won a bronze medal at an exposition for this well-known and still-existing French firm of clockmakers.

DUTCH CLOCK FROM FRANCE

I recently purchased this Dutch windmill clock. The case looks like Delft—blue-on-white porcelain—with no marks of identification. The movement, we were told, is not original, but is by Étienne Maxant, made for J. E. Caldwell & Company. Can you furnish further data on the clock?

A.E.R. — *Stamford, Conn.*

Since the Delft style case bears no pottery marks, we cannot trace its maker. Étienne Maxant was a Paris clockmaker in the last quarter of the nineteenth century. The words "Made in France" indicate that the movement was made after 1890, when according to the McKinley Tariff Act, all imported articles shall be plainly marked in legible English words so as to indicate the country of their origin. Brevette is the French word for patented or registered. J. E. Caldwell and Company have been leading Philadelphia jewelers and silversmiths from 1839 to the present day. Their merchandise enjoys a fine reputation.

HOLLAND CLOCK

The auction brochure for this clock I purchased states: "Very rare antique walnut High Case Dutch clock with musical attachments, by Otto Van Meurs, of Amsterdam (who made only three clocks in his lifetime)." When was it made?
A.B.S. — Meadowbrook, Pa.

Otto Van Meurs worked in Holland from 1730 to 1780. During fifty years he must have made many clocks. But you do have a fine antique by a well-known maker.

NAPOLEON III MANTEL CLOCK

We would appreciate any comments on our French black marble clock. It weighs approximately 40 pounds. The only markings are on the movement: "A.D. Mougin," a printed star beneath, "deux Médailles," and the number "411" below.
R.J.F. — Pawcatuck, Conn.

Your mantel clock is of the Napoleon III period, 1852–1870. The maker, A. D. Mougin, was a Paris clockmaker; "411" was the design number. Two of his designs won medals at expositions.

VIENNESE MANTEL CLOCK

My clock came from my mother's estate in Austria. Its chimes sound every quarter hour; it also indicates the day of the month. "Johann Rau, Wien," is the name on the rear plate. Would you consider this clock an antique?
H.R.E. — Hempstead, N.Y.

You have an excellent antique mantel clock. Johann Rau was a well-known clockmaker of Vienna during the middle part of the nineteenth century.

SWISS REGULATOR CLOCK

My friend recently became the owner of this clock, originally a wall clock. There are no markings on the movement, and the base has been added. Could you approximate its age?
M.J.M. — Terre Haute, Ind.

The movement for your clock is definitely pre-World War I and probably dates from around the turn of the century. These Swiss Regulators, noted for their accuracy, were always wall clocks. From about the mid-nineteenth century they were generally made in France. Typical features include a sweep second hand that jumps ahead one second with each swing of the large compensated pendulum.

SWISS REGULATOR CLOCK

I would appreciate some information about this unusual clock.
N.S.M. — Croswell, Mich.

You have a Swiss Regulator wall clock with a compensated pendulum, made about the mid-nineteenth century. These clocks are well made and easy to maintain.

GERMAN REGULATOR CLOCK

How old would you judge our chiming wall clock to be? It is 53 inches tall, has a porcelain face, and "Made in Germany" stamped on the back. The eagle on top looks handcarved.

H.B.S. — Racine, Wis.

Your pendulum wall clock was probably made after 1890, when many such clocks were exported to this country. Their pendulums were equipped with regulators that helped keep them on time. With no maker's mark on the dial or the movement, we cannot trace it further.

FRENCH WAG-ON-THE-WALL CLOCK

Can you possibly date this French country clock? The white porcelain face is signed: "Le Tessier à Martigne sous Mayenne." It is a calendar clock that strikes and has a 34-inch pendulum.

W.J.R. — Palos Verdes Estates, Cal.

Your French provincial clock, popularly called a wag-on-the-wall clock, probably dates around 1830–1860. The inscription on the face generally refers to the seller, not the maker. The question of whether this most interesting type of French wag-on-the-wall clock was or was not intended to be placed in a tall case will probably never be settled to everyone's satisfaction. The clock was finished in such a manner that a case was not necessary. On the other hand, the status of a tall case clock as a visible sign of wealth in the eyes of a provincial housewife may well have been the main reason so many of these clocks ended up in cases.

FRENCH WAG-ON-THE-WALL CLOCK

We feel that this wall clock, which we bought last summer in southern France, is very old. The face is surrounded with brass, and the weights are extremely heavy. What can you tell us about it?
F.L.C. — APO, New York

Your clock, of French provincial origin, was probably made around 1830–1850. The compensated pendulum is interesting. It was supposed to take care of the variation in temperature and thus increase the accuracy of the timepiece.

BELGIAN WAG-ON-THE-WALL CLOCK

What are the origin and age of my clock? "Leken-Herstal" is written on the face. It has been in my family for close to 100 years.
O.T.C. — Plainview, Tex.

Your wag-on-the-wall clock is Belgian and probably dates about 1830–1850. Like all clocks of this kind, it was designed to be fitted into a case, but such cases are rarely seen. Despite this, there is a growing interest among antique collectors in clocks of this type.

FRENCH EMPIRE CLOCK

I would like very much to know the age and origin of this clock, which has been in my family for several generations. The base is ebony and the case tortoise-shell inlay. The movement is marked on the back "Vincent."

E.H.H. — *Augusta, Me.*

Your lyre-shaped clock covered with a glass dome appears to be French of the Napoleonic period. The maker, Vincent, is listed as working in Paris in the year 1812.

GERMAN WATCH

The watch I sketched was brought from France after World War II. It is handmade, ornately engraved, has no jewels in the movement, and is wound and set with a key. It has a double back, and the marks appear on the outer back. Can you tell me its age?

M.E.H. — *Wenatchee, Wash.*

The marks indicate that your watchcase is silver and was made in Germany around the 1880s.

SWISS REPEATER WATCH

I would like to know the origin of this chiming watch in a 14-karat gold case, said to be 100 years old. What do the words "Le Phare" on its face mean?

K.T.P. — *Chicago, Ill.*

"Le Phare" is French for "The Lighthouse," and chiming repeater watches were often owned by blind men. Yours was made by A. Vulle of Montreux, on Lake Geneva, about 1870–1890. Very few repeaters are made today.

TURKISH-TRADE WATCH

I bought this watch in Turkey, but was told it had been made in London by Edward Prior especially for trade with Turkey and other Moslem countries. Its mechanism is driven by a small link chain similar to a bicycle chain. The watch is enclosed in two cases, the inner elaborately engraved silver, the outer tortoise shell. Would it be possible to date the watch?

Mjr. W.E.A. — APO, New York

Edward Prior was a fine watchmaker in London from 1800–1868. The double case would date your watch about 1800–1820. Instead of the customary Roman numerals, the numerals are modern Arabic and totally different from ours, which derive from the Hindu-Arabic.

WATCH HOLDER

I've spent fifteen years searching for information about my singing-bird watch holder. You pull the side lever and a bird pops up, spins around, flaps his wings, and sings. The watch is removable. The case has the number "800" on the underside. Can you tell me anything about it?

J.E.K. — DeKalb, Ill.

Your decorative case with the singing bird and timepiece is German in origin, probably dating around the end of the nineteenth century. The metal is silver — the "800" indicates that out of 1,000 parts, 800 are silver. German silver has less silver content than sterling, having 925 parts fine silver.

VICTORIAN WATCH HOLDER

Can you tell me what this small bronze stand, about a foot high, was used for? Is it very old?
E.H.W. — *Greensboro, N.C.*

You have a watch holder and trinket box of mid-nineteenth-century European manufacture. The watch holder was a popular Victorian accessory in the bedroom, because the watch could be in full view and there was no need to fumble for it beneath the pillows. A cherub in Indian costume was a favorite European exotic motif and was forever turning up in the most unexpected places.

CLOCKS
AND WATCHES
English

ENGLISH BRACKET CLOCK

Enclosed with the snapshot of my English bracket clock is a freehand facsimile of the name engraved on the face and on the back plate of the works. Can you date this clock?

J.D.R. — Alexandria, Va.

Samuel Atkins (1697–1768) was an eminent London watch- and clock-maker. He worked at his trade from about 1733 to 1765. His bracket clocks, such as this one, are well known to collectors.

ENGLISH TABLE CLOCK

I own a very old English clock which I would like your help in dating. The case is mahogany veneer; the face is brass, inscribed "Robert Wood— London."

P.G.C. — *Pleasant Valley, N.Y.*

Robert Wood, who made the works for your fine table clock, was active in London around 1780–1800.

ENGLISH TABLE OR BRACKET CLOCK

The engraved back plate of my bracket clock is inscribed: "Richard Baker, Exchange Ally, London." I would appreciate any information you can give me about the clock.

C.P. — *Fort Wayne, Ind.*

You have a fine English table, or bracket, clock made by Richard Baker, a clockmaker of high repute. It was made between 1685 and 1710, the year of Baker's death. After the introduction of the short pendulum by Fromanteel in 1658, considerable attention was given to the production of so-called bracket, or table, clocks, spring-driven and wood-encased. Clocks such as yours, having a square-fronted "squat" case with a domed top in either wood or metal, and provided with a top handle to make them portable, were introduced around 1685.

SCOTTISH TALL CASE CLOCK

My in-laws sent this clock to us from Scotland. It had been in their family for many years. "Alexander Brand, Edinburgh" is inscribed on the face. How old do you think this clock might be?

S.M.J. — Merion Station, Pa.

Alexander Brand, clockmaker, worked in Edinburgh from about 1711 to 1757. The broken scroll-shaped pediment filled with pierced tracery is a feature of the Chippendale style and suggests that the tall case probably dates about the third quarter of the eighteenth century.

SCOTTISH GRANDFATHER CLOCK

I'd like to trace the history of my mahogany grandfather clock. The name "J. Breakenrig, Edinburgh," appears on the face.

L.B. — Mountainside, N.J.

J. Breakenrig, who worked in Edinburgh from 1767 to 1800, made the clock's movement. The scrolled ogee pediment, or "horn top," surmounting the hood flanked by colonettes was much favored in the late eighteenth century.

EIGHTEENTH-CENTURY CLOCK

Our grandfather clock has the inscription "Sam Cox, Long Acre, London" on its face. The walnut case seems to be original and the brass hinges handwrought. What is its approximate age?
D.J.J. — APO San Francisco, Cal.

The movement for your tall-case clock was made by English clock-maker Samuel Cox, who was working at Long Acre, London, in 1770. The arched panel of the trunk door following the arched top of the clock is a characteristic feature of that period.

WELSH CLOCK

Can you identify this tall case clock? "Richd. Griffith, Denbigh" appears on the dial.
W.H.W. — Cedar Rapids, Iowa

It is an English clock made by Richard Griffith, who worked at Denbigh, Wales, from 1770 to 1800. The case with a scrolled ogee pediment was widely popular in the late eighteenth century.

ENGLISH TALL CASE CLOCK

I purchased this clock at auction and would especially like to know how old it is. The name "Jn Fernal Wrexham" is on the face. Also, would you know what type of ornaments were on the top of the clock?

J.Z. — Nampa, Idaho

The movement of your tall case clock was made by John Fernal, who was active at Wrexham, England, around 1770. Clock faces at that time were often made of tin or iron lacquered cream-white and gaily painted with pastoral subjects or, like yours, with flowers and birds. The three ornaments on top were frequently in the form of brass balls.

GOTHIC CLOCK

Is this a cathedral clock? My mother's uncle bought it many years ago and we know it is not an antique, but the shape seems unusual. It is marked "Elliot of London" on the dial.

V.Y. — Narberth, Pa.

If your tall case clock of Gothic design has chimes, it can be called a cathedral clock. F. W. Elliot, in London, has been making such clocks for about sixty years. His slogan is "Designed by experts, built by craftsmen."

FLAT-TOPPED TALL CASE CLOCK

The brass dial of our tall case clock bears the name "Ninyon Wilmshurst" and the place "Brighthelmstone" (now Brighton, England). Can you help us date the clock?

M.VS. — Fallsington, Pa.

The flat-topped hood and square dial flanked by colonettes indicate a date between 1690 and 1715, the period when this general type of clock was popular.

REGENCY WALL CLOCK

"Elliott" and "Clerkenwell" appear on the dial of this English clock I recently acquired. The inlays on the case are brass. Who made it and how old is it?

W.N.J. — Silver Spring, Md.

John M. Elliott probably made the works of your wall clock in his shop at Aylesbury Street, Clerkenwell, around 1804. Brass inlaid decoration was widely used during the English Regency period, about 1795 to 1820.

SCOTTISH CLOCK

Recently this clock, a family heirloom, was brought to this country from Ireland. On the brass dial is the name "Robt Knox, Paisley." Is he the maker?

S.M.B. — Pittsfield, Mass.

Robert Knox was the maker of the movement for your tall case clock. He worked in Paisley, Scotland, from 1820 to 1837. The case was undoubtedly made by a local cabinetmaker.

SCOTTISH GRANDFATHER CLOCK

"Wm. Harvey, Stirling" is marked on the face of this clock I recently purchased. The case, which opens on the side, is solid rosewood. Any information you can furnish will be appreciated.
                    R.S. — Pennsauken, N.J.

The movement and dial are the work of William Harvey of Stirling, Scotland, who worked there as a clockmaker from 1810 to 1830. The blocklike character of the tall case shows the influence of the English Regency style and was probably made by a cabinetmaker from Edinburgh.

SCOTTISH CLOCK

How old would you judge our tall case clock to be? The name "J. & C. McNab" is very faint on the face. The antique dealer said it was English.
                    M.H. — Los Angeles, Cal.

J. & C. McNab, clockmakers, worked in Perth, Scotland, from 1790 to 1800. The tall case has a high base and stunted trunk door. A longer trunk door usually gives more pleasing proportions.

MUSICAL INSTRUMENTS

PORTABLE HAND ORGAN

My hand organ has no mark, but the rolls it plays read: "Aeolian Music Company." I wrote the Aeolian Company of Rochester, and they knew nothing about such an instrument. Can you help me?

R.F.L.—Glen Cove, N.Y.

The Aeolian Music Company that made your organ was in business at Syracuse, New York, from 1905 to 1907 only. The Rochester company manufactures pianos exclusively.

AMERICAN PARLOR ORGAN

Would you please give us whatever information you can about this organ? The only identification are the words above the keyboard: "Cornish Co., Washington, N.J., U.S.A."

J.C.F. — Batesville, Ind.

The Cornish Company was active at Washington, New Jersey, from 1879 to 1922. It was a mail-order house that started out as organ builders. Your organ probably dates around the end of the nineteenth century.

ENGLISH SHERATON-CASED PIANO

I would like some information about this piano. It has sixty-eight keys, and the hammers inside hit upward. The marks are: "John Broadhood & Sons, makers to His Majesty and Princesses, Great Pulteney, London, Golden Square."

J.B. — New York, N.Y.

The Broadhood firm was established in 1723 and continued in business until 1903. Your piano, in Sheraton style, dates between 1800 and 1825.

OHIO PARLOR ORGAN

Can you approximate the age of my organ? It is marked: "A. B. Chase, Norwalk, Ohio, No. 22039."

J.F.M. — Lancaster, Cal.

The style of the case indicates your organ dates about 1880–1885. The Chase Company was founded in 1875 at Norwalk and made both organs and pianos.

PIANO BY MORGAN DAVIS

The name "Morgan Davis" appears on the back of my piano. Any further information will be appreciated.

H.M.N. — Upperco, Md.

New York City directories list Morgan Davis, piano maker, at 63 Barclay Street, 1812–1833. He is also listed at other addresses until 1841. Your piano, judging from the style of the case and the acanthus-leaf leg carvings, was made on Barclay Street.

AMERICAN DULCIMER

Can you identify this musical instrument, which looks like a zither?

L.G.S. — Holly Hill, Fla.

This is a dulcimer, played by striking the strings with two light wooden hammers. It is early Victorian, 1850–1860, and is probably American.

DUNHAM SQUARE PIANO

This solid rosewood piano has the nameplate "Dunham of New York." I can find nothing in reference books about this make of piano. Could you give me any information?

J.W.F. — Durham, N.C.

It is known that John Dunham made pianos in New York City about 1850 to 1865, but there is no other recorded data about him. From the style of the case, especially the octagonal, baluster-shaped legs, I would date your instrument as having been made before 1860.

EMERSON SQUARE PIANO

We assume our square piano, made by the Emerson Piano Company of Boston, dates back to 1880, for behind the keyboard is the mark "A.C.-1880." Does this really date the piano, and are the initials those of a workman?

K.L.M. — Aberdeen, S.D.

William P. Emerson built pianos in Boston from 1849 to 1871. In 1879 the Emerson Piano Company was organized. Your piano was made in 1880. "A.C." are the initials of the man who made the final adjustment on the action before it left the factory.

GIRAFFE PIANO

I know my piano is called a giraffe piano and that it was made in Amsterdam about 1800. What else can you tell me about this kind of instrument?
R.S. — San Francisco, Cal.

The giraffe, a kind of upright pianoforte, enjoyed a certain popularity, especially in Germany and Austria, in the early nineteenth century. The case stood on the floor, and the upper part of the case followed the natural curve of the strings. The action was below the keyboard. Your piano is Biedermeier in style.

ENGLISH REGENCY PIANO

We purchased this piano in the East. The name above the keyboard is: "Goulding & Company, 20 Soho Square, London." Can you tell us anything about it?

K.J.H. — China Lake, Cal.

The fine mahogany and satinwood case of your piano belongs to the Regency period, between 1811 and 1823. Goulding & Company was a leading English music publisher and occupied the Soho Square address from 1811 to 1858. Goulding did not make pianos, just sold them.

ENGLISH PIANO

Our piano has been in the family for seventy years, but we have no idea how old it actually is. Can you tell us? The plate reads: "Gunther and Horwood, Pratt Place, Camden Town, London."
D.H. — Aptos, Cal.

The style of the case, with its eight turned and reeded legs, is typical of the Sheraton period of design, between 1810 and 1825. The makers were a well-known nineteenth-century firm.

HALE SQUARE PIANO

The label on my rosewood square piano reads, "J. P. Hale & Co., New York," and the serial number is "616070." When I bought it twenty years ago it had an ebony finish. I would appreciate any information you can give me on this piece.
J.B.D. — Haskell, Tex.

Joseph P. Hale established his piano factory in New York City about 1865. He was very successful, and in time his factory produced 100 instruments a week. From the style and serial number of your square piano, I would date it around 1870–1875.

FRENCH UPRIGHT PIANO

My small rosewood piano bears the name of the maker, Henri Herz, on a certificate on the inside. This certificate also states that Mr. Herz won the Medal of Honor award in Paris, 1855; a prize medal, London, 1862; and an Exposition Universelle, 1867. I would like to know if his descendants are still in business and when this particular piano was made.

F.S.B. — Eastsound, Wash.

The style of the case dates your piano between 1860 and 1870. Mr. Herz was a leading manufacturer and made pianos for such royalty as the King of Portugal and Empress Eugénie of France. After his death in 1888, the Herz piano factory of Paris was closed.

CHICAGO MELODEON

We would appreciate learning more about the history of our melodeon marked: "W. W. Kimball, Chicago, Illinois."

R.G. — Virginia, Ill.

William W. Kimball started his factory shortly after the famous fire of 1871, and it became the largest maker of melodeons in the Midwest, producing 4,000 a year. The case style dates yours about 1875.

MANDOLIN

The label in my mandolin reads: "Angelo Mannello, Mandolins, Mandolas and Guitars. Highest Awards at the World's Columbian Exposition." Who was he?

K.K. — San Francisco, Cal.

Angelo Mannello, an Italian-trained maker of musical instruments, came here in 1890. He exhibited his beautiful works at the Columbian Exposition of 1893. Your mandolin dates soon after that year.

AMERICAN MILITARY DRUM

Could you tell the approximate age of this drum I recently acquired? Except for ropes and leather pulls, it is original, with natural maple shell, red hoops, shield and eagle decoration. Inside it is labeled: "William Kilborn, successor to George Kilborn, No. 7 Clinton Ave., Albany, N.Y."
G.A.S. — Northampton, Mass.

Since William Kilborn's shop was located at 7 Clinton Avenue between 1864 and 1869, your drum must have been made during that time. The Kilborns were drum makers from 1839 to 1891. William succeeded his father, George, in 1860. The eagle and shield mark it as a National Guard drum of the late Civil War period.

CYCLOID PIANO

I would appreciate any information about this piano I've owned for twenty years. Above the keyboard it is marked "Lindeman & Son, New York," and below that "Cycloid Grand." Its history has been lost.
S.V.L. — Eaton, Colo.

The cycloid was a compromise between a square piano and a concert grand. William Lindeman, who came from Germany, began making pianos in New York in 1836. (His son joined the firm in 1858.) He invented this type of piano in 1860, but made few, because of the Civil War.

MUSICAL AUTOMATON

I would like to know more about our glass-domed music box. There is a handpainted seascape on the back of the glass dome, with a castle in the foreground made of cardboard, and foliage of dried weeds. The sailing ship rocks and the little soldier circles the turret as the music plays. A sticker on the inside states the following: "Musique à 2 Airs Les Cloches de Dorneville Valse Pagues Pleuries Coupler 232 No. 485124."

C.F.P. — Grosse Pointe, Mich.

Apparently you have an antique French musical automaton of about 1850. "No. 485124" was the serial number; the maker cannot be traced. You are lucky to have one in running condition.

AMERICAN SQUARE PIANO

I am interested in information about our piano, which has been in my family for over 100 years. It is made of rosewood, and the keyboard section lifts free of the legs. The maker's name on a metal plate is "R. Nunns, Clark & Co., New York."

E.M.C. — Charlotte, N.C.

You have an unusual and very interesting type of American square piano. R. Nunns, Clark & Company opened their piano factory about 1845. In 1851 they were one of the few American piano makers who exhibited at the Crystal Palace in London.

MUSICAL INSTRUMENTS

POLYPHON MUSIC BOX

We would appreciate any information you can give us on the history of this music box.

J.P.L. — *Durham, N.H.*

Your music box was made by the Polyphon Company of Leipzig, Germany, after 1885. A partner of the company came to the United States in 1886 and established the Regina Music Box Company in Rahway, New Jersey.

REGINA MUSIC BOX

All of the metal playing disks for my beautiful Regina music box are marked in the 1700s and 1800s. Could these numbers refer to when it was made?

J.C. — *Sarasota, Fla.*

The numbers on the disks identify the musical selections and have nothing to do with the date of the instrument. The Regina Music Box Company of Rahway, New Jersey (1886–1915), introduced their Regina Automatic about 1900. It played twelve disks, the diameter of which varied. Today every kind of American music box is widely popular with collectors.

Enclosed is a drawing of the metal plate on my small piano. I bought it from one of the oldest families in the county. Can you tell me if it is an unusual piano?

S.G. — Leesburg, Va.

It is certainly an unusual piano. Johann Andreas Stein made pianos as early as 1770 at Augsburg and later in Vienna. Mozart played concerts on a piano made for him by Stein.

VICTORIAN CONCERT GRAND

Our Steinway concert grand has a rosewood case. We have seen one like it in a Lincoln museum. The number on the sounding board is "10625." Can you tell how old it is?

S.E.B. — Washington, Ga.

Your piano is typical of one of Henry Engelhard Steinway's early instruments. The design of the case contains many common elements of the Victorian style. Steinway's records of the Grand Style III piano with your serial number show it was first sold in 1866 and resold in 1900 to the Standard Auction Rooms of New York City. Steinway celebrated their one-hundredth anniversary in 1953.

MUSICAL INSTRUMENTS

SWISS CHAIR WITH MUSIC BOX

Can you tell me when and where my hand-carved musical chair was made? The design is inlaid, and the seat conceals a music box that plays when sat upon. The only marking is "Patd. Nov. 23, 1862" on the music box.

K.W.P. — Sharon, Conn.

The Swiss made many things with music boxes—including chairs like yours—during the latter half of the nineteenth century. This chair dates between 1875 and 1890. Traveling Americans brought home such chairs as souvenirs. They are much more rare than the usual Swiss cuckoo clock.

AMERICAN SQUARE PIANO

We should like to know the age of our piano. The case is rosewood and the signature above the keyboard is "Horace Waters & Co., New York."

E.W. — Matawan, N.J.

Horace Waters & Company established their piano factory in New York in 1845. The style of your piano's square rosewood case with carved cabriole legs dates it between 1860 and 1870.

SQUARE PIANO

*My piano has the words "Weber, New York" on
the center panel above the keyboard. Can you
give me its approximate age and any other information you may have about it?*

F.A.J. — Grand Rapids, Mich.

Your square piano was made by Weber & Company of New York
between 1860 and 1875. The openwork music support, lyre-form pedal
frame, and massive cabriole legs are typical of this period.

UKELIN

*What can you tell me about this musical instru-
ment? The label inside reads: "Ukelin — sole distributor $35.00, International Musical Corpora-
tion, 14th Street and Bloomfield Sts., Hoboken,
New Jersey."*

G.W. — Floral Park, N.J.

The ukelin — a kind of cross between a violin and a ukulele — was
patented in 1926. It is played on the lap by plucking zither type
strings with one hand and simultaneously bowing an entirely different set of strings with the other. The International Musical Corporation, the sole manufacturer of this unique instrument, discontinued them in 1963.

PICTURES

EARLY COPYRIGHT

My Centennial picture, 30 by 24 inches, bears the inscription: "Entered according to Act of Congress in the year 1876 by D. T. Ames, Library of Congress." I would like to know why it took an act of Congress to have this picture printed.
                    W.E.S. — *Tuscola, Ill.*

It did not take an act of Congress to print this particular picture. But before the current copyright laws were passed, a 1790 act of Congress required all copyrighted material to bear an inscription stating that it was entered according to this act in the clerk's office of a district court. In 1870 the act was amended, giving the Library of Congress sole authority to issue copyrights. Thus your inscription. Today all that is required is a "c" in a circle, the year in which the work was first issued, and the name of the copyright proprietor.

CURRIER & IVES PRINT

I have what I think is an authentic Currier & Ives print. It was a wedding gift to my grandmother in 1875. The caption reads, "Charlie Is My Darling." I have never seen another copy, nor is this print listed in my Currier & Ives book. Is it authentic?

A.H.H. — Topeka, Kan.

Yes, you have a real Currier & Ives print, published in 1872. It is listed in *Currier & Ives Prints, An Illustrated Check List,* by Frederick A. Conningham, 1949. A revised edition of this catalogue of Currier & Ives prints was published by Crown, New York, 1970.

CURRIER & IVES MOTTO

We have been searching for information on this Currier & Ives print of a quotation from Lincoln. Could you assist us?

C.C.G. — Norfolk, Va.

The quote is from Lincoln's second inaugural address, March 4, 1865. Currier & Ives published it as a small folio motto in 1875.

DAGUERREOTYPE CASE

I would like to know the age and origin of this case, which contains a picture tinted and framed in gold.

J.C.D. — Pacoima, Cal.

PICTURES

As a rule the daguerreotype was mounted in a case, frequently with the picture framed in gold-colored metal and the case lined with velvet. Your case, probably dating from the third quarter of the nineteenth century, was made of gutta-percha, a tough plastic substance from the latex of several Malaysian trees resembling rubber but containing more resin. Gutta-percha was exhibited at the Great Exhibition held in London in 1851 and became a popular material for daguerreotype cases.

BRITISH PHOTO FRAME

Can you tell from this sketched mark when and where my frame was made? It is gold-plated bronze designed like a gate, has a latch, and when open it holds four photos.

H.K. — Elmhurst, N.Y.

Your bronze frame is English. The mark indicates that C. Betdenann & Sons registered the design at the British Patent Office on September 29, 1846.

SPORTING PRINT

This racing print painted by Harry Hall and engraved by Charles Hunt commemorates a race run at York, May 13, 1851. Can you tell me more?
V.A.P. — Massapequa, N.Y.

Charles Hunt was a well-known English engraver, and Harry Hall specialized in painting race horses. Your engraving dates a year or two after the race.

FRANKLIN AT THE FRENCH COURT

Has this picture of Benjamin Franklin at the French court any historical value? The colors are magnificent. It was engraved by W. D. Geller, London, and painted by Baron Jolly, Brussels, but published by William Jay, Charles J. Hedenberg, and William H. Emerson, Philadelphia, Pennsylvania.

G.F.H., Jr. — Wilmington, Del.

Collectors would consider your handcolored steel engraving to be of distinct American interest. It was published sometime between 1845 and 1855.

WASHINGTON MEMORIAL PICTURE

Is it possible to estimate the age of the picture sketched here? Executed on light-blue silk, it has a painted background, while grass, trees and figures are embroidered. It says: "In Memory of Geo. Washington — Sarah H. MaGinley."

E.C.B. — Forty Fort, Pa.

Memorial pictures with Mount Vernon in the background were a popular subject for American amateur artists shortly after Washington's death, about 1800–1810.

PICTURES

LITHOGRAPH

What can you tell me about this picture? The colors are very delicate.
                    R.D.H. — *Crystal Lake, Ill.*

This print, copyrighted 1848, was made by Nafis & Cornish, New York lithographers. Little is known about them other than that they printed title pages and frontispieces for books and sheet music.

GENRE PICTURE

What information can you give me about this lithograph? It is marked: "Louis Moeller, N.A.; copyright 1902 by Taber-Rand Art Co."
                    L.M.J. — *Tacoma, Wash.*

It is a handcolored lithograph of a painting by Louis C. Moeller (1855–1930), a member of the National Academy of Design, whose forte was genre paintings like yours.

NEEDLEWORK MAP

My needlework map of England and Wales is signed "Ann Hathaway." Is this the Ann Hathaway who was Shakespeare's wife?
                    G.D.B. — *West Palm Beach, Fla.*

The map is a good example of the pictorial embroidery done by young women in England and America from about 1780 to 1840. Many signed their work. This Ann Hathaway was not Shakespeare's wife, for he was married in 1582, two centuries before pictorial needlework came into fashion.

POKER ETCHING

We have a lovely picture called "Potato Gathering." It was done by Lew Pennington, a jeweler of Natick, Massachusetts. It is identified on its back as a "poker etching." What does this mean?
P.L.H. — Chatham, Mass.

Poker work, or pyrography, as it is more commonly known today, is the art of etching designs in wood, ivory, leather, etc., by means of a heated metallic point. Examples of poker work have been found among primitive cultures and also highly sophisticated ones such as those of ancient Egypt and Rome. Many designers and artists of the nineteenth century made use of this technique. Today electric pyrography sets are sold in most artists' supply stores. Your etching dates about 1900.

COPY OF WASHINGTON PORTRAIT

I have been trying for a long time to identify the artist who did this oil portrait of George Washington, probably about 1840. Can you help?
H.K. — Bay Shore, N.Y.

This is a copy of one of the portraits painted from life by Gilbert Stuart. Without the artist's signature, there is no way of establishing his identity.

AMERICAN PRIMITIVE

Can you identify the enclosed picture?
J.M. — Pittsburgh, Pa.

Your portrait of universal charm is probably the work of an unknown itinerant artist, dating around 1830–1860.

COLONIAL SILHOUETTE

The name inscribed on the sleeve of this gilded silhouette-on-glass portrait of my great-great-grandfather is "C. P. Polk." Please tell me what you can about this artist.

M.F.K. — Ridge, Md.

Charles Peale Polk was born in Maryland in 1767. Orphaned in 1777, he grew up in the home of his famous uncle, the artist Charles Willson Peale (1741–1827). Trained by Peale, Polk first advertised as a portrait painter in 1785 in Baltimore; then in 1787 at Philadelphia as a house, ship, and sign painter. From 1791 to 1793 he again painted portraits in Baltimore. Polk died in 1822.

AMERICAN PORTRAIT

I would appreciate any information on my portrait, which is unsigned and undated.
A.E.I. — Winchester, Mass.

Your portrait, like many commissioned in pre-Civil War days, is by an itinerant American artist. From the sitter's formal pose, the coat style and black cravat, the portrait probably dates around 1835–1850.

STEVENGRAPH PURE SILK WOVEN PICTURES.

The following subjects can be had beautifully illuminated in 10 or 12 colours:

THE GOOD OLD DAYS (Royal Mail Coach) | THE START (A Race Scene)
THE PRESENT TIME (Railway Train) | THE STRUGGLE (Companion to above)
TURPIN'S RIDE to YORK (The Toll gate Leap) | THE LAST LAP (A Bicycle Racing Scene)
FULL CRY (A Hunting Scene) |

THOMAS STEVENS Sole Inventor and Manufacturer,
STEVENGRAPH WORKS. COVENTRY.

STEVENGRAPHS

*I am enclosing snapshots of my silk pictures,
woven in beautiful colors. They are 5 by 8 inches,
including mat, and have descriptive material on
the back. Can you tell me anything about them?*
M.K.B. — Denver, Colo.

These pictures, woven in silk on a Jacquard loom, were known as
Stevengraphs, after their originator Thomas Stevens (1828–1888). They
were produced at his plant in Coventry, England, in the form of
panels, bookmarks, and greeting cards. The subjects varied — com-
memorations of current events, portraits, local scenes, etc. Stevens'
first picture was dated 1863, and yours were registered in 1879.
Stevengraphs are now considered collectors' items. For further information you can write Stevengraph Collectors Association, Lewis
Smith, President, Daisy Lane, Irvington, N.Y., 10533.

SCULPTURE

I obtained this terra-cotta bust from a Paris dealer. It is supposedly of a French actor and is 2 feet high, with marble base. The inscription reads: "Buirette de Belloy par son amy J. J. Caffieri, 1771." I will be most grateful for any information about the sculptor and subject.

W.N.B., Jr.—Newnan, Ga.

This is a portrait bust of Pierre Laurent Buirette, an actor and dramatist, friend of the prominent sculptor J. J. Caffieri. The actor's stage name was Belloy Dormonte. Monsieur Caffieri (1725–1792) executed a number of busts of this kind.

PLASTER SCULPTURE

*I have been unsuccessful in finding out the name
of the artist who did these sculptured heads. They
are plaster of Paris and almost life-size. What was
their original purpose?*

J.L. — Stamford, Conn.

Your plaster sculpture, which probably was intended for bronze casting, is the work of a talented sculptor. It was not uncommon during the first decade of the twentieth century for wealthy American parents to commission these likenesses of their children. The sculpture was meant to be placed on a pedestal.

"LES TROIS AMIS"

*I would like to know about this bronze statue inscribed "Les Trois Amis" on the front and "J. B.
Edix 1855" on the back.*

S.K.C. — Bethany, Ohio

The bronze statue of two small boys and a dog — "The Three Friends" — is French, but J. B. Edix, the sculptor, is not listed in books on that period. An overwhelming interest in art that tells a story is a marked feature of Victorianism.

BOY WITH ROOSTER

*In 1958 we purchased in France this bronze
sculpture of a small boy attempting to hold onto
a rooster. The inscription on the base reads:
"L'enfant au Coq par Adriano Cecioni." When
and where did the sculptor live, and what is the
date of the figure?*

C.F.S. — Fayetteville, N.C.

SCULPTURE

Italian sculptor Adriano Cecioni (1838–1886) was a student at the Academy in Florence. He then moved to Paris and exhibited there his "L'enfant au Coq" at the Salon of 1872. You have a reproduction of the original, which is in the Gallery of Modern Art in Florence.

DOG OF FO

Can you help me to find out more about this pair of stone Moon Dogs? They are about 4 feet tall. One has his paw on a carved ball, the other on a young dog. They were brought from China and supposedly are very old.

M.B. — Red Bank, N.J.

The Dog of Fo, a Chinese animal figure, was widely used in ceramics, sculpture, and painting. He is actually a lion, and was generally depicted in pairs — one playing with a ball, the other with a lion cub. The very large figures were placed as guardians at the entrance gates of Buddhist temples; smaller ones were used as incense holders on altars. Your stone sculptures, either from a temple or palace, date from the eighteenth century, because at that time the curls of the mane were made to resemble snail shells. In the nineteenth century the curls were loose.

VICTORIAN BUST

We wondered if this bust portrays some historic figure. The markings on its back read: "Haseltine-Rome-1872."

R.C. — Jersey City, N.J.

Your portrait bust was done by the American sculptor Henry James Haseltine, who was born in Philadelphia, fought in the Civil War, and settled in Rome in 1867. It was fashionable in those days for Americans making the "grand tour" to patronize American artists working abroad. They often commissioned portrait busts of themselves, frequently in the classic toga. These had snob appeal and gave status to the Victorian parlor they graced.

BRONZE DIANA

I am enclosing a photograph of my bronze statue, which is approximately 2 feet high. On its base over other marks is the name "Houdon." Can you give me any information about the statue?

J.C. — Memphis, Tenn.

Your statue is a commercial copy, probably late nineteenth-century, of "Diana" by the French sculptor Jean-Antoine Houdon (1741–1828). It is interesting to note that the original was refused by the jury for the exhibition at the Salon of 1781 because they alleged that a statue of Diana must be draped. However, a bronze reproduction of the statue is now in the Louvre in Paris.

KOREAN HEAD C. A.D. 1000

This stone head is 11 inches tall and is carved from a single piece of black stone. I brought it from Korea and would like to know more about it.

F.K. — Stockton, Cal.

It seems to be an authentic Korean head carved from black marble, dating about A.D. 1000, and done in the Chinese style of the T'ang dynasty (618–906).

MOON BOY

A Russian friend in China gave me this figure in 1948. Can you tell me anything about it?
V.J.N. — Honolulu, Hawaii

The subject of your late Chinese Ming bronze sculpture is Liu-chu, the Moon Boy with Toad. It dates from the late sixteenth or early seventeenth century and is a popular Chinese motif.

MALINES MADONNA

This Flemish Madonna and Child will be a highlight of a group of dealers' personal collections at the Canadian Antique Dealers Association's first Antiques Fair in Toronto. It is a carved and polychromed wood statuette, about 14 inches tall, the colors being muted blue and gold. Can you give us any additional information about it?
T.B. — Oakville, Ontario, Can.

Your statuette of the Madonna and Child was made in the Flemish city of Malines around the mid-sixteenth century. Many of these small-scale Malines figures, popular with collectors, have the mark of the city of Malines or the letter "M" incised in their backs.

NEPALESE BUDDHIST FIGURE

I purchased this metal-and-lacquered Buddha in Central China many years ago. The figure is five inches high. Can you tell me anything about the age and origin of the figure and scrolls?

P.A.S.—Seattle, Wash.

Your beautiful Buddhist figure is Nepalese, late sixteenth- or early seventeenth-century. The hands are in the position of Giving and Teaching. Generally a Buddhist monk wrote the votive prayers kept in these figures, which were placed on the family altar.

COPY OF THORWALDSEN SCULPTURE

Could you identify this wooden plaque that originally decorated a bed?

P.G.P.—La Marque, Tex.

Your carving is a reproduction of a widely copied marble plaque by the Danish sculptor Albert Thorwaldsen (1770–1844), entitled "Night with Her Children Sleep and Death." The companion sculpture is entitled "Aurora with the Genius of Light." Both were modeled in 1815.

ITALIAN SOLDIER OF FORTUNE

Will you please tell me when this bronze statue was made and where? Can you identify the subject and maker?

J.C.J. — Whittier, Cal.

Your statue is a copy of one of the best equestrian statues in existence. The statue of Bartolommeo Colleoni (1400–1475), Italian soldier of fortune, was made by Verrocchio and Leopardi at Venice and cast in 1496. It stands before the church of Santi Giovanni e Paolo in Venice. This statue characterizes with remarkable realism that haughty and formidable mercenary soldier, and has been copied countless times throughout the centuries.

BUST OF LINCOLN

I am enclosing a picture of a life-size bust of Lincoln that I own. I know it was done by L. W. Volk, who also made a bust of Stephen Douglas. The bust is signed, but has no date. Could you add to my information?

S.D. — Lima, Ohio

The American sculptor Leonard Wells Volk (1828–1895) was born in Wellstown, New York. Stephen Douglas was his wife's cousin and helped him to study sculpture in Rome. Volk's studio was in Chicago, and he made the portraits of Lincoln and Douglas during the debates of 1858.

LIGHTING

SET OF MANTEL CANDELABRA

What can you tell me about my candle holders? The Colonial metal figures stand on a marble base and are covered with a gold wash. Each holder has ten hanging crystals. The single holders are signed "Cornelus & C" and dated "April 18, 1848." The centerpiece has the same signature but is dated "Dec. 5, 1848."

W.L.O. — Highland, Cal.

This type of candelabra mantel set consists of a three-branched candlestick for the center of the mantel and a single candlestick to match on either side. A complete set of three in good condition is well worth collecting. Cornelius (not Cornelus) & Company of Philadelphia was one of the foremost manufacturers of lighting devices in the United States during the nineteenth century.

FRENCH CANDELABRA

These heavy brass candelabra are marked: "Barbedienne, Paris, 1869." Who was Barbedienne?
E.S. — Walla Walla, Wash.

François Barbedienne was an important nineteenth-century French founder. His excellent craftsmanship was fully recognized, for he was the recipient of several medals and the Legion of Honor.

VICTORIAN CANDELABRUM

My guess is that this candelabrum was brought from abroad by my aunt previous to 1900. Can you give me any further information?
W.S.H. — Avon, Ill.

Your three-branched candlestick with cut-glass pendants, a figural gilt metal standard, and marble base probably dates around 1840–1860, and could be either of English or American manufacture. The use of cut-glass lusters for lamps and candlesticks was very widespread during this period and gave a feeling of lightness and delicacy to objects that might otherwise have been a trifle too heavy and solid.

GLASS LUSTERS

I am curious about the origin of my blue luster glass candlesticks. Can you give me any information?
J.S.G. — Houston, Tex.

Lusters made of glass and hung with prisms were a popular type of Victorian mantel garniture. By inserting a candle, the luster became a candlestick. While many lusters were made in England and France, they were also made at American glassworks, and the prisms also were cut in American shops. Your lusters are probably European in origin, dating around 1870–1890.

BRASS CANDELABRUM

*My husband found this candelabrum in the base-
ment of an old building. When we cleaned it, we
discovered it was made of brass and onyx, with the
name "James W. Tufts" under the base. Can you
trace it?*

R.S. — Great Falls, Mont.

Tufts manufactured mostly plated silver at 33 Bowker Street, Boston,
Massachusetts, from about 1875 to before 1915. Your brass candelabrum dates about 1890.

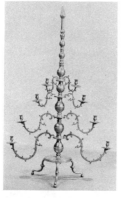

STANDING CANDELABRUM

*About where and when was my brass candelabrum
made? It is five feet, two inches high. Did it belong
in a church?*

P.T. — New York, N.Y.

Your brass standing candelabrum of important size was probably
made in eastern Germany in the second half of the eighteenth century.
It is probably one of a pair and was intended for domestic use, perhaps
on a large sideboard table in the dining room, or on a pedestal.

TIFFANY STUDIOS CANDELABRUM

*I'm interested in learning more about my candela-
brum. "Tiffany Studios, New York" is on the base.*
T.D.A., Jr. — APO New York, N.Y.

Louis Comfort Tiffany opened his studios about 1900. His craftsmen
made handtooled metal candelabra, stained glass and other art objects.
The studios closed in 1933.

NATURALISTIC CANDLESTICKS

I would like information about these 20-inch bronze candlesticks. One has a mouse looking into a nest of hatchlings, the other a bird bringing them a worm. "Cain" is the name marked plainly on each base.

E.D. — *East Hampton, N.Y.*

Your candlesticks were made about 1860 by Auguste Nicole Cain (Paris, 1822–1894), who had been a pupil of Rude and was known as a sculptor of animals. His work can be seen in the Luxembourg Gardens, Tuileries, and Trocadéro.

DOLLY MADISON'S GIRANDOLES

This pair of sconces has been handed down in my family for many years, along with the story that they were originally given to my great-great-great-great-grandmother by Dolly Madison and once hung in the White House. Can you authenticate this?

L.T.S. — *Granville, Ohio.*

Your girandoles appear to be English, dating between 1790 and 1810, so they could have been used in the White House during President Madison's administration, 1809–1817. Although considerable research has been compiled on the furnishings of the White House before it was burned by the British in 1814, there is no way of verifying your family story of their use there. They might have come from the Madison estate at Montpelier, Virginia.

JAPANESE FOLDING CANDLESTICK

My son bought this candlestick in an antique shop while he was with the Army of Occupation in Japan. Can you tell me something about it?
C.W. — Los Angeles, Cal.

This type of folding brass candlestick was intended for use in traveling, as it was easy to pack. It is Japanese in origin, probably dating from the nineteenth century.

"CRANE AND TORTOISE" CANDLESTICK

This candlestick was brought from China by my husband's uncle many years ago. Could you tell me the approximate date? What is the significance of the turtle and the crane?
M.K.M. — Tacoma, Wash.

The tortoise with a long, wide tail is the Japanese symbol of longevity. It is usually shown with a crane, when the combination is known as "crane and tortoise." Your candlestick is Japanese in origin and is probably less than one hundred years old.

VICTORIAN GIRANDOLE

Can you date this gold-leaf-finished brass girandole, which is one of a pair? On the marble base it is marked "Fleete Brothers."
A.W.H. — San Marino, Cal.

Your girandole, or candelabrum, is Victorian, dating about 1840–1860. Fleete Brothers, the makers, operated a brass foundry in Birmingham, England. The use of cut-glass pendants, drops and prisms was first introduced by the glassmakers of England and Ireland, and was copied here in our glassworks.

TÔLE CANDLESTICKS

I would like to know the age and any other pertinent facts about this pair of antique tole candlesticks with gold-leaf trim.

A.B. — Boston, Mass.

Your candlesticks are French, judged from the stenciled gilt decoration, probably of the Napoleonic period, the early nineteenth-century. The French word *tôle* is a short form for *tôle peinte,* or painted sheet-metal used decoratively, such as for lamp shades, bases and the like. During the First French Empire it was used with notable success.

LOUIS XV STYLE SCONCES

Can you tell me whether my gilt-bronze sconces are antiques or merely copies?

D.S. — Washington, D.C.

Without examining the workmanship closely, the condition of the metal, and other factors, it is practically impossible to determine the approximate age of your sconces. However, their asymmetrical and capricious shapes readily identify them as being in the Louis XV style, very handsome and ornamental.

CANDLE LAMPS

Please tell me about when and where these candle-sticks were made and if oil was used to light them? They are pressed glass, 10 inches high.

R.W.McC. — Rhône, France

Your candle (not oil) lamps mounted on a standard are fashioned on the same principle as Clarke's fairy lamp. In fact, Clarke patented a type of candle lamp mounted on a standard under the name Cricklite lamps, which he advertised as charming lamps for lighting the dinner table. Your lamps, a variant of Clarke's Cricklite, are of late-nineteenth-century English manufacture.

ENGLISH SHIP LANTERN

This lantern of brass and copper with red glass globe was salvaged in Alaska about 1910–1920. It is marked: "Grieve & Gillespie, Bedford Street, North Shields." What was its use?

R.L.E. — Riverside, Cal.

You have a ship's portside running lamp, dating about 1880–1900. The makers were English, of the seaport town of North Shields in Northumberlandshire. The lantern might have been lost from a small ship that foundered in Alaskan waters during a storm.

BETTY LAMP

We found this rusty iron scooplike object among attic treasures. What was it used for?

R.W.D. — Decatur, Ill.

You have a Betty lamp. At least one Plymouth colonist brought one with him. The saucer was filled with fish oil; a twisted rag served as the wick. It hung on the wall and gave a feeble light. Betty lamps were also made in this country, 1700–1800.

EMPIRE OIL LAMPS

We bought this pair of oil lamps twenty years ago in Mountainburg, Arkansas. The photograph shows the component parts. Can you identify them further?
R.O. — Shreveport, La.

The chimneys and bases of your oil lamps are typically continental, most likely of French manufacture, dating around the time of the Second French Empire, 1852–1870.

FRENCH OIL LAMPS

Can you tell us something about our oil lamps? We bought a pair of them some years ago from a New England estate.
H.J.G. — Parkersburg, W.Va.

The gilt-bronze tripod stand that holds the bowl of your oil lamp was adapted from an eighteenth-century Louis XVI style *brûle-parfum,* a kind of incense burner. Your lamps are probably French, dating perhaps from the Second Empire, 1852–1870. Made in pairs, these burners were costly, and lamps made from them were considered elegant accessories.

EUROPEAN OIL LAMP

I would appreciate any information you can give me about my antique solid-brass lamp that was bought over fifty years ago in Berlin. The handle of the lamp ends in a dog's head; the handle of the stand ends in a hand clutching a snake.

M.S. — *Glen Cove, N.Y.*

Oil lamps such as yours were made in Europe during the eighteenth and nineteenth centuries, and copies are still being made. These lamps were adapted from those used in very ancient times.

AMERICAN KEROSENE LAMP

This lamp belonged to my great-grandmother. I would appreciate anything you can tell me about it.

H.B.N. — *Baton Rouge, La.*

Your glass kerosene lamp is typically American, of a type used between 1870 and 1890. Such lamps generally stood on parlor center tables to give a clear light for the assembled family to sew or read by. Your American kerosene lamp dates from around the 1870s.

Kerosene was by far the most efficient and inexpensive illuminant up to this time. Supplies became abundant and cheap after 1859, the year of Colonel Drake's successful boring for petroleum in Titusville, Pennsylvania. The first American kerosene lamp was patented in 1859, along with forty others, and for the next two decades the patents averaged eighty a year. However, it was not until 1880 that a satisfactory burner using kerosene was constructed and came into general use.

POSTBELLUM LAMP

What information can you give me about my lamp?

M.F.O. — *Stratford, Conn.*

Your parlor lamp was perhaps the most popular form of kerosene lamp used in America during the 1880s and 1890s. The globe-shaped shade and font were usually decorated with flowers treated in a naturalistic manner.

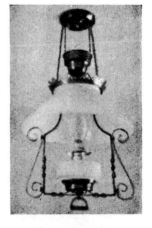

KEROSENE HANGING LAMP

When the family home in Maine was torn down last year this lamp was found behind a partition. We would appreciate any information about it.

P.R. — *Minneapolis, Minn.*

Brass, or copper-and-brass lamps like yours were made by a number of American manufacturers in considerable quantity for well-equipped farm and village homes from around the 1880s. They were the favorite lamps for living and dining rooms.

AMERICAN OIL LAMP

If you can give me any information about this lamp, I would appreciate it.

W.M.F. — Allentown, Pa.

Your oil lamp appears to be American in origin, dating from about 1840. It is a fine example of its class.

DOUBLE STUDENT OIL LAMP

Was this ornate student lamp produced in any quantity? I am curious, for I have never seen one like it.

D.O. — San Luis Obispo, Cal.

Many twin and single student lamps were made by American manufacturers about 1875–1890. They were superior reading lamps for household use. The student oil lamp with one or two arms was popular in America late in the nineteenth century. It was a fine reading lamp, and this fact explains its name. Your double student lamp probably dates around 1890–1900.

SCHNEIDER HANGING LAMP

This is a signed Schneider lamp, and the glass is blue, shading into red. Could you tell us more about its background?

B.L.G. — Springfield, Mo.

Gustav Schneider was Viennese. His shop was in Vienna, but his work was sold through a French representative. He was active from 1900 until World War I, and his glass artifacts are highly regarded as period pieces. Your lamp was probably made between 1900 and 1910. The coloring is quite unusual for a Schneider lamp.

OLD MINE LAMP

We found this old boxlike lamp in Indiana. It is copper with a silverlike metal overlay. The handle appears to have been resoldered. How was the lamp used, and when?

A.F.W. — Louisville, Ky.

It is a mid-nineteenth-century mine lamp. The device at the left is for the wick, and the round center hole for fuel. But the fuel-pan lid is lost.

RUSHLIGHTS

This mysterious pair of objects were found in a hundred-year-old house in Lake Geneva, Wisconsin. The bases are wood, the rest iron, including little cups embedded in the wood. Can you identify them?

H.E.H. — New York, N.Y.

They are rushlights, a primitive lighting device comprising a simple iron clamplike piece mounted on a wood block or tripod base. After dipping the pith of the soft rush in melted fat, the rush was secured in the clamp and lighted. For centuries they were used in British cottages for ordinary illumination, and undoubtedly the English colonists brought rushlights with them to this country.

TIFFANY TABLE LAMP

Any information you can give me concerning my beautiful Tiffany lamp will be appreciated. It has a metal base and an 18-inch glass shade in many colors, with the mark: "Tiffany Studios, New York."

K.R.H. — Palmdale, Cal.

Tiffany Studios, organized by Louis Comfort Tiffany, made your table lamp with a leaded-glass shade and bronze base in the early twentieth century. Tiffany lamps were never cheap — not even copies of them. Today again they are in great demand, and for this reason they are expensive.

TIFFANY TABLE LAMP

We recently bought this lamp, marked on the bottom: "Tiffany Studios, New York." It has a leaded-glass shade and base. Can you tell us more about it?

E.G. — Muskogee, Okla.

At the Paris Exposition, 1900, Tiffany exhibited his Dandelion lamp and Dragon Fly lamp, each having a leaded-glass shade and bronze base. Because of their overnight success, this type of lamp was copied both in America and abroad. The bronze bases and leaded-glass shades varied in design. Your Tiffany lamp belonging to this class of lamps is early twentieth-century.

AMERICAN POLE LAMP

An old blacksmith's shop sold us this kerosene oil street lamp. It is marked "Dietz Inc." When was it in use?

B.J. — *Wausau, Wis.*

Dietz, established in 1840, is still in business in Syracuse, New York. This type of oil lamp was probably in general use from around 1880 on.

HEATING
EQUIPMENT

ANTIQUE AMERICAN BRASS ANDIRONS

The dealer assured me these brass andirons were American and handmade not later than about 1830. To substantiate this, he showed me the hand-filed thread of the wrought-iron uprights on which the ball finials screwed. Some friends have questioned their age. Who is correct?

E.J.W. — Burbank Cal.

The dealer was correct. Besides the hand filed threads, you will find on looking closely that the ball finials were cast in two parts. Finials in one piece were made considerably later.

AMERICAN ANDIRONS

We recently purchased these solid-brass andirons, which bear the name "John Molineux—Boston." How old do you think they are?
R.W.LV.—Columbus, Ohio

According to the 1810 Boston City Directory, John Molyneux (also spelled Molineux) was a founder in Boston, and your andirons date around that time. The heavy ball finials are typical of andirons bearing his name.

ANTEBELLUM ANDIRONS

Could you tell the period and origin of our brass andirons? I took one apart to show the hand-wrought iron upright.
W.R.M, Jr.—Newtown Sq., Pa.

Your andirons are entirely handmade, apparently by a skilled brass founder, who probably worked in one of our important cities about 1815–1830.

TILED GRATE

This tiled ship's stove has brass trim. On the back is written: "Murdock Parlor Grate Co., Boston Ms." Please let me know what you can find out about this stove.
F.McL.—New York, N.Y.

Tiled grates of this type were popular for household use around 1880–1890. They required an outlet or chimney and were often attached to the fireplace. Your grate suggests English rather than American manufacture. It was probably imported and sold by Murdock of Boston.

COAL HOD

I have what I think is a foot warmer. It is cast iron with porcelain insets. Is it really a foot warmer, and how old is it?

D.D. — *College Station, Tex.*

You were close. Your article does have to do with heat, but it is a coal hod, or fuel box, made for holding and carrying coal. It is probably of European manufacture, and dates between 1880 and 1890.

HOD FOR CANNEL COAL

Can you give the name, original use and approximate date of this fairly heavy metal container?

A.M.M. — *Gladwyne, Pa.*

It is a hod for cannel coal, which was widely used both here and in England from 1850 to 1890 in fireplaces fitted with basket grates. The hods' stencil decoration made them attractive hearthside containers.

IRON FIREPLACE GRATE

I purchased this small stove from a western New York State dealer, who said it was a French antique. Is it French?

M.K. — *North Hollywood, Cal.*

Yes, your coal-burning grate is of French manufacture and probably dates from around the Second French Empire, 1852–1870. It was designed for a fireplace opening and derives in principle from the Franklin stove.

FRANKLIN STOVE

We bought a house that had this old stove in it. What can you tell us about it?

N.T. — Waccabuc, N.Y.

You have a Franklin stove. They were invented by Benjamin Franklin in 1742 to solve the heating problem. These cast-iron fireplaces in which the fire burns on an iron hearth were originally meant to be set partly inside an already built fireplace. Franklin soon discovered that they operated more efficiently outside the fireplace or where they could be joined with a chimney.

Your model is especially attractive because of the brass mounts. It probably dates from early in the nineteenth century, when manufacturers along the eastern seaboard were kept busy making them. There were many kinds of Franklin stoves. Your stove is apparently of the type described as "open fireplace stove with andirons." Otherwise the small scale of the andirons could be quite a problem, unless made to order.

PARLOR STOVE

Can you give me any information about this old stove made by Chaney-Hunter of Rochester, New York — and perhaps its age?

E.S.H. — Aiken, S.C.

Your decorative, four-column, wood-burning parlor stove dates around the 1840s. The columns, which support a horizontal piece with an opening for a stovepipe, help spread the heat. Recently an amazing number of people have become interested in the more elaborate examples of parlor stoves because of their ornamental appeal.

SIX-PLATE BOX STOVE

This little cast-iron stove is only 24 inches long. It has ship designs on the side and is marked on front and top: "1839 Plymouth, Vt. — No. 7 — Tyson Furnace."

A.G. — Bay Port, Mich.

This class of wood-burning parlor stove was called a six-plate box stove because the heating apparatus is in the form of a box made of six separate plates. Iron was discovered in Plymouth Mountains in 1835, and the Tyson Furnace was under construction by 1837. Perhaps the first stoves were made in 1839 and the manufacturer regarded this historically as a "Second Plymouth." Hence the ships. Presuming this to be a fact, it would be a sort of commemorative stove, and these are not common.

CADET STOVE

I would appreciate any information about my little stove, 22 inches high. It is marked, "Charles Fawcett, Limited, Sackville, N.B.," and the word "Cadet" is on the top.

DeW.R. — Tacoma, Wash.

Many stove foundries made such small stoves from 1875 to 1900. The Canadian firm of Charles Fawcett Ltd. is now the Enamel & Heating Products Ltd. Cadet stoves appeared in the firm's 1895 catalogue.

AMERICAN STOVE

The door of this potbelly stove reads: "Joker No 6 Southard, Robertson & Co., Water Street and Peck Slip, New York." How old is it, and where was it used?

J.E.O. — Mt. Prospect, Ill.

Stoves like yours date 1870–1890 and were used in country railroad stations, one-room schools and some farmhouses. They were often given whimsical names, such as Jolly Companion, Little Ferdy, and Joker.

TEN-PLATE IRON BOX STOVE

My wood-burning stove has the name "Jefferson Furnace" across the top. Where was Jefferson Furnace, and how old is the stove?

J.R., Jr. — Richwood, N.J.

The ten-plate parlor box stove was adopted from the six-plate box stove to permit the insertion of a small oven for baking. Four more plates were necessary; top and bottom plates for the oven, and two doors, one on each side. The majority of these box stoves appear to date from around the early Victorian era, though still earlier examples are known.

AMERICAN COOK STOVE

Can you tell me when and how this little stove was used? On the front are the words "Comet National, Excelsior Stove Mfg. Co., Quincy, Ill."
J.M.P. — Dayton, Ohio

From about 1875, American stove works made these single-oven cook stoves. The Excelsior Stove Company was incorporated in 1893, but may have been a going concern before that date. It closed in 1954.

TOYS
AND GAMES

END-OF-THE-CENTURY DOLL HEAD

When my stepmother was young her aunt gave her this doll head, which she said came from Sweden and had been in the family for many years. We would like to learn more about it if possible.
D.D.L. — Evanston, Ill.

Your doll head dates from before 1891, as after that date the country of origin was required to be stamped on the head. The sweet expression on the doll's face, however, dates it no earlier than 1890, since doll features were slightly sterner before the 1890s. It is difficult to place the country of origin, but many doll heads like yours were made in Germany.

JUMEAU MECHANICAL DOLLS

Can you date these Jumeau musical dolls? The girl plays castanets and the boy a mandolin.
R.O. — San Anselmo, Cal.

The Maison Jumeau, founded in Paris about 1843 by Pierre François Jumeau, made musical dolls of a very fine grade. Your dolls date between 1900 and 1910.

GERMAN TURN AROUND DOLL

This doll on a stick plays what I think is an old German tune when you twirl the stick. It is marked "Simon Halbig." Is it a collector's item?
R.J.R. — Yakima, Wash.

Some doll collectors would welcome a turn-around doll as a novelty, especially if the music box still plays. The doll was exported by Simon Halbig's German doll factory around 1900–1910.

MUTT AND JEFF, THE COMIC-STRIP DOLLS

What can you tell me about this set of Mutt and Jeff dolls? They are wearing their original clothes.
H.L.M. — Sioux Falls, S.D.

These dolls were probably made between 1910 and 1920. Cartoonist Bud Fisher's comic-strip pair, on which they were modeled, first appeared in newspapers in 1905, and soon after became national celebrities.

NINETEENTH-CENTURY DOLL CARRIAGE

Can you furnish any information about this doll carriage that belonged to my mother? Body, wheels, spokes, and axle are wood. The top, which folds, is leather, and the body is lined with leather.
C.G. — *Newport News, Va.*

Your doll carriage appears to be of mid-nineteenth-century American manufacture. We are inclined to believe that this class of small-scale carriages was the work of talented makers of full-sized ones, who perhaps made these toys as gifts for family members or on special order for affluent customers.

MINIATURE FIREPLACE

This cast-iron "thing" was supposedly used in the home of my great-grandfather, who came to America from England as a boy. Can you help me find out just what it is?
C.J.S. — *Fort Dodge, Iowa*

You have a small-scale model fireplace. It is one of a type believed to have been made for doll houses and dates about 1850. The model is almost certainly of English workmanship.

TOY STOVE

The words "Favorite Stove & Range" are on the oven door of my small stove, and "Dollys' Favorite, Piqua, Ohio" on the side. Can you tell whether this is a toy stove or a manufacturer's sample? And how old is it?

R.U.—Moberly, Mo.

The words "Dollys' Favorite" on your miniature stove suggest that it was intended to be a toy. It probably dates around the 1880s. A manufacturer's sample was always an absolute replica of the large stove it represented and really worked, whereas a toy stove had only to look like a stove.

COMMEMORATIVE BANK

This cast-iron bank is inscribed: "Birthplace of American Independence," and on the bottom, "Enterprise, Mfg. Co Philada, Pat. Sep. 14, 1875." What is its background?

J.O'C.—Gap, Pa.

Your cast-iron bank in the form of Independence Hall was made to commemorate the one-hundredth anniversary of American independence, and its value is enhanced by its historical significance. This type of coin bank is known as a "still bank"—in contrast to the mechanical banks with moving parts.

NINETEENTH-CENTURY HINDU TOY

Can you possibly give me any information about this object? It is of solid brass, 14 inches tall, 10½ inches wide, with moving wheels. I wish especially to know its origin.

S.M. — Baltimore, Md.

Animals like this, with wheeled base and rider, were made in India as children's toys during the last half of the nineteenth century. Wholesalers in Hindu antiques occasionally imported a few such brass toys about thirty years ago. They are rare now.

AMERICAN KALEIDOSCOPE

On the frame of my kaleidoscope it states: "C. C. Bush & Co., Prov., R.I., Pat. reissued Nov. 11, 1873." How old is it?

B.L.G. — Indialantic, Fla.

Since patents are issued for periods ranging from three to fourteen years, your kaleidoscope would date somewhere between 1873 and 1887. After Sir David Brewster invented the kaleidoscope in 1817 it became a very popular optical toy all over Europe and America. Some had stands like yours.

FRENCH RACING GAME

I believe this is a French game, as the plate reads: "Jeu de Course—M. J. & Cie." Could you tell me anything about it?

H.B.—New York, N.Y.

Your game is French and dates about 1880–1900, but we cannot trace the maker. The label means "The Racing Game." A very similar American game was called "The Steeplechase."

VICTORIAN CARD GAMES

Our son recently acquired two old English card games—"Counties of England" and "Proverbs." The cards are beautifully printed and tinted. Can you give us any idea as to when these games were played?

S.K.W.—Ellicott City, Md.

The cards were printed sometime between 1840 and 1870. These games were similar to American card games such as "Authors" and "Old Maid" and were especially popular with Victorian parents, who considered them instructive to their children.

ON WHEELS

CONNECTICUT BABY BUGGY

This odd-looking baby carriage has an apparently hand sewn top and hand turned wheels. We can't imagine its age. Do you know?
                    W.D.S. — *Lakeville, Conn.*

We think that this baby carriage is a miniature of the famous American buggy, and would date it between 1835 and 1860. Three similar carriages were found in Connecticut, so it was probably made there. One is in the collection of the New Haven Historical Society.

AUTHENTIC BABY BUGGY

Can you judge the age of this carriage? It is made of wood and leather. There are no marks on it.
R.D.A. — *New Brunswick, N.J.*

I would date your American-made baby carriage around 1850–1870. With its collapsible top and leather-covered dashboard, it is an exact copy in miniature of the one-horse buggy, and was probably made by some carriage builder of that era.

LATE VICTORIAN BABY CARRIAGE

Could this baby carriage be called an antique? We bought it in a used-furniture store. It is all wood, with metal rims on the wheels and S-shaped metal springs.

A.E.B. — *Houma, La.*

Your American baby carriage was made about 1880–1890. (After 1895 they had rubber tires.) It is not a true antique.

ON WHEELS

PONY-CART CARRIAGE

Any information you can give me about the history and origin of my carriage would be appreciated.

A.W. — Detroit, Mich.

Your unusual child's-carriage with hobbyhorse mounted over the front wheel was made by an American carriage company. The wire-spoked wheels, rubber tires and wicker body date it 1895–1905.

POPCORN WAGON

Please tell me whatever you can about this old popcorn wagon. I don't know the make.

R.W. — Sacarro, N.M.

Wagons like this were built to order by local wainwrights for popcorn men from about 1880 to 1910. Carnivals, county fairs, and band concerts were not complete without the little glass house on wheels dispensing fresh popcorn.

AMERICAN WATER WAGON

Can you tell me the year this water wagon was made and by whom?

E.J.F. — Stamford, Conn.

Water wagons date back to the eighteenth century. This one is like those used on large farms and construction jobs and by circuses from about 1880 to 1910. The running gear for such water wagons was made in a local wagon shop, the circular tanks by coopers. Earlier examples had smaller wheels.

WEAPONS

BOWIE KNIFE

Can you tell me the history or the age of this antique knife recently found near an Indian battleground? The handle is carved bone; the blade appears to be handforged steel.

C.R.A. — Thermopolis, Wyo.

Judging from the picture and description, you have a bowie knife made between 1830 and 1870, and named for James Bowie, who died during the siege of the Alamo. Such hunting knives were very popular; no cattleman was without one.

CARBINE OF THE CIVIL WAR ERA

Our old gun looks like a cavalry rifle. The stock is marked: "Burnside Rifle Co., Providence, R. I." and "Burnside Patent March 25, 1856-33765." Was it used in the Civil War?

> *H.W.L. — South Meriden, Conn.*

The Burnside Rifle Company was organized in 1860 and took over the patent for this rifle from a Bristol, Connecticut, company. During the Civil War Burnside delivered 55,567 of these carbines to the War Department to be issued to cavalry regiments. It may be of that issue.

CHINESE MINIATURE CANNON

A friend of mine dug up this miniature cannon in the old Chinese area of Helena, Montana, which was a mining camp around 1780. It is 8 inches long, with handcarved fire-breathing dragons and floral and bamboo patterns. The material feels like jade. To date, eight have been found in the area, each of a different caliber. Where did they come from? How old are they?

> *W.A.B. — Riverside, Cal.*

Your small-scale fortress cannon made of steatite (the real name for soapstone) was made in China early in the nineteenth century. It illustrates well the Chinese zest for copying and the extent to which they carried it. Much more commonly found are the examples made of metal.

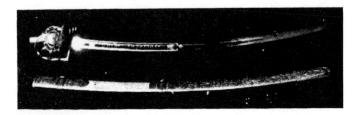

FRENCH OFFICER'S SWORD

I would appreciate your comments on this sword. There is an "N" on the guard, the words "Garde Imperiale" on the blade, and "Coutaux Frères, Klingenthal" on the back of the blade. A Hippocratic symbol is engraved on the scabbard.

E.J.C. — Miami, Fla.

Your sword dates between 1810 and 1840 and was carried by an officer of the famous Garde Imperiale, which Napoleon established as Emperor of France. Coutaux Frères made fine sword blades in Klingenthal, Saxony, a small city noted for its cutlery factories. The Hippocratic symbol on the scabbard indicates the sword originally belonged to a medical officer.

SWORD ORNAMENTS

My son bought these small metal ornaments in an antique shop in Kyoto. The dealer said each pair was part of the fittings on a Japanese sword. Can you tell me more about them?

M.W. — Armonk, N.Y.

Pairs of these ornaments, which the Japanese call menuki, were placed on each side of the sword hilt. Generally a matched pair, they are held in place either by a projecting pin or by braid wound around the hilt. Fine examples of menuki worked in gold and other metals are remarkable for their jewellike quality. Judging from the snapshot, yours most likely date from the late nineteenth century.

JAPANESE SWORD GUARD

My nephew bought this object in Kobe, Japan. The dealer told him it was part of a Japanese sword. Can you tell me more about it?

J.L.H. — Hackettstown, N.J.

This metal disk, known as a tsuba, is the guard on a Japanese sword and the most important fitting, because the metalworker lavished such skill on it. The openings on either side of the tang (blade opening) were for the *Kozuka* (small knife) and *Kogai* (skewer) to pass through. Your iron tsuba with eight openwork designs in brass and an over-all brass inlaid ground dates from the eighteenth century.

PEPPERBOX PISTOL

My old six-shooter pistol has a caplike hammer and revolving barrel. The mark reads: "Allen Thurber & Co., Worcester, Mass." How old is the pistol?

H.T. — Kansas City, Mo.

Thurber & Company was in business only two years, 1855 and 1856. A revolving barrel pistol was called a pepperbox.

FOOD SERVICE

FIREPLACE GRILLE

This wheel has a round pot, or bowl, at the outer edge. The wheel rotates on an axis, which is set on three short legs. The spokes are grooved and drain into the round pot. Do you have any idea what it could possibly have been used for?

R.G. — Suffern, N.Y.

Your device was used as a grille for cooking food over an open fire, and probably dates around the second half of the nineteenth century.

EUROPEAN COFFEE MAKER

My grandfather was given this strange-looking coffee maker in the mid-1880s by an English sea captain, and it still works. I haven't been able to track down its origin. Can you help me?

E.M.N. — Wilmington, N.C.

You have one of the many unusual devices developed in Europe in the nineteenth century for brewing coffee. Yours is notable because it is complete and still in working condition.

ITALIAN COFFEEPOT

Can you help me identify this brass pot? The only mark is an "8" on the hinged upper lip of the pouring spout. The interior is somewhat like that of a modern percolator, and the burner looks as if it is for alcohol.

B.S. — Palo Alto, Cal.

You have an upside-down coffeepot, or *macchinetta* (little machine), probably made in Italy around 1900 and designed for the preparation of espresso, the Italian version of drip coffee. You put water in the lower container and very finely ground coffee in the perforated middle container. When the water boils, you turn the pot upside down to let it drip through. Your brass model was intended for use in the dining room; simpler versions were made — and are still made — for use directly on the kitchen stove.

ENGLISH BRAZIER

Can you tell me anything about my antique copper-and-brass brazier? It is unmarked.
D.H. — Rutland, Vt.

Your brazier is English, dating about the middle of the eighteenth century. Such braziers were placed on marble-topped service tables, filled with charcoal, and lighted to keep serving dishes warm. The piercing of the bowl allowed the entrance of air, needed for the charcoal to burn.

EDWARDIAN FISH-AND-FRUIT SERVICE

I found this wonderful fish-and-fruit set at Goodman's in Memphis. They think it turn-of-the-century, but since it came from a very old plantation, could it be antique?
H.A.B. — New York, N.Y.

The dealer is right, it is not an antique, but an Edwardian service, probably Sheffield. Charming sets such as this one, in handsome silk- or velvet-lined boxes, were very popular as presents for weddings or other occasions in the 1890s.

FOOD SERVICE

BRONZE FRUIT KNIVES

On the blades of my ivory-handled fruit knives is the inscription "Uchatius-Bronce." About when and where were they made?

R.A.B. — Cairo, Ill.

The inscription stands for Uchatius bronze, a steel bronze invented by an Austrian general, Franz Baron Uchatius (1811–1881). Your knives are European, perhaps German or Austrian, and date around the latter part of the nineteenth century.

ENGLISH FLATWARE

My parents' chest of forks and knives with ivory handles are marked "RFM+S." The date on the chest is "25th Jan. 1888." Can you trace them?

R.J.D. — Safford, Ariz.

They were probably made in Birmingham, England, in 1888, but the full name of R.F.M., who made them, can't be traced further.

INGENIOUS FRUIT KNIFE

The fruit knife I have sketched is one of a set of ten. Their handles are a deep sea-green ivorylike material, which has small cracks throughout. The rim and blade appear to be a light brass. Can you tell me their approximate age?

E.M.O. — Lake Bluff, Ill.

Fruit knives such as yours were very popular in the last quarter of the nineteenth century. The ski-shaped blade with its center slit made the knife useful for coring as well as paring.

I hope you can tell us what this copper thing is and how old it might be. We bought it from an English lady, who said it had been in her family in the Midlands as long as she remembered.

G.A.S. — St. Paul, Minn.

You have a British copper bombe mold used for frozen desserts such as a mousse or ice cream. The pyramid form is unusual; cylindrical bombe molds are far more common. There was a great interest in all kinds of molded foods during the last quarter of the nineteenth century and throughout the Edwardian decade (1901–1910), so your mold was probably made sometime during this period.

VICTORIAN KNIFE CASE WITH SLOPING LID

Could you tell me the age of the inlaid-design knife box I bought in a North Carolina antiques shop? Since the only utensils that fit the box with the lid closed are spoons, why should it be called a knife box?

G.E.S. — Arlington, Va.

Your knife case is English Victorian, dating from the second half of the nineteenth century, and apparently was intended for some kind of short-handled knife. Knife cases, usually in pairs, stood on the buffet or side table in the eighteenth-century English dining room. They were a necessity, as the fashionable dining room furniture possessed no cutlery drawers until the introduction of the sideboard, about 1780. The interior of the knife case was divided into many small, rectangular partitions; the knives and forks were inserted handles upwards; the spoons inserted bowls upwards. Apparently they were always known as knife cases.

UTILITY ITEMS

ALPHABET PADLOCK

Do you have any idea of the age and origin of the padlock I have sketched? It has movable combination brass rings marked with letters of the alphabet. When manipulated to spell "Fulton," it unlocks.

E.L.F. — Belleville, Ill.

From your sketches and explanation, I would say you have an alphabet padlock, American, made about 1840. These padlocks were set to unlock by spelling a word or name.

BUTTER CHURN

Can you tell me where my old butter churn was made, and how long ago?

N.R.W. — *North Boston, N.Y.*

You have an American splash butter churn, and judging by its excellent condition, I would say it was made after 1885. Without maker's name, the exact geographical origin cannot be traced.

BUTTER WORKER

Can you identify this implement and its purpose? The paddle wheel moves back and forth.

L.P. — *Drexel Hill, Pa.*

It is a butter worker, designed to remove excess moisture from freshly churned butter—which is quite wet—until it reaches the desired consistency.

COBBLER'S BENCH

I recently purchased this cobbler's bench complete with tools. Can you tell me anything concerning its age?

R.C. — *Chicago, Ill.*

Its size and design indicate it is an American cobbler's bench of the sort in use from about 1850 to 1880. Tools, nails and lasts were arranged in the tray top, leather in the drawer.

COFFEE GRINDER

Did this large coffee grinder have a brass eagle on top originally? It is marked: "Star Mill, Philadelphia; Henry Troemner, Maker."
                    N.W. — *Glendora, Cal.*

Yes, the lid of the canister probably had a brass spread-eagle finial. Henry Troemner, a manufacturer of precision laboratory balances and weights and a wide line of other products, made Star coffee mills between 1882 and 1926.

STORE COFFEE GRINDER

How old would you judge this coffee mill to be? It is marked: "Enterprise Mfg. Co., Philadelphia, U.S.A."
                    J.A. — *Radcliff, Ky.*

It is a store-size coffee grinder and dates between 1880 and 1900. The Enterprise Company was a leading maker of such grinders.

MILKING STOOL

Although in fine condition, this milking stool is said to date about 1820. It is of pine, with no nails or screws. Your comments would be appreciated.

R.F.S. — Amissville, Va.

Such a milking stool could have been made between 1810 and about 1850. The workmanship suggests a country cabinetmaker. The pine indicates that it came from the South.

BRASS BALANCE SCALE

We are interested in learning the age of and any other information about our 40-inch scale. I am enclosing a sketch of the marks on the crossarm.

B.S. — Miami, Fla.

The mark "ER" beneath a crown indicates that your brass balance scale was tested for accuracy since Elizabeth II was crowned in 1953. The number "248" is that of the sealer of weights who tested it, and "85117" is the serial number of Anderson Brothers.

ENGLISH BALANCE SCALE

Can you tell me the approximate age of my brass balance scale? It has two marks: the first, "C.W.S. Makers Manchester"; the second, a lead seal with a crown and "ER II 58" below it.

H.G.J. — Framingham, Mass.

The design is that of an English Victorian balance scale dating around 1860–1880. The first mark refers to the Cooperative Wholesale Society Makers, Manchester. The second mark shows the scale was tested and passed by a sealer of weights and measures after the coronation of Queen Elizabeth II in 1953.

ITALIAN SCALE

*We recently purchased this old brass scale and are curious about its origin. The base is marble, the weight arm a gray dull metal, and stamped on the round end is "A * 1867 * gr. *R."*

J.E.Y. — San Rafael, Cal.

Your scale, of unusually forceful and imaginative design, was made and registered in Florence, Italy, in 1867 or shortly thereafter.

EARLY SEWING MACHINE

Please tell me what you can about this sewing machine. The brass plate on it reads: "Grover & Baker S.M. Co., Boston, U.S.A., Howe's Patent, Sept. 10, 1846."

J.R. — Pulaski, Tenn.

Elias Howe patented his sewing machine in 1846, and the patent expired in 1867, so your machine was made sometime during this period. It was manufactured by a company that paid royalties to Howe for the use of his patent.

EARLY CASH REGISTER

I bought this cash register years ago from a man who owned a tavern near Flushing, New York. He had bought it secondhand at the turn of the century. Can you tell me where it was made and how old it is?

W.R. — Franklin Square, N.Y.

You have a very early and interesting example of a primitive cash register. It is American in origin and in all probability dates around the last quarter of the nineteenth century.

ENGLISH SHEARS

These shears, marked "Mottram & Sons, Sheffield," are said to have been brought here by my first ancestor before the Revolutionary War. Can you date them?

J.C.B. — Mesa, Ariz.

Mottram & Sons were well-known English cutlers about 1830–1880. Design of the shears dates them about 1840.

AMERICAN SPINNING WHEEL

Could you possibly tell me where, when, and by whom this old spinning wheel was made?

H.E.K. — Fresno, Cal.

Your flax spinning wheel is American and was made between 1780 and 1830. Few makers of such spinning wheels put their names on their handiwork.

LINEN SPINNING WHEEL

What information can you give me about this spinning wheel? All the wooden pegs are removable. The peg at the far left screws into the wood, adjusting the part that spins the thread.
R.J.M. — Palos Park, Ill.

You have an American spinning wheel of the small size for spinning linen thread. The turned details of legs, spokes, wheel supports and comb frame indicate that it was made by a spinning wheel maker working somewhere in this country about 1800–1830.

CANADIAN FLAX WHEEL

My grandmother owned this spinning wheel in Nova Scotia. The name "R.S. Stewart" is marked on it. Can you identify it for me?
M.H.T. — Tacoma, Wash.

You have a small flax wheel, the kind used to produce linen thread. It was made in the late eighteenth or early nineteenth century. Stewart may have been the name of the original owner.

ENGLISH SPINNING WHEEL

Can you help me identify my mahogany spinning wheel? It has ivory buttons and hand-wrought screws. On the top is a copper cup and a movable holder, which seems to be for a candle.
M.S.E. — Philadelphia, Pa.

Your finely tuned spinning wheel appears to be of English origin, dating from the late eighteenth century. The holder held the distaff on which the flax was placed before spinning. The cup held water with which the spinner could moisten her fingers and thus handle the flax better.

LINEN SPINNER

What was spun on this small (30") spinning wheel bought in France? The bolts that hold the four uprights are carved of wood.
I.L.H. — Mineral Wells, Tex.

From design and construction, it appears that yours is a typical European spinning wheel used to spin linen thread. It probably dates from the late eighteenth or early nineteenth century.

SPINNING WHEEL

All parts of my spinning wheel are in working condition. I believe it dates back to about 1850. Would it be considered valuable?
R.G.B. — APO 132, N.Y.

Your spinning wheel is of European provenance, probably German or Swiss, and dates from the late eighteenth or early nineteenth century. Yes, spinning wheels like yours, complete and in working order, are collectible antiques and can be considered valuable.

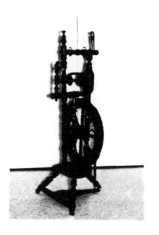

GERMAN SPINNING WHEEL

My wife's grandmother brought this spinning wheel to America from Germany in 1874. It is mostly pegged together with hand-fashioned wooden dowels. The few metal parts are crudely made of brass or bronze. Can you tell us anything about its history? It has no mark.

J.A.K. — Tucson, Ariz.

Yours is a typical German spinning wheel of the eighteenth and early nineteenth centuries. This kind of wheel is used in the "Spinning Song" when the opera *Faust* is performed.

SPINNING WHEEL

This spinning wheel belonged originally to my mother's family. I've only seen one like it — at the Cabildo in New Orleans. What type is it, and when was it made?

T.C.W., Sr. — Pearlington, Miss.

Judging from the picture, you have a small upright flax spinning wheel with a distaff, probably made in Holland in the latter part of the eighteenth century.

SNOW-BIRD EAGLE

This metal eagle is marked: "Patented July 22, 1900." I was told it was used as a snow bird. Can you explain?

L.D.B. — Tulsa, Okla.

Throughout New England, in sections where heavy snowfall was expected, rows of cast-iron eagles like this one, 4 to 6 inches high, were mounted on sloping roofs to help retard snow slides.

EARLY-AMERICAN SPECTACLES

I would like some information about this pair of eyeglasses. The frames are made of copper and have sliding bows. I have seen the same type in a picture of Benjamin Franklin.

G.M. — Union City, Tenn.

A portrait of Benjamin Franklin as an elderly man, painted from life by Charles Willson Peale, does show him wearing spectacles with octagon-shaped lenses and sliding bows. Similar frames, of 18-karat gold, were made by American goldsmiths in the late eighteenth and early nineteenth centuries. Those of copper or steel date from about 1840 to 1870. They had sliding or folding bows.

AMERICAN LEATHER-COVERED TRUNK

My black leather-covered trunk has a dome top and is lined with thin light-blue paper. It measures 24" long, 13" deep and 10" high. Any information will be appreciated.

D.M.T. — Schenectady, N.Y.

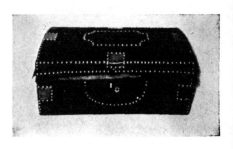

Small leather trunks like yours are American; many of them were made in New England. Some of them were lined with newspapers (1810–1830); yours might be of that vintage.

IRON-BOUND TRUNK

I would like information about my small pine trunk banded in iron, with handmade nails and brass ornaments. There is evidence that it was originally covered with tooled leather.

D.R. — Visalia, Cal.

Your trunk is American, made between 1835 and 1850. Such trunks usually were covered with tooled leather; sometimes the studs were arranged in floral designs.

SARATOGA TRUNK

We purchased this charming little leather-inlaid trunk at a sale and are curious to know more about it.

H.N. — White Bear Lake, Mich.

From the picture, I'd say you have an American trunk of the kind generally called a Saratoga trunk, dating about 1875–1890.

OLIVER TYPEWRITER

My father-in-law owns this Oliver typewriter. I saw one like it in a museum. Does it rate as an antique?

D.G.T. — *Portland, Ore.*

The Oliver typewriter was invented by Reverend Thomas Oliver, a Methodist minister, in 1896. The Oliver was entirely original in design, using a type-bar similar to an inverted "U" and having new features in the carriage mechanism. The Oliver Typewriter Company was active in Chicago, Illinois, from 1896 to 1928. The Carl P. Dietz Collection of Typewriters at the Milwaukee Public Museum contains four models. To be regarded as antique, an article must be no less than 100 years old.

HAND-POWERED VACUUM

Several months ago I found an old vacuum cleaner in the basement of a building I rent. It is marked: "Regina Pneumatic Cleaner, Chicago, Ill." How old is it?

G.T., Jr. — *Selma, Ala.*

This vacuum cleaner must have been bought from the Chicago distributor of the Regina Company, Rahway, New Jersey, around 1900. Regina had made music boxes until Edison's phonograph crippled their sales. Then they switched to vacuums, hand-powered at first. Today the Regina Corporation makes only electric vacuum cleaners; their principal model bears the trade name "Electrikbroom."

EARLY WASHING MACHINE

Could you approximate the age of this washing machine? It is labeled "Improved Whirl." What is the kind of wood used?

E.T. — Kenosha, Wis.

This is an early kind of American washing machine, probably dating about the 1890s. In the Sears, Roebuck catalogue of 1902 they mention that they have found that "the yellow cottonwood grown in the lowlands of Arkansas and Mississippi is the best lumber for washing machines."

EARLY HAND IRONS

These old hand irons are on display in our school library. Can you date them and tell us how they were used?

L.C.L. — Buras, La.

Your sadiron, top, one of the first flatirons, dates from the late nineteenth century. "Sad" in this case meant "heavy." The iron was heated by red-hot pieces of iron put into it. The box iron, bottom, also dates from the second half of the nineteenth century, and contains an enclosed space for live coals to keep it hot.

WINE-BOTTLE CORKER

What was the use of this implement made of hard maple? The knob on top moves the metal-tipped spindle up and down.

J.H. — Lunas, N.M.

This gadget was used to cork bottles. During Prohibition, when many Americans made their own wine, they used an implement like this.

DECORATIVE
AND USEFUL
OBJECTS

ALABASTER GARNITURE

I would appreciate any information on this carved object, which I think is of alabaster. It is about 27 inches tall.

F.H. — Grand Rapids, Mich.

Your ornately carved garniture was undoubtedly created in Italy. A typical trophy of the "grand tour," it probably dates around the third quarter of the nineteenth century.

GIBSON GIRL SILVER BELT

This is a sterling silver belt with a loop behind each head for running ribbon through. Could you tell me during what period this type of belt was worn?

M.A.M. — Norfolk, Va.

Such belts were very fashionable between 1900 and 1910, worn with a shirtwaist and skirt. This was the Gibson Girl era. The heads on the belt are copies of Charles Dana Gibson's drawings.

BALLOT BOX

We would appreciate any information on this maple-wood machine. A small ball drops through the bowl section into the neck, then a brass spring clip opens to let the ball drop out onto the saucerlike base.

V.P. — Monterey, Cal.

Your device is a nineteenth-century ballot box. The word "ballot" is derived from the Italian *ballotta* (small ball), and early votes used to be cast in urns, or boxes, like yours, a white ball for "yes," a black for "no." Ballot boxes were also used for drawing lots. The bowl was filled with balls, then rotated to shuffle them, and when the spring was released, the lucky ball dropped to the bottom.

FLEMISH COAT-OF-ARMS BADGE

This engraved brass oval has two raised loops on the back, one at the top and the other at the bottom. Was it some sort of badge worn on a soldier's uniform?

L.S. — Haverford, Pa.

Yes, the raised loops are the clue to its use as a badge on a uniform. The coat of arms is that of Her Majesty Prochie of Ruysselede (a principality of Flanders, now part of Belgium). The badge was probably engraved in Holland in 1773.

WELSH WHEEL BAROMETER

On the face of my barometer is the name "A. Taroni, Llanelly." I believe the instrument came from England, and would like to know its age and any other pertinent facts.

D.T.F. — New Rochelle, N.Y.

You have a type of siphon barometer called a wheel barometer, first made in 1665. The elaborate case dates it in the last half of the eighteenth century, when barometers were considered important pieces of furniture. Llanelly, where the maker of your barometer apparently lived, is a seaport situated in Carmarthenshire, Wales.

CLASSIC CAMEO BROOCH

What information can you give me about this pure-white cameo?

C.C.M. — *Canajoharie, N.Y.*

From the classic design and fineness of workmanship, we would judge that it was probably cut in Italy. The style of the gold mounting dates the cameo between 1845 and 1860.

CURRENCY BUST

I have a 4-inch-high bust of Lincoln made entirely of ground-up currency. It had a sticker on the back, with "$75,000" written in old script. What is its origin?

W.H.T. — *Monroe, N.Y.*

Between 1876 and 1928, worn-out and mutilated currency returned to the U.S. Treasury Department was macerated to pulp and sold to the contractors who offered the highest bids. They had it made into busts of prominent Americans and replicas of national monuments, which were sold in Washington as souvenirs. Since the sale of the pulp was discontinued in 1929, your bust would date between 1876 and 1929. The "$75,000" sticker on the back might have been meant to suggest the amount of currency it contained—but this would have been impossible to estimate once the paper had been macerated.

VICTORIAN SHELL BASKET

My shell basket was brought here from France in the mid-nineteenth century. Anything you can tell me about this kind of work will be appreciated.
M.H.H. — North Plainfield, N.J.

Shell work was one of the fashionable "art recreations" of the Victorian lady. Shells were gathered at the seaside or bought. Shell-work baskets were often charming and elaborate and were set under a glass dome and placed on a mantel for decorative purposes.

CLOISONNÉ VASE

There is no mark on my beautiful 5-foot cloisonné vase. It has been in my home for thirty-five years. Can you give me any idea of its origin?
W.L.M. — Los Angeles, Cal.

Most likely your vase is of Japanese manufacture, dating around the late 1890s or early 1900s. Cloisonné enamel, in which Japan excels above all other Far Eastern countries, was perfected by Kaji Tsunekichi about 1838. Generally the base of this work is of thin copper. The cloisons, which are delicate ribbonlike pieces of metal, are laid on the surface in the desired designs. The colored enamels are then applied to the open surface.

BLACK-CAT SALESMAN

Will you tell me who or what this boy repre-
sented? "Onyx Black" is lettered in gold on the
lapels of his coat. I believe the material is plaster
of paris.

A.A.R. — *Racine, Wis.*

About 1900, life-sized seated figures depicting a grinning black boy
were given to retail clothing stores as advertising display for Black
Cat hosiery. This was a leading brand of boy's long black cotton
stockings, manufactured in Kenosha, Wisconsin.

VICTORIAN RENAISSANCE EWERS

Our metal urns are about 19 inches high. I be-
lieve they are pewter, with evidence of some gild-
ing. We were told they are altar urns. Can you
give me any information about them?

M.E.G. — *Austin, Tex.*

Your ewers are not altar urns but copies of sixteenth-century Renaissance silver urns used to pour rose water over the hands of diners.
They usually came with a matching basin to catch the water. The
Victorians were enamored with the Renaissance style and copied it
frequently. In all probability, your ewers are white metal and were
made in Europe in the second half of the nineteenth century.

COLUMBUS STATUE

I picked up this plaster-of-paris statue in a flea market. Inscribed in the base is "Christopher Columbus Rum." What was its use, and when was it made?

G.T. — Homewood, Ill.

The statue was used to advertise rum in a Chicago liquor store at the time of the Columbian Exposition in 1893. The Exposition celebrated the four-hundredth anniversary of the discovery of America by Columbus.

AMERICAN FLAG, 1796 DESIGN

This is a picture of a large old flag I own. I would appreciate knowing something of its history.

L.O'M. — Belmont, Cal.

Until about 1810 the flag of the United States had a field of thirteen stars and added a stripe as each new state was admitted. After that the design was changed to thirteen stripes for the original states, and a star to represent each state. This flag, with thirteen stars and sixteen stripes, dates from 1796, when Tennessee was admitted to the union as the sixteenth state. Your flag could be of this time or it might possibly be a later copy.

JAPANESE GONG

There are no identifying marks on my gong. It looks like brass, with birds and flowers in the border design, and has a beautiful tone. Can you trace it?

W.C.A. — *Pomona, Cal.*

The decoration proves it to be Japanese, made between 1890 and 1910. Many such gongs were imported, usually in sets of diminishing size.

SPANISH WAX JACK

On a trip to Spain we got this antique candle. Our Spanish is fragmentary, but we understood that it is old. How old? And what was its use?

R.S. — *Hollywood, Cal.*

Your wax jack, or taper jack, is of late-nineteenth-century manufacture of European, perhaps Spanish, origin. It was used to seal letters with wax. The end of the coil of wax taper passes through a narrow opening at the top of the frame and is lit. Holding sealing wax to flame, you let the sealing wax drip onto the envelope to be sealed. The cone-shaped snuffer extinguishes the flame.

QUILL-PEN INKWELL

We were told our American inkwell is over 100 years old. It is wood, with glass containers and three holes for quills. Where does it come from?
J.M.M. — East Norwich, N.Y.

It was made by the Silliman Company of Chester, Connecticut, about 1850–1870. This type was called a countinghouse. It was made of hand-turned wood and was hand-finished.

JAPANESE INRO

My aunt, who spent much of her life in Japan, willed me this fine piece of lacquerwork. It is called an inro and is signed "Chohei Saku." Please tell me just what an inro is.
J.D. — San Francisco, Cal.

The inro is a miniature medicine case that Japanese gentlemen carried suspended from the obi, or girdle. In its fully developed form it is composed of a nest of from three to five tiny boxes fitted tightly into each other and held in place by a silk cord. Above the top of the inro, the cord passes through a sliding bead (*ojime*), which keeps the boxes secure. The ends of the cord are finally knotted into the toggle, *netsuke* (in this case in the form of a fish), which keeps the inro securely suspended from the girdle. Your inro, a collector's piece, dates from the eighteenth century.

GERMAN MEERSCHAUM PIPE

I would like to know the age and origin of this pipe with an armored knight on the bowl and castle in the background. The brass cap is marked "F.B."

R.W. — Benton, Ill.

The carved meerschaum bowl, brass cap, and wooden stem of your pipe indicate that it is German, dating after 1875.

JAPANESE NETSUKE

Recently I inherited some Japanese art objects from an uncle who had lived in Japan for a number of years. This is a snapshot of a carved wood netsuke signed "Tomokazu." Can you tell me how it was used?

C.M. — Ballard, Wash.

As the Japanese native costume, the kimono, was not provided with either pockets or pouches, it was necessary for a gentleman to carry small objects, such as a money or tobacco pouch, pipe case and inro (medicine case), slung by a cord to his obi, or girdle, like a chatelaine. The ends of the cord were knotted into the netsuke, which kept these pieces securely suspended from the obi. The finest examples of netsuke date from the Edo period (1615–1868) and were made for an inro, which was incomplete without its cord and netsuke. The principal materials used for this creative miniature sculpture, which generally averages about one and a half inches in length, were ivory and wood. Your collectible netsuke, which depicts a monkey eating loquats, dates from around 1800.

ENGLISH HUMIDOR

My oak and silver cabinet is a humidor made in England. Below the doors on the front is the serial number "Rd231621." Does this help date the piece?

V.G. — Parma, Ohio

According to the registration number, the manufacturer registered the pattern for your humidor at the London Patent Office in 1894. The simple form reflects the English Arts-and-Crafts Movement.

PAUL-AND-VIRGINIA STATUE

Can you tell me the age or anything else about this statue? It seems to be made of plaster and clay painted in natural colors. The title, "L'Orage," and signature of the artist, "Buicha," is on a brass plate.

G.O. — New York, N.Y.

Your statue most likely dates from the turn of the century. The figures are based on a painting, "L'Orage" (The Storm), by Pierre Auguste Cot (1837–1883), which is now in the Metropolitan Museum of Art. This painting in turn was based on Bernardin de Saint-Pierre's celebrated novel of unhappy lovers, *Paul et Virginie* (1788). We are unable to trace the artist Buicha.

ORNAMENTAL PIPE RACK

*My pipe rack is made of unglazed plaster of paris,
and the faces are very lifelike. I would appreciate
any information about it.*
R.C.M. — *Arlington Heights, Ill.*

Your rack was made in America and dates somewhere between 1895
and 1915. Such racks were very popular and were made by a number
of firms specializing in figures and ornaments.

RINCEAU PANEL

*I recently acquired a mantel from an early-
nineteenth-century house. After removing several
layers of thick paint I found this intricately carved
oak panel. Can you tell me anything about this
type of design and the panel's approximate age?*
R.G.H. — *East Longmeadow, Mass.*

A fanciful panel design such as yours is called a rinceau. These designs usually consist of elaborate leaf scrollwork mingled with real or
mythical birds or animals placed symmetrically on each side of a
central figure, such as a mask, cherub, or vase. The rinceau motif
was widely used in Renaissance Italy and spread throughout Europe.
Since these designs continued to be used long afterward, you would
have to consult an expert to determine the panel's age.

FRENCH STEEL PURSE

*How old would you say this little steel purse is?
It has been in my family for a very long time. The
decoration is bright steel wire, the frame marked
"Breveté."*

J.B.S. — *New Orleans, La.*

Your purse is French and was made about 1810. The word *breveté*
means "patented." Steel jewelry and accessories were first made in
England as early as 1760. By the Napoleonic era they were in vogue
in Paris, and some were brought to America.

TIFFANY BRONZE PLATES

*These plates were purchased from an antique
shop in Baltimore that specializes in bronze. I
sent them away for cleaning and the company
returned them saying that they were gold. After
cleaning, the marks "Tiffany Studios, New York
1708" were legible. Might you know anything
about them?*

A.P.F. — *Washington, D.C.*

Tiffany Studios, essentially an outgrowth of Tiffany and Associated
Artists, was started by Louis Comfort Tiffany around 1900 and continued in business until 1933, so your plates date somewhere between
these years. Tiffany made decorative objects of brass, copper, and
bronze, all of above-average quality, but since the studios did not
work with precious metals, your plates are probably not gold. The
number "1708" is the pattern number.

CHINESE WATER DROPPER

In our small library we have limited resources, and we're trying to identify this bronze turtle, handcarved, with a hole in the center top.

W.C., Librarian — Cairo, Ga.

Your turtle is a Chinese water dropper, a very important part of the calligrapher's equipment, as he had to drop the water on the ink stone to make ink. It looks like a rather nice one, probably eighteenth-century.

JAPANESE YATATE

Can you tell me what this iron object was used for? It has become quite a conversation piece in our family.

S.L.S. — Tenafly, N.J.

Your wrought-iron device, a container for writing equipment, was carried by Japanese men at the girdle and is called a *Yatate*. It consists essentially of two sections — a small, round, shallow, bowl-shaped inkwell with a hinged lid, and a long hollow stem in which the writing brush is carried. The writing ink was first ground and diluted and then soaked into an absorbent substance to prevent spilling. Your *Yatate* probably dates from the Edo period, the eighteenth century, when it was an indispensable article for almost all classes of people.

Bibliography

A short selection of interesting and standard reference books relating to antiques and the arts of decoration.

GENERAL

The American Heritage History of American Antiques from the Revolution to the Civil War. American Heritage, New York, 1968.

The American Heritage History of Antiques from the Civil War to World War I. American Heritage, New York, 1969.

The American Heritage History of Colonial Antiques, 1607–1785. American Heritage, New York, 1967.

The Art-Journal Illustrated Catalogue. (London, 1851.) Unabridged paperback reprint. Dover Pubns., New York, 1970.

Bénézit, E. *Dictionnaire des Peintres, Sculpteurs, Dessinateurs et Graveurs.* New ed., 8 vols., Librairie Gründ, Paris, 1948.

Boger, Louise Ade, and H. Batterson. *The Dictionary of Antiques and the Decorative Arts.* Enlarged ed., Charles Scribner's Sons, New York, 1967.

Comstock, Helen, ed. *The Concise Encyclopedia of American Antiques.* Hawthorn Books, New York, 1965.

Edwards, Ralph, and L. G. Ramsey, eds. *The Connoisseur's Complete Period Guides.* Bonanza Books, New York, ND.

Encyclopaedia Britannica, 11th ed., 29 vols. University Press, Cambridge, England, 1900–1911.

Kinard, E. *The Care and Keeping of Antiques.* Paperback. Hawthorn Books, New York, 1971.

Lichten, Frances. *Decorative Art of Victoria's Era.* Charles Scribner's Sons, New York, 1950.

McClinton, Katherine Morrison. *Collecting American Victorian Antiques.* Charles Scribner's Sons, New York, 1966.

Museums Directory of the United States and Canada. 2d ed. American Association of Museums and the Smithsonian Institution, Washington, D.C., 1965.

BOOKS IN PRINT

Books in Print: author-title-publisher index to books currently in print, hardbound and paperback. Annual, 2 vols.: Vol. I—authors, Vol. II—titles and publishers. R. R. Bowker Co., New York.
Paperbound Books in Print: author-title-subject index to paperback books currently in print. Biannual. R. R. Bowker Co., New York.
Subject Guide to Books in Print: subject index to books currently in print, hardbound and paperback. Annual, 2 vols. R. R. Bowker Co., New York.
Australian Books in Print: author-title-subject index to Australian books currently in print, hardbound and paperback. Annual. D. W. Thorpe, Melbourne. Distributed by R. R. Bowker Co. in the United States and Canada.
British Books in Print: author-title-subject index to British books currently in print, hardbound and paperback. Annual, 2 vols. J. Whitaker & Sons, London. Distributed by R. R. Bowker Co. in the United States and Mexico.
German Books in Print (Verzeichnis Lieferbarer Bücher): author-title index to German books currently in print, hardbound and paperback. Annual. Verlag der Buchhändler & Vereinigung & Verlag Dokumentation, Munich. Distributed by R. R. Bowker Co. worldwide, excluding Europe.
Italian Books in Print (Catalogo dei Libri Italiani in Commercio): author-title index to Italian books currently in print, hardbound and paperback. Prepared by the Italian Publishers' Association in Milan. Distributed by R. R. Bowker Co. in the United States, Canada, and Latin America.
Libros en Venta: author-title-subject index to Spanish books currently in print, hardbound and paperback. Published in the Americas and Spain by R. R. Bowker Co., Buenos Aires, 1964 and yearly supplements.

FURNITURE

Andrews, Edward D. and Faith. *Shaker Furniture: The Craftsmanship of an American Communal Sect.* Paperback reprint. Dover Pubns., New York, 1950.
Aslin, Elizabeth. *Nineteenth Century English Furniture.* Robert MacLehose & Co., Glasgow, 1962.
Bishop, Robert. *Centuries and Styles of the American Chair, 1640–1970.* E. P. Dutton & Co., New York, 1972.
Bjerkoe, Ethel Hall. *The Cabinetmakers of America.* Doubleday & Co., New York, 1957.
Blackie and Son. *Victorian Cabinet-Maker's Assistant.* Paperback reprint. Dover Pubns., New York, 1970.
Boger, Louise Ade. *The Complete Guide to Furniture Styles.* Enlarged ed. Charles Scribner's Sons, New York, 1969.
———. *Furniture Past and Present.* Doubleday & Co., New York, 1966.
Cescinsky, Herbert. *The Gentle Art of Faking Furniture.* Paperback reprint. Dover Pubns., New York, 1967.
Chippendale, Thomas, *The Gentleman & Cabinet-Maker's Director.* Paperback reprint of 3d ed. (1762). Dover Pubns., New York, 1966.
Comstock, Helen. *One Hundred Most Beautiful Rooms in America.* Rev. ed. Viking, New York, 1965.

Constantine, Albert, Jr. *Know Your Woods*. Charles Scribner's Sons, New York, 1959.

Cornelius, Charles Over. *Furniture Masterpieces of Duncan Phyfe*. Paperback reprint. Dover Pubns., New York, 1969.

Edwards, Ralph. *The New Shorter Dictionary of English Furniture: From the Middle Ages to the Late Georgian Period*. Country Life, London, 1964.

Fales, Dean A., Jr. *American Painted Furniture*. E. P. Dutton and Co., Inc., New York, 1972.

Hayward, Helena, ed. *World Furniture*. Hamlyn Publishing Group, London, 1965.

Heal, Sir Ambrose. *The London Furniture Makers from the Restoration to the Victorian Era, 1660–1840*. Paperback reprint. Dover Publications, New York, 1972.

Hepplewhite, George. *The Cabinet-Maker and Upholsterer's Guide*. Paperback reprint of 3d ed. (1794). Dover Pubns., New York, 1969.

Hope, Thomas. *Household Furniture and Interior Decoration of the Regency Period*. Paperback reprint of 1807 ed. Dover Pubns., New York, 1971.

Joy, E. T. *English Furniture, A.D. 43–1950*. Arco Publishing Co., New York, 1962.

Kettell, Russell Hawes, ed. *Early American Rooms, 1650–1858*. Paperback reprint of 1936 ed. Dover Pubns., New York, 1967.

———. *The Pine Furniture of Early New England*. Reprint of 1929 ed. Dover Pubns, New York, 1949.

Kinney, Ralph Parson. *The Complete Book of Furniture Repair and Refinishing*. Rev. ed. Charles Scribner's Sons, New York, 1971.

Kovel, Ralph and Terry. *American Country Furniture*. Crown Pubs., New York, 1965.

Miller, Edgar G., Jr. *American Antique Furniture*. 2 vols. Paperback reprint of original 2-vol. work (1937). Dover Pubns., New York, 1966.

Nutting, Wallace. *American Windsors*. Paperback reprint. Cracker Barrel Press, Southampton, Long Island, N.Y., ND.

———. *Furniture of the Pilgrim Century*. 2 vols. Paperback reprint of rev. and enlarged ed. of 1924. Dover Pubns., New York, 1965.

———. *Furniture Treasury*. 2 vols. Macmillan Co., New York, 1948.

———. *Furniture Treasury*. Vol. III. Macmillan Co., New York, 1949.

Praz, Mario. *An Illustrated History of Furnishing: From the Renaissance to the Twentieth Century*. Translated from the Italian by William Weaver. Braziller, New York, 1964.

Sweeney, John A. H. *The Treasure House of Early American Rooms*. Viking Press, New York, 1963.

Toller, Jane. *Antique Miniature Furniture in Great Britain and America*. G. Bell & Son, London, 1966.

Viaux, Jacqueline. *French Furniture*. Translated by Hazel Paget. G. P. Putnam's Sons, New York, 1964.

POTTERY AND PORCELAIN

Altman, Violet and Seymour. *The Book of Buffalo Pottery*. Crown Pubs., New York, 1969.

Barber, Edwin Atlee. *Marks of American Potters*. Paperback reprint. Cracker Barrel Press, Southampton, Long Island, N.Y., ND.

———. *The Pottery and Porcelain of the United States*. G. P. Putnam, New York, 1909.

————. *Tulip Ware of the Pennsylvania German Potters*. Paperback reprint of 1926 ed. Dover Pubns., New York, 1970.

Barret, Richard Carter. *Bennington Pottery and Porcelain*. Crown Pubs., New York, 1958.

Boger, Louise Ade. *The Dictionary of World Pottery and Porcelain*. Charles Scribner's Sons, New York, 1971.

Bristowe, W. S. *Victorian China Fairings*. Enlarged ed. A. & C. Black, London, 1971.

Burton, William, and Robert L. Hobson. *Handbook of Marks on Pottery and Porcelain*. Macmillan & Co., London, 1928.

Chaffers, William. *Marks and Monograms on European and Oriental Pottery and Porcelain*. European and Oriental section edited by Frederick Litchfield and R. L. Hobson; British section edited by Geoffrey A. Godden. 15th rev. ed., 2 vols. William Reeves Bookseller Ltd., London, 1965. U.S. ed., Dover Pubns., New York, 1965.

Charleston, Robert J., ed. *World Ceramics*. McGraw-Hill Book Co., New York, 1968.

Danckert, Ludwig. *Handbuch des Europäischen Porzellans*. Prestel-Verlag, Munich, 1954.

Garner, Sir Harry Mason. *Oriental Blue and White*. Faber and Faber, London, 1954.

Godden, Geoffrey A. *Encyclopaedia of British Pottery & Porcelain Marks*. Crown Pubs., New York, 1964.

————. *An Illustrated Encyclopaedia of British Pottery & Porcelain*. Bonanza Books, New York, ND.

Hannover, Emil. *Pottery and Porcelain: A Handbook for Collectors*. Translated from the Danish by W. W. Worster; edited with notes and appendices, by Bernard Rackam. Vol. I, *Europe and the Near East Earthenware and Stoneware*; Vol. II, *The Far East*; Vol. III, *European Porcelain*. Charles Scribner's Sons, New York, 1925.

Henzke, Lucile. *American Art Pottery*. Thomas Nelson, Camden, N.J., 1970.

Hobson, Robert Lockart. *Handbook of the Pottery and Porcelain of the Far East*. 3d ed. London, 1948.

Honey, William Bowyer. *European Ceramic Art: From the End of the Middle Ages to About 1815*. 2 vols. Faber and Faber, London, 1952.

Hyde, J. A. Lloyd. *Oriental Lowestoft*. (Chinese Export Porcelain.) 2d ed. Newport, Monmouthshire, England, 1954.

Ketchum, William C., Jr. *The Pottery & Porcelain Collector's Handbook: A Guide to Early American Ceramics from Maine to California*. Funk & Wagnalls, New York, 1971.

Larsen, Ellouise Baker. *American Historical Views on Staffordshire China*. 2d rev. ed. Doubleday & Co., New York, 1950.

Newman, Harold. *Veilleuses, 1750–1860*. A. S. Barnes, South Brunswick, N.J. 1967.

Parsons, C. S. M., and H. Curl. *China Mending and Restoration*. Faber and Faber, London, 1963.

Penkala, Maria. *European Pottery*. Charles E. Tuttle Co., Rutland, Vt., 1968.

Ramsay, John. *American Potters and Pottery*. Hale, Cushman and Flint, Boston, 1939.

Scott, G. Ryland, Jr., and Cleo M. *Antique Porcelain Digest*. Ceramics Book Co., Newport, Monmouthshire, England, 1961.

Wakefield, Hugh. *Victorian Pottery*. Thomas Nelson & Sons, New York, 1962.

Wynter, Harriet. *An Introduction to European Porcelain*. Thomas Y. Crowell Co., New York, 1972.

SILVER

Bigelow, Francis Hill. *Historic Silver of the Colonies and Its Makers*. Macmillan Co., New York, 1917.

Bradbury, Frederick. *History of Old Sheffield Plate*. Reprint of 1912 ed. Macmillan & Co., London, 1969.

Clayton, Michael. *The Collector's Dictionary of the Silver and Gold of Great Britain and North America*. U.S. ed. World Pub. Co., New York, 1971.

Davis, Frank. *French Silver, 1450–1825*. Praeger, New York, 1970.

Ensko, Stephan G. C. *American Silversmiths and Their Marks*. Paperback reprint of 2d ed. (1937) Cracker Barrel Press, Southampton, Long Island, N.Y., ND.

Fales, Martha Gandy. *Early American Silver*. Funk and Wagnalls, New York, 1970.

Flynt, Henry N., and Martha Gandy Fales. *The Heritage Foundation Collection of Silver*. Heritage Foundation, Old Deerfield, Mass., 1968.

Fredericks, J. W. *Antique Dutch Silver*. 4 vols. The Hague, 1952–1965.

French, Hollis. *A Silver Collector's Glossary and List of Early American Silversmiths and Their Marks*. Reprint of 1917 ed. Da Capo Press, New York, 1967.

Hayden, Arthur. *Chats on Old Silver*. Rev. paperback reprint. Dover Pubns., New York, 1969.

Hood, Graham. *American Silver, A History of Style, 1650–1900*. Praeger, New York, 1971.

Hughes, Graham. *Modern Silver Throughout the World, 1880–1967*. Crown Pubs., New York, 1967.

Jackson, Sir Charles J. *English Goldsmiths and Their Marks*. Reprint of original 1921 work. Dover Pubns., New York, 1964.

———. *An Illustrated History of English Plate*. 2 vols. Reprint of original 1911 work. Dover Pubns., New York, 1969.

Langdon, John E. *Canadian Silversmiths, 1700–1900*. Toronto, 1966.

Oman, Charles. *English Silversmiths' Work, Civil and Domestic*. Her Majesty's Stationery Office, London, 1965.

Pyne Press, compiled by the Editors of the. *Victorian Silverplate Hollowware*. Pyne Press, Princeton, N.J., 1972.

Rainwater, Dorothy T. *American Silver Manufacturers*. Everybody's Press, Hanover, Pa., 1966.

———. *American Silverplate*. Everybody's Press, Hanover, Pa., 1971.

———. and Donna H. Felger. *American Spoons, Souvenir and Historical*. Everybody's Press, Hanover, Pa., and Camden, N.J., 1969.

Rosenberg, Marc. *Der Goldschmiede Merkzeichen*. Frankfurt am Main, 1922–28; reprinted 1964.

Roth, Henry Ling. *Oriental Silverwork, Chinese and Malay*. University of Malaysia Press, Kuala Lumpur, 1966.

Wardle, Patricia. *Victorian Silver and Silver Plate*. U.S. ed. Universe Books, New York, 1970.

Wyler, Seymour B. *The Book of Old Silver*. Crown Pubs., New York, 1937.

———. *The Book of Sheffield Plate*. Bonanza Books, New York, ND.

PEWTER

Cotterell, Howard H. *Old Pewter: Its Makers and Marks in England, Scotland, and Ireland*. Reprint of 1929 ed. Charles E. Tuttle Co., Rutland, Vt., 1963.
Jacobs, Carl. *Guide to American Pewter*. Medill McBride Co., New York, 1957.
Kerfoot, J. B. *American Pewter*. Crown Pubs., New York, 1942.
Laughlin, Ledlie Irwin. *Pewter in America, Its Makers and Their Marks*. 2d ed. Reprinted by Barre Pubs., Barre, Mass., 1969.
Rogers, M. A. *American Pewterers and Their Marks*. Paperback reprint. Cracker Barrel Press, Southampton, Long Island, N.Y., ND.

GLASS

Bergstrom, Evangeline H. *Old Glass Paperweights*. Privately printed. Lakeside Press, Chicago, Ill., 1940.
Elville, E. M. *A Collector's Dictionary of Glass*. Country Life, London, 1963.
Gardner, Paul V. *The Glass of Frederick Carder*. Crown Pubs., New York, 1971.
Kampfer, Fritz, and Klaus G. Beyer. *Glass: A World History: The Story of 4000 Years of Fine Glass-Making*. Translated and revised by Edmund Launert. New York Graphic Society, Greenwich, Conn., 1967.
Klamikin, Marian. *The Collector's Book of Bottles*. Dodd, Mead & Co., New York, 1971.
Koch, Robert. *Louis C. Tiffany: Rebel in Glass*. Crown Pubs., New York, 1964.
Lee, Ruth Webb. *Early American Pressed Glass*. Enlarged and rev. ed. Printed by the author, Northboro, Mass., 1946.
————. *Sandwich Glass*. Enlarged and rev. ed. Lee Pubns., Wellesley Hills, Mass., 1966.
————. *Victorian Glass*. Printed by the author, Northboro, Mass., 1944.
————. and James H. Rose. *American Glass Cup Plates*. Printed by the author, Northboro, Mass., 1948.
McKearin, Helen and George S. *American Glass*. Crown Pubs., New York, 1941.
Melvin, Jean S. *American Glass Paperweights and Their Makers*. Thomas Nelson & Sons, New York, 1967.
Papert, Emma. *The Illustrated Guide to American Glass*. Hawthorn Books, New York, 1972.
Pepper, Adeline. *The Glass Gaffers of New Jersey*. Charles Scribner's Sons, New York, 1971.
Robertson, R. A. *Chats on Old Glass*. Rev. paperback reprint. Dover Pubns., New York, 1969.
Van Rensselaer, Stephen. *Early American Bottles and Flasks*. Paperback reprint. Cracker Barrel Press, Southampton, Long Island, N.Y., ND.
Vavra, Jaroslav R. *5000 Years of Glass-Making: The History of Glass*. Translated by J. R. Gottheiner. Artia, Prague, 1954.
Wakefield, Hugh. *Nineteenth Century British Glass*. Faber and Faber, London, 1961.
Weiss, Gustav. *The Book of Glass*. Translated by Janet Seligman. Praeger, New York, 1971.
Wilson, Kenneth M. *New England Glass & Glass-Making*. Thomas Y. Crowell Co., New York, 1972.

CLOCKS AND WATCHES

Baillie, G. H. *Watchmakers and Clockmakers of the World.* 3d ed. Thomas Nelson and Sons, London, 1951.

Bassermann-Jordan, Ernst von. *The Book of Old Clocks and Watches.* 4th ed. Revised by Hans von Bertele. Allen and Unwin, London, 1964.

Britten, F. J. *Old Clocks and Watches and Their Makers.* 7th ed. by G. H. Baillie, C. Clutton, and C. A. Elbert. E. P. Dutton and Co., New York, 1956.

Mody, N. H. N. *Japanese Clocks.* Reprint of 1932 ed. Charles E. Tuttle Co., Japan, 1967.

Palmer, Brooks. *The Book of American Clocks.* Macmillan Co., New York, 1966.

———. *A Treasury of American Clocks.* Macmillan Co., New York, 1967.

OTHER SUBJECTS

Angione, Genevieve. *All Bisque & Half-Bisque Dolls.* Thomas Nelson & Sons, Camden, N.J., 1969.

Benham, W. Gurney. *Playing Cards.* Spring Books, London, N.D.

Blair, Claude. *European and American Arms, 1066–1880 A.D.* Batsford, London, 1962.

———. *European Armour, 1066–1700.* Batsford, London, 1968.

———. *Pistols of the World.* Batsford, London, 1968.

Boehm, Max von. *Dolls.* Unabridged paperback reprint of the first portion of *Dolls and Puppets,* originally published as a separate book in German. Translated by Josephine Nicoll. Dover Pubns., New York, 1972.

———. *Puppets & Automation.* Unabridged paperback reprint of "Part II: Puppets" of the one-volume English translation of *Dolls and Puppets* originally published by David McKay, Philadelphia, Pa., ND. Dover Pubns., New York, 1972.

Boger, H. Batterson. *The Traditional Arts of Japan.* Doubleday & Co., New York, 1964.

Brockhaus, Albert. *Netsuke: Versuch einer Geschichte der Japanischen Schnitz-kunst.* Leipzig. 1901. Abridged ed. translated from the German by M. Watty. London, 1969.

Buday, George. *The History of Christmas Cards.* New ed. Spring Books, London, 1964.

Bushell, Raymond. *Collectors' Netsuke.* John Weatherhill, Tokyo, 1971.

Caulfield, S. F. A. *Encyclopedia of Victorian Needlework.* 2 vols. Unabridged paperback reprint of 6 vols. of 2d ed. 1887; formerly entitled *The Dictionary of Needlework: An Encyclopedia of Artistic, Plain and Fancy Needlework.* Dover Pubns., New York, 1972.

Coleman, Elizabeth A. *Dolls, Makers and Marks.* Rev. paperback ed. Published by Dorothy S. Coleman, Washington, D.C., 1966.

Conningham, Frederic A. *Currier & Ives Prints, An Illustrated Check List.* Updated by Colin Simkin. Crown Pubs., New York, 1970.

Cooper, Grace Rogers. *The Invention of the Sewing Machine.* Smithsonian Institution, Bulletin 254, U.S. Government Printing Office, Washington, D.C., 1968. (NB: The main library in most large cities has a Government Depository Library.)

Davenport, Millia. *The Book of Costume.* Crown Pubs., New York, 1964.

Eastlake, Charles L. *Hints on Household Taste.* Paperback reprint. Dover Pubns., New York, 1972.

Entwistle, E. A. *A Literary History of Wallpaper.* Batsford, London, 1960.

———. *Wallpapers of the Victorian Era.* F. Lewis, London, 1964.

Eras, Vincent M. *Locks and Keys Throughout the Ages.* H. H. Fronczek, Amsterdam, 1957.

Erdmann, Kurt. *Seven Hundred Years of Oriental Carpets.* Edited by Hanna Erdmann and translated by Mary H. Beattie and Hildegard Herzog. University of California Press, Berkeley, Cal., 1970.

Forrer, Leonard S. *The Art of Collecting Coins.* Citadel Press, New York, 1955.

Garner, Sir Harry Mason. *Chinese and Japanese Cloisonné Enamels.* Rev. and enlarged ed. Faber and Faber, London, 1971.

Glissman, A. H. *The Evolution of the Sad-Iron.* P. O. Box 215, Carlsbad, Cal., 1970.

Godden, Geoffrey. *Stevengraphs and Other Victorian Silk Pictures.* Barrie & Jenkins, London, 1971.

Groves, Sylvia. *History of Needlework Tools and Accessories.* Country Life, London, 1966.

Hayward, Arthur H. *Colonial Lighting.* 3d enlarged paperback ed. Dover Pubns., New York, 1962.

Herrl, George. *The Carl P. Dietz Collection of Typewriters Catalogue.* Milwaukee Public Museum, Milwaukee, 1965.

Hunter, Genze Leland. *Decorative Textiles.* J. B. Lippincott, Philadelphia, 1918.

———. *The Practical Book of Tapestries.* J. B. Lippincott, Philadelphia, 1925.

Ickis, Marguerite. *The Standard Book of Quilt-Making and Collecting.* Paperback reprint. Dover Pubns., New York, 1970.

Jacobs, Flora Gill. *A History of Dolls' Houses.* Charles Scribner's Sons, New York, 1965.

John, W. D., and A. Simcox. *Pontypool and Usk Japanned Wares.* Rev. ed. Ceramic Book Co., Newport, Monmouthshire, England, 1965.

Jonas, F. M. *Netsuke.* London and Kobe, 1928. Reprinted by Charles E. Tuttle Co., Japan, 1960.

Kauffman, Henry J. *Early American Copper, Tin and Brass.* Medill McBride Co., New York, 1950.

MacSwiggan, Amelia E. *Fairy Lamps.* Bonanza Books, New York, 1962.

McClelland, Nancy. *Historic Wall-Papers.* J. B. Lippincott, Philadelphia, 1924.

McClintock, Marshall and Inez. *Toys in America.* Public Affairs Press, Washington, D.C., 1961.

Meyer, Franz Sales. *Handbook of Ornament.* Unabridged paperback reprint. Dover Pubns., New York, 1957.

Meyer, John D. *A Handbook of Old Mechanical Penny Banks.* Privately printed, Tyrone, Pa., 1948.

Michel's Piano Atlas. Published by N. E. Michel, Pico Rivera, Cal., 1961.

Morris, Ernest. *Tintinnabula: Collecting Small Bells.* Robert Hale, London, 1959.

Penzer, Norman Mosler. *The Book of the Wine Label.* Home and Van Thal, London, 1947.

Pinto, Edward H. *Treen and Other Wooden Bygones.* G. Bell & Son, London, 1969.

Powys, Marian. *Lace and Lace-Making.* Charles Branford, Boston, 1953.

Pyne Press, compiled by the Editors of the. *Lamps & Other Lighting Devices, 1850–1906.* Pyne Press, Princeton, N.J., 1972.

Relling, Ray. *The Powder Flask Book.* Bonanza, New York, N.D.

Rhead, George Wooliscroft. *The History of the Fan.* London, 1910.

Robins, Frederick William. *The Story of the Lamp and Candle.* Oxford University Press, London, 1939; reprinted 1971.

Sexton, Carlie. *Early American Quilts*. Reprinted by the Cracker Barrel Press, Southampton, Long Island, N.Y., ND.

Simkin, Colin, ed. *Currier and Ives' America*. Crown Pubs., New York, 1952.

Snowman, A. Kenneth. *Karl Gustavovich Fabergé, 1846–1920*. Faber and Faber, London, 1953.

Sonn, Albert H. *Early American Wrought Iron*. Charles Scribner's Sons, New York, 1928.

Springer, L. Elsinore. *The Collector's Book of Bells*. Crown Pubs., New York, 1972.

St. George, Eleanor. *The Dolls of Yesterday*. Charles Scribner's Sons, New York, 1948.

Symonde, Mary, and Louisa Preece. *Needlework Through the Ages*. Hodder & Stoughton, London, 1928.

Toller, Jane. *Papier-Mâché in Great Britain and America*. U.S. ed., C. T. Branford Co., Newton, Mass., 1962.

Webb, Ruth Lee. *A History of Valentines*. Studio Publication in association with T. Y. Crowell, New York, 1953.

White, Gwen. *Antique Toys*. Arco Pub. Co., New York, 1971.

———. *Dolls of the World*. Mills & Boon, London, 1962.

Whiting, Gertrude. *Old-Time Tools and Toys of Needlework*. Paperback reprint. Dover Pubns., New York, 1971.

Whiting, Hubert B. *Old Iron Still Banks*. Forward's Color Productions, Inc., Manchester, Vt., 1968.

Wilder, F. L. *How to Identify Old Prints*. G. Bell & Sons, London, 1969.

ABOUT THE AUTHOR

Louise Ade Boger is a native of Williamsport, Pennsylvania. She received a B.S. in Latin from the University of Pennsylvania and then went on to take her M.A. in history. With her late husband, H. Batterson Boger, she lived and traveled all over the world, including three years in postwar Japan. They collected furniture and other treasures, and at the same time built up an invaluable reference file. The first result was their collaboration on *The Dictionary of Antiques and the Decorative Arts*. Since then, Mrs. Boger herself has produced three other acclaimed reference works: *The Complete Guide to Furniture Styles, Furniture Past and Present,* and *The Dictionary of World Pottery and Porcelain*. Mrs. Boger makes her home in New York City.